Also by Frank Calkins

ROCKY MOUNTAIN WARDEN

This is a Borzoi Book
Published in New York
by Alfred A. Knopf

JACKSON HOLE

Frank Calkins

JACKSON HOLE

Alfred A. Knopf
New York
1973

THIS IS A BORZOI BOOK
PUBLISHED BY ALFRED A. KNOPF, INC.

Library of Congress Cataloging in Publication Data

Calkins, Frank, date
  Jackson Hole.

  Bibliography: p.
  1. Jackson Hole, Wyo. 2. Grand Teton National Park. I. Title.
F767.T3C25   917.87′55   72-11030
ISBN 0-394-47437-6

Manufactured in the United States of America

FIRST EDITION

This book is for my father

Contents

Sixteen pages of photographs follow page 114

Acknowledgments

This first part of a book is actually written last. It is the capstone a writer puts on his pile of manuscript before he mails it to the publisher. Finishing a book is a very happy time for any writer, and one that should be shared. So, until a better moment arises, I would like to have this page serve as a celebration at which I can introduce and thank everyone who contributed to the completion of the book.

To reach this finishing place there had to be an inception. It happened in the East; Alfred A. Knopf, Paul R. Reynolds, Jr., John W. Hawkins, and my editor, Angus Cameron, all contributed to the idea for this book. The four make up an awesome quartet in American letters, and I hope they find their trust in me well placed.

My other guests at this appreciation were helpful in more ways than I have space to list. I thank them all very much: John W. Cornelison, research historian, Wyoming State Archives and Historical Department; L. D. Frome, outfitter, Afton, Wyoming; Gene M. Gressley, director of the Western History Research Center at the Coe Library, University of Wyoming; Mike Hanson, U.S. forest ranger, Caribou National Forest, and pack trip companion; Darrel Jenkins, my neighbor and also a pack trip companion; George Kaminski, I & E division chief, Wyoming Game and Fish Commission; Mrs. Jean Kirol, librarian, Teton County Library; Miss Patti Kopf, Western History Research Center; W. C. "Slim" Lawrence, regional historian and owner of the Jackson Hole Museum.

My thanks also go to Gerald N. Lehan, records administrator, Idaho State Penitentiary; Mrs. Eleo Mettler, co-owner of the Moose Head Ranch; Don Redfearn, superintendent of the National Elk Refuge; Charles G. "Chuck" Roundy, research historian, Western History Research Center; Mrs. Eunice

Spackman, Western History Research Center; Jim Straley, big game biologist, Wyoming Game and Fish Commission; Edith M. Thompson, Midwest, Wyoming, for permission to use portions of "Beaver Dick's" writings.

In addition, I was given a great deal of all sorts of help by employees of the Teton National Forest. The staff at Grand Teton National Park was extremely generous and helpful, and a number of them have been specifically mentioned in the book. It must be understood, however, that the interpretations of data supplied by anyone mentioned directly or indirectly are my own, as are any errors.

It has taken more than two years to compile the information and then write this book. There has not been a day in that time when my wife, Rodello, did not in some way help me. She also helped to edit and type the final manuscript. Most difficult of all for her, she stayed home alone, in the big, Wyoming dark, for what added up to months while I was away collecting material. Thank you, Rodello.

Thank you all.

F.C.

Freedom, Wyoming
May 1972

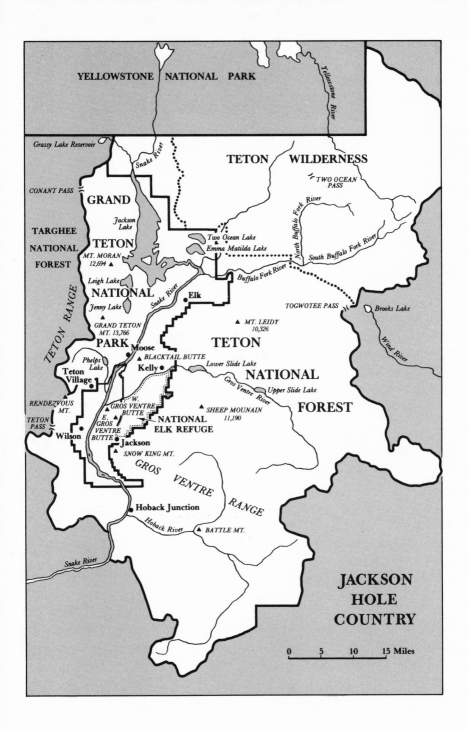

JACKSON HOLE

*Yonder is Jackson Hole. The last
of the Old West.*

FAMILIAR HIGHWAY SIGN

1 / *First Time Through*

Jackson Hole was dark and dripping wet. A light rain began falling during our drive through Yellowstone Park and pursued us all afternoon. I remember the steady throb of the windshield wipers and the way the window glass fogged tightly all around the space reclaimed by the defroster.

It was shortly after the close of World War II, and the road south from Flagg Ranch was rough and very muddy. Our tires spewed out a thin slurry of it that floated up behind us, bespattering our own car as well as those few we passed. Like apprehensive animals they were hastening through the chill gloom toward cover. My mother and I, finished with staring out at the dark landscape, sat and waited for the trip to end. My father was hurrying, too, tired and concerned about finding accommodations for us in Jackson.

Moran, then Moose, appeared—window-sized shafts of yellow lamplight that flashed momentarily and were gone. It was dark by the time we reached Jackson, and what I saw of the tiny town was only a thin spatter of rain-washed lights twinkling in a sodden void.

The first real warmth and concentration of light we found in the town was in the lobby of the old Wort Hotel. But we were able to enjoy it just long enough for my father to be told that the hotel was full. He took us through it, though, to see the famous Silver Dollar Bar and to try unsuccessfully to pick up some of the 2,032 silver dollars imbedded in it. Somewhere near the bar I saw a slender young woman with a pale, impassive face dealing blackjack amidst the whirr and *chunk, chunk, chunk* of the slot machines. Jackson had wide-open, illegal gambling then, which for some reason seemed to inordinately bother some newspaper men three hundred miles away in Salt Lake City.

We stayed that night in a log cabin auto court on the south end of town. The room was large, warm, and agreeably rustic. Today that establishment is closed and a family lives in its main building. No longer on the edge of town, it has been engulfed by an eager business district that has all the personality of the porcelain-faced blackjack dealer.

During the night the rain stopped and the dripping clouds drifted east across the valley, leaving behind them a glistening morning of limpid blue. Outside, our breath steamed in the snap of cold air. We went back to the Wort for breakfast, and then my father drove us up the Gros Ventre River road toward Lower Slide Lake. In an open stand of aspen trees we saw a leggy young moose that fled from us with the swinging, ponderous gait that is the moose's nearest approach to grace. The dirt road ahead was still slippery from the rain, so my father turned around and drove back down into the valley for a head-on look at the Tetons.

I had never seen such mountains before, and it would be nice to recall that I was awed and moved by them. But I was not. Most kids are unimpressed by the scenery their parents haul them hundreds of miles to see, and I was one of these. Still, during the ensuing years, whenever I read or heard about Jackson Hole the image of those tall, fiercely lustrous mountains came first to mind.

Jackson Hole lies immediately south of Yellowstone Park in the northwestern corner of the state of Wyoming. If you were to make a map tracing of this valley, running your pen along the lower slopes of the surrounding mountain ranges, the result would look something like a sea horse. This sea horse faces east, its nose pointing toward Togwotee Pass, while its tail balances at Jackson Hole's southerly tip, where the Hoback River enters the Snake River. The valley is about sixty miles long and up to twenty miles wide.

The western side of Jackson Hole is walled in by the abruptly rising Teton Range. Its sharp, central peaks are the ones that have been assailed by every possible superlative in the English language. The highest of these is the Grand Teton; it rises 13,766 feet. I have seen people scratch their privates and eat popcorn while gaping up at it. I do not think it gives a damn.

Across the valley to the southeast is the Gros Ventre (pronounced "grow vaunt") Range. Its mountains flow northward into the Mount Leidy highlands, beyond and somewhat north of which is the Washakie Range and the Pinyon Peak highlands, which are north-northeast of Jackson Hole. No one, not even Jackson Hole's biggest booster, has ever been able to push the valley's northern end beyond Yellowstone's Pitchstone Plateau.

The tracing of the sea horse occupies only about a third of the mountainous area surrounding and draining into Jackson Hole. Still, it includes all of the Grand Teton National Park, over 300,000 acres; the National Elk Refuge, 23,754 acres; and most of the Teton National Forest, upwards of 1,700,000 acres. Private lands amount to less than 60,000 acres. The cash value of this private land, depending upon its location, ranges from $5,000 to more than $25,000 an acre. The number of farms and ranches is slowly decreasing. Today there are less than ninety in all of Teton County.

Recently I met a native-born cowboy who told me about a neighboring farmer who had once offered to sell him land in Jackson Hole for a few hundred dollars an acre. "I was going into the army, though, and couldn't be bothered."

When the cowboy came home the farmer again offered him the land for a very reasonable price. "I turned him down that time, too. Told him I'd rather take the money and throw a big drunk." Soon afterward the boom started and the farmer began selling off an acre or two at a time, at five thousand an acre. "Every time the old boy sold some land," the cowboy said, "he'd take me into town, get me drunk, and then laugh like hell."

Jackson Hole is as much a state of mind as it is a specific area. Some people see it all in an afternoon, while others need a lifetime. But no matter how you look at it, the town of Jackson takes up just a speck, maybe two square miles, couched in a mountainside near the southern end of the big valley. Some people consider the town and its immediate surroundings as Jackson Hole, and if you address a letter to someone in "Jackson Hole, Wyoming" it will be delivered to the town post office in Jackson.

The town of Jackson does burgeon and glitter from a "hole," as the mountain men described it, but only figuratively. Jackson, Wyoming, is 6,234 feet above sea level. Until the end of World War II it was one of the most remote county seats in the West, but in the years since the war its population, and sophistication, has ballooned; the population of Teton County is around four thousand, and over half of these people live in and around Jackson.

Jackson is backdropped by Snow King and other mountains to the south and east, and it is effectively screened from the valley itself by a couple of buttes. Immediately west of the town is East Gros Ventre Butte. On a slope facing Jackson, it is a treeless, sausage-shaped pile that rises as much as a thousand feet above the town. Mule deer ply these steep hillsides looking for food during the winter and early spring. Jackson is one of the nation's only towns where you can sit in your car and count deer while your wife visits some rather exclusive shops. The butte extends north of town about four miles, acting with the mountains south and east to hold the town in a U-shaped alcove. Near the top of the U, to the northeast, Miller Butte rises as another barrier between the town and the valley. These buttes and the town's buildings cut much of Jackson off from even the slimmest glimpse of the Grand Teton.

Lying west of Jackson, though shielded from its view by intervening buttes, is the smaller community of Wilson. It is an old, log cabin and pole fence settlement that is being increasingly beseiged by ticky-tack trailer houses, prefabs, and slab-sided A-frames.

A few winters back my wife and I drove out with two other couples to a recommended eating place near Wilson. The building, when we arrived, was attractively banked with deep snowdrifts that shone blue-white in the darkness. We entered the dimly lit building and then stood puzzled and alone in a set-up but completely empty dining room. Eventually a man emerged from a darkened side doorway. He told us the dining room was closed because "We've had a little death."

We muttered our not entirely heartfelt sympathies and turned to leave, only to be told by our would-be host, "The bar's open, though."

Outside someone said, "I guess it takes a pretty *big* death to close a bar in Jackson Hole."

North of Wilson, on the slopes of the Tetons, is the relatively new community of Teton Village. It is a skiing place with pseudo-chalets, cliff dwellings, and business establishments whose names end in "haus" rather than "house." One evening I took my wife and a friend into a picturesque bar there, and we all decided to have a Dubonnet on the rocks. The bartender hadn't any Dubonnet, so we changed our orders to Bristol Cream sherry. It was duly served—on the rocks!

From the highway turnoff to Teton Village it is about twelve miles north over a narrow but charming secondary road to Moose. Some call it Moose Village. Moose is headquarters for Grand Teton National Park. There is employee housing here, and a large combination museum and park office building. In winter the kids from outlying ranches ride snowmobiles to this building and wait in its warmth for their school bus.

Many visitors to park headquarters at Moose want to know why all the trees are dying. Specifically it is the lodgepole pines that are turning brown and making a rusty smear of some formerly green stands of timber. These trees are dying, and will continue to die, because they are old. In their senility they have become easy prey for the pine bark beetle, who burrows happily through the lodgepoles' cambium layers and strangles them. Control programs were tried for years, but none succeeded in saving many trees. In the end the failure of the chemical sprays and spraying proved not only an almost complete waste of tax money but an injury to the environment as well. Nature is already replacing the dying pines with young spruce and fir.

Across the valley, east of Moose, is the tiny community of Kelly. Any claims it aspired to as a leading town—even the county seat—were all washed away in the famous flood of 1927. The only establishments of note today are the Slide Inn and an old log church that has long served more secular needs as a post office and store. In the summer of 1971 the latter building caught fire and was partially burned. The efforts of the volunteer firemen to control the blaze were made even livelier by the popping of the store's ammunition stock. After the fire the owner expressed plans to repair the damage and remain in business.

Farther up the valley to the north there used to exist a rustic resort community called Moran. It lay below the long, low reclamation dam that spreads across the outlet of Jackson Lake. Moran eventually grew a bit untidy, and most of it was then torn down or moved away by the Park Service, with the approval of the Rockefellers, who owned it. All that remains of Moran now are a few log cabins that are variously used as a biological station and housing for employees of the sprawling Jackson Lake Lodge. This lodge may be reached either by following the highway north or tramping upstream from the big sewage lagoons that are adjacent to the lodge complex.

Jackson Lake constitutes most of the aforementioned sea horse's head. The lake, which covers about 25,000 acres and has depths to 400 feet, draws its moods from the weather and the season. On a blue-sky summer day its beauty is incomparable. In winter it can be a bleak Siberia of ice and wind-driven snow. On a cold and cloudy spring day it turns a vomitous gray-green. Semisubmerged deadheads often wallow evilly in the lake's cold waters, and on windy days they can arm the vicious, chopping waves with sodden battering rams.

Due east of Jackson Lake are Two-Ocean and Emma Matilda lakes. Each of these long, narrow lakes is about two miles in length and up to half a mile wide. The name Two-Ocean is a misnomer, for the drainage of this lake is into Pacific Creek, and then, classically, the Pacific Ocean. Today its waters more likely end up in Idaho irrigation ditches.

Arrayed south of Jackson Lake along the steep Teton flanks are six more popular lakes: Leigh, String, Jenny, Bradley, Taggart, and Phelps. These are all glacial lakes with the exception of String Lake, which is more accurately just a widening and slowing of the Leigh Lake outlet.

There is a developed picnic ground at String Lake. Its parking area serves both the picnickers and hikers who leave their cars here when they start out on the trails that head nearby.

One afternoon in late June I was sitting in my car in the parking lot waiting for a naturalist's hike to begin when a family of four came tramping back to their huge Winnebago motor home. (I have a readily admitted loathing for these motorized motels.) The leader, and father, was a well-bellied man about my age. He burst out of the trees ahead of his wife and two preteen kids and marched straight for his behemoth home on wheels.

"There's too many bugs around here," he said. "Keep the screen door closed!" The door was immediately closed, but I could still hear him. "What's all this crap around here? Git this stuff cleaned up. Git the Six-Twelve! Where did you put it? Don't sit in the sun. Even if you sit in the shade, you'll sweat."

Until this unhappy man told his children what a horrible place they were in, I think the kids had been having fun. I overheard the little boy relate excitedly how he and his sister had "crawled and walked on logs!"

String Lake empties into Jenny Lake on the south. Jenny covers about 1,300 acres and is just as lovely as everyone says— and just as crowded.

Bradley and Taggart lakes are almost halfway between the larger Jenny and Phelps lakes. These two small lakes are favorite turnaround points for Park Service nature hikes.

Phelps Lake, because of the location of the trails leading to it, is the least accessible of the six lakes. The JY Ranch, a big Rockefeller property, is situated on the southeast end of Phelps Lake. I must assume that the Rockefellers have a better view up the lake, toward the Tetons, than the hiking public has down the lake, toward the Rockefeller's pine-veiled lodge.

There are about a hundred more lakes in the Jackson Hole country. Some are little more than weedy ponds deep in the timber, while others are lovely, lost jewels hidden near lonely divides. Some have never been officially named.

The majority of these lakes and ponds give rise to tributaries of the great Snake River, which bisects Jackson Hole north and south. The Snake rises in south-central Yellowstone Park. It grows rapidly and its size is further augmented by the Lewis River near the south entrance of Yellowstone Park. The Snake's pace is leisurely as it winds down between willow banks and marshy meadows to the inlet at the north end of Jackson Lake.

This meandering resumes once the stream emerges again from the dam at Moran. It wanders along past great spruces and stands of cottonwood, often dividing itself into a multiplicity of channels. But once the stream reaches the narrowing defiles below South Park in southern Jackson Hole it is through meandering. It overwhelms the smaller Hoback River at its mouth and drives the Hoback's waters against the far, southeast shore. The combined streams then surge down the Grand Canyon of the Snake in an obvious display of the reason mountain men called it the Mad River.

As the Snake flows through Jackson Hole it gathers water from numerous creeks and springs together with the outpourings of the Buffalo Fork and Gros Ventre rivers. The Buffalo Fork originates in the Teton Wilderness northeast of Jackson Hole, while the Gros Ventre begins far up in the mountains of the same name southeast of Jackson Hole.

And here, probably, is where Jackson Hole ends for most of the millions who pour through it all summer. They buy wool felt cowboy hats, T-shirts for the kids emblazoned "Jackson Hole, Wyoming," complain about the high price of the gasoline, and then roar off to get a bumper sticker at the "Reptile Gardens"—wherever they may be.

2 / No Stone Unturned

There are three beautiful valleys in northwestern Wyoming that, when considered together, form a rough triangle. Jackson Hole is at the northern apex; Star Valley, where I live, is south; and the valley of the Green lies to the southeast. Each of the valleys is beautiful, but for different reasons. The Green River Valley is not only verdant, in its season, but it is uncluttered and free-looking. Star Valley has been divided into medium-sized farms, and in summer their cultivated, green swards blend pleasantly with the surrounding foothills and timbered mountainsides.

The floor of Jackson Hole, on the other hand, is only verdant in places. The valley has an intense beauty, although much of the central part of it is covered with gray-green sagebrush. Formerly cultivated areas are being permitted to revert to their former wild somberness by the National Park Service. Parts of the floor of Jackson Hole are not particularly beautiful, and some people even wonder why these areas are in a national park. The gravelly soil is so porous near the surface that water practically gushes down through it. This tendency for the land to dry out quickly is a condition that sentenced many of the early homesteaders to lives of near poverty. Unless it can be well irrigated, much of this potentially green land soon turns brown. It is one of the valley's anomalies, then, to find that basements aren't generally dug here because of the high water table. Many of the early settlers' wells were brought in simply by driving thirty feet of pipe down into the ground.

It is another irony of nature to know, too, that much of this dry, rocky soil is flecked with gold. As much as two-thirds of Jackson Hole may be underlain with the precious metal. The estimated value of this buried treasure is staggering. The only thing that has saved the valley's beauty from the far-flung despoilation of the miner is the character of the gold itself. It is "float" gold, metal so fine that no way has yet been found to mine it economically. I have seen this stuff glittering on top of the ground, but at the same time I saw that collecting a substantial amount of it would be heartbreaking toil. Nevertheless, there have been many attempts, even to the present day, to mine or, more commonly, to claim the land under the guise of mining it. Happily these attempts have all either failed or been thwarted by a resolute citizenry.

Gold has been known to exist in the area since early days, but it took a trained geologist to estimate the extent of the valley's gold deposits. For years many other geologists have been probing and drilling in and around Jackson Hole in their incessant search for oil and natural gas. There seem to be few altruistic geologists. The great things they have taught us about our planet are often just extraneous facts picked up during their quest for riches.

Still, it must be thrilling for a geologist to be able to look at cliffs, and peaks, and even mute little pebbles and understand how the surrounding landscape was formed. One of the small but really intriguing things I learned in Jackson Hole occurred on a Park Service nature walk. The site was Blacktail Butte, a curious formation rising from the valley floor due east of Moose. A cold, raw wind was blowing that morning, and it held the number of hikers to two, plus the ranger-naturalist, who turned out to be an attractive, blond girl in her early twenties.

Connie Meyers was her name, and despite the really unpleasant weather she resolutely led her other charge and me
to the top of the butte. On the way we turned off the trail and
walked over the rough ground to a grayish outcropping of
rock, about the size of a large coffee table. On the side of this
rock were some cylindrical things an inch or so long and
joined together in a sort of honeycomb. It looked like petrified grouse crap to me, but I kept that thought to myself while
Miss Meyers explained that it was organ-pipe coral—or, rather,
a petrifaction of what had once been organ-pipe coral under
an ancient sea. I found the idea of an ancient sea covering
Jackson Hole so fascinating that whenever I have gone back
to Blacktail Butte I have walked over to see that coral again. It
is a sort of touchstone in the midst of an eternity I do not begin
to comprehend.

This lack of comprehension was developed in college, where
the geology professor's usual lot was that, in explaining his
subject to me, he ossified my brains and petrified my butt.
How I used to ache and yearn for those interminable lectures
to end.

I once had a geology professor who, on field trips to a particular canyon, broke away from his newest class and crying,
"Oh! God! I can't stand it any longer!" would leap into the
abyss. His classes would barely have time to react to this with
their mixture of fright and sadistic delight when their professor's shiny, bald head would pop up from behind the edge
of the brink over which it had so recently disappeared. Then
the gleeful little man would clamber up and launch himself
into a geologic moral about knowing what to expect although
we couldn't see it at the moment. I learned to expect that the
professor's hidden ledge below the rim would one day erode
away, but I also was taught to expect it not to happen soon
enough to save me from the man's class.

My feelings about geologists help to explain the reluctance
with which I decided to attend a park naturalist's lecture on
Teton geology at the Jenny Lake Amphitheater. And I only
attended this particular lecture because I had gone on an es-

pecially enjoyable nature hike with the speaker, Don Ester. Like most park employees, Ester only had a seasonal job at Grand Teton. During most of the year he teaches at a college in northern California. And I suspect that the coeds flock to his lectures because he is not only a charming man but a handsome one, too. He looks something like Milton Caniff's comic strip hero, Flip Corkin, in a Smokey the Bear hat.

While people filed in and arranged themselves on the low wooden benches, Don built the traditional bonfire at one side of the amphitheater's pit. By the time the first flames subsided an audience had assembled, and it was dark enough to begin the slide-illustrated lecture. There was reason in Don's words, and the reason cemented the facts both shown and spoken into a brief but enthralling experience.

For the first time I got a clear idea of how the Tetons, still dimly outlined in the dark sky above, got there. And Ester told the story in such a way as to make his audience care—even about such complicated things as radioactive "clocks." By the use of these instruments scientists are able to determine with considerable accuracy the age of various kinds of rocks. The theory is simple enough: certain elements decay in time to form new elements. This decaying time is constant, so by calculating what's left of an element in a mineral crystal against the decay materials it has produced, the age of the crystal may be estimated. It's like knowing that a man with a hammer can break a certain-sized rock into gravel in an hour. If he's found with half the rock and some gravel it's obvious he's been working half an hour. In the same way, but over millions of years, uranium decays and becomes lead and potassium turns into argon. Carbon 14 becomes nitrogen in about forty thousand years, thus providing a sort of decimal system for the seven-league boots of the other radioactive clocks. The point of it all is to derive a starting point from which the various types of rock in a formation may be aged and then mapped throughout the area.

Much of the rock in the ruggedest part of the Tetons is granitic. It isn't granite exactly; rather the rocks are gneisses and shists, hard, noncrumbling rocks that mountaineers find the safest to climb. The granitic rocks of the Tetons have been estimated to be from two and one-half to three billion years old. These are the ancient ones, the rocks by which others are appraised. For instance, rock containing fossils must be much younger than the granite stone because the earth revolved many times before any life occurred that could later be fossilized.

Geology takes on considerably more life if you get into the mountains and see it for yourself. For example, here are some notes from a trip to the treeless summit of Rendezvous Peak via the Teton Village overhead tram: "After some waiting, Ranger Don Ester led us aboard the tram for our $2 ride to the top . . . I noted that the car—a standing-room-only conveyance carrying up to 62 passengers—had been made in Switzerland. It runs rather smoothly except for a mild upward and downward roll as it passes each of the five suspension towers. I could not help thinking that we were not far enough off the ground to cause instant death in case of a crash.

"At one point the motorman announced that we were hanging on the world's longest stretch, one mile, of unsupported cable. I was impressed, but not in the way I was supposed to be impressed. The safety features apparently consisted of a short ladder for reaching the car's roof and a couple of radios. The fellow who seemed to be in charge in the glassed-in control house on the ground didn't appear to me to be any more skillful than the average streetcar conductor.

"The boy said the tram operated until the outdoor wind speed exceeded 45 mph. The speed of the car itself was 11 mph, and it seemed an eternity to me before we reached a rather hesitant landing at the platform on the mountaintop. I did not enjoy the ride a bit. At one point a great, monstrous rock wall looms in front of the car, and it does not seem possible that the struggling car can clear it. At this place the car is at its highest point off the ground—over 300 feet— enough, I thought, to ensure a quick death.

"The supporting towers are enormous, ugly red structures,

and they detract materially from the appearance of the mountain.

"It was very cold on the barren mountaintop, an icy wind was blowing that cut easily through my down vest and set me shivering. The view of the surrounding area was good, but this point does not offer the best view of the Teton peaks.

"We started down the trail, a new rough one . . . The area was wide-open alpine canyon country with typically barren ridges and mountaintops all around. We descended the long switchbacks to a cirque where Ester stopped to explain the ice ages—a glacier having been 'born' in this cirque . . .

"At this cirque (about 10,000 feet high) there was much sedimentary rock that contained fossils. There was coral and also brachiopods (shells) and crinoids, organisms that floated in the water like pond lilies but were animal rather than vegetable. The brachiopod lives in warm, shallow, salt seas. It is an important part of a geological record here that goes back about 600 million years."

A few nights later, at Jenny Lake, Ester explained how marine fossils got to the top of the Tetons. The rock in the Tetons' crags is very old, but the mountains themselves are comparatively young, much younger than the Rocky Mountains. The Tetons were formed about ten million years ago, yesterday in geologic time, but of rocks that were already more than two billion years old. These old rocks had been covered in past ages by ancient seas, lakes, and even tropical jungles. We were told how, when the Tetons rose, some of the fossilized rocks rose with them, piggyback. Young molten rock invaded the older rock and solidified as whitish, intruded stripes or as dark dikes, such as the one rising on the side of Mount Moran.

Geologists theorize that volcanic activity beneath the present site of the Tetons resulted in the flow of vast quantities of lava northward. This outward flow created an imbalance in the earth's crust and set the stage for faulting—the action that creates mountains. The Teton and Gros Ventre ranges began to rise, while the area that is now Jackson Hole started sinking.

The Tetons probably rose to well over twenty thousand feet. In fact, they are still rising at the general rate of one foot every five hundred years. Small earthquakes tremble throughout the mountains almost every day, and occasionally a big jolt such as the 1959 Yellowstone quake occurs to emphasize this internal movement.

As the mountains rose they carried with them the marine fossils that had once lived on the shores of ancient seas. But, as graphically illustrated in Ester's talk, the Tetons rose as vast rounded mounds—and they probably looked a lot more like *tetons* then than they do today. Then, some two hundred thousand years ago, the first of what were to be three glacial periods began in Jackson Hole. After the first subsided with returning warmth, another began some eighty-five thousand years ago and still another occurred just ten thousand years ago. This one was so "recent" that primitive men may have seen the last of it.

Some of the most dramatic of Ester's slides demonstrated how ice formed on the once-round Tetons and then, through freezing and thawing, carved the pinnacles we see today.

Huge glaciers filled Jackson Hole with hundreds of feet of ice and ice-borne rock. They also carved the rounded canyons, scoured the valley floor, and streamlined its buttes as the glaciers flowed south past them. If you get up high on the slopes of the Tetons you can see how the buttes in the valley below have been worn into slim, vessel-like shapes by the ice grinding along their sides. The buttes survived as mute monuments to the passage of the ice, and they clearly show which way it passed.

As the glaciers receded from the canyons they left behind amphitheater-like cirques at the bases of the high peaks. There are still some small glaciers reclining in little cirques high up in the Tetons. When these, and other, glaciers began to melt and then recede they left behind moraines, huge windrows of rubble and boulders, that mark the limits of their progress. Most of the present lowland lakes are surrounded by these moraines, and, indeed, the lakes are offspring of the old glaciers.

Part of the evidence of succeeding ice ages is in the "hanging" canyons of the Tetons. Cascade Canyon, straight west from Jenny Lake, has the typical U shape of a glaciated canyon. But its mouth does not open out onto the valley floor. It was cut off, leaving the upper end of the canyon hanging hundreds of feet up on the mountainside. This surgery was done by a later glacier that moved along the Teton face and ground away what had been the lower end of Cascade Canyon.

The glaciers have left some softer-looking tracks, too. One day I hiked to the top of a low ridge on the Gros Ventre side of the valley. From it I had a super view of Jackson Lake and the strangely dimpled plain that lies southeast of it. This sage-covered area is called the Potholes. From a distance it looks like an old-fashioned quilt. Each quilted dimple in it is where a great block of glacial ice was buried by debris at the time of glacial retreat. When these buried blocks finally melted, the ground where they had been was left pockmarked.

The ridge I was on is near Spread Creek, not too far from Moran Junction. Spread Creek is unusual in that it runs over a gravelly flat, sending its bright streamers of water here and there all over the wide creek bottom. It is a stream so new that it has not yet had time to cut itself a channel. When you approach Spread Creek from the north you must go *up*hill to cross it. The same is true of the Gros Ventre River; you drive uphill from the town of Jackson to reach the Gros Ventre.

Even the old Snake River, whose meanders through Jackson Hole have already been mentioned, does not yet run through the lowest part of the valley. It is slowly working its way west toward the Tetons and the lowest part of Jackson Hole. The highway bridge over the Snake near Wilson is higher than the community itself. A secondary purpose of the irrigation dam on Jackson Lake is to curtail flooding around Wilson. The river has also been diked to at least slow its inexorable march to the mountains.

At one time my wife and I considered buying some meadow land in the Wilson area. Hearing of it, a friend who lives in Jackson chided us that the land would probably be washed away in five hundred years. My personal intimations of immortality were not strong enough to be affected, although the knowledge has made me feel better about all the trailer houses that are being installed near Wilson.

And the Gros Ventre Range has long been a spectacular refutation of the old sermonizer's intonations about being "in the shadow of the everlasting hills." In a small collection called *Old Time Stories* in the Coe Library's Pioneer Archives is this one:

"Mr. S. N. Leek tells of a startling experience which happened to him several years ago when he was guiding a pack outfit in the Eastern Highlands. The country was familiar to him . . . But suddenly confronting him was a great crack in the earth . . . worthy of being called a canyon. On previous visits . . . it had not been there.

"He made his way with some difficulty down into the crevice and so on along the bottom of it. Then, he said, on looking up he was horrified to see hundreds of tons of earth reaching out into space over his head. . . . He lost no time in getting out. . . .

"A year or so afterward . . . Mr. Leek decided to explore further. He went to the place where the earth was laid open in that great crack only to find that all trace of it had vanished."

Some of the reasons for this and the many earth slides or "slumps" along the highways in the Jackson area are the fine texture of the soil and shales, plus the pitch of the slopes where these finely textured materials are. In places thick layers of rock overlie very unstable substrata, and an increase in soil moisture turns this lower material into a greasy roller coaster. Road building and clear-cutting of timberlands speeds up the rate of the slides.

One fellow, caretaking on a remote estate deep in the Gros Ventre, was terrified by the nightly earthquakes that vibrated through his room. Not only did they move his bed around, but they made unsettling noises that "went bump in the night." These geological phenomena are said to have resulted in a high turnover in caretakers.

Understanding some of Jackson Hole's geology could help to allay such ignorant fears, but it could also help a person to develop some worse, real apprehensions. Over half the acreage of the Teton Forest has been rated as unstable. A lot of it is just waiting to tumble or slide away. People who plan to build in Jackson Hole would be wise to check the stability of the sites they select before going ahead.

This basic instability of the land may also clash with some staid, Anglo-Saxon notions of order. Because, while there is a natural order in Jackson Hole, there is also a great natural disorder. The deep, deep bedrock under the valley floor is the same primeval rock that shimmers regally at the top of the Grand Teton. In this respect the mountain is not unique. The whole area is strewn with bits and pieces of material of vastly varying ages. Blacktail Butte, for example, is a giant jigsaw puzzle of rock that geologists still do not completely understand. The round quartzite boulders that litter the floor of Jackson Hole were washed down some seventy million years ago from what is now Montana, and you can still see the bangs and bumps the trip left on the surface of many of them. They have persisted through all manner of cataclysms, and the camper who imperiously lobs one of them out of his campsite probably has no inkling of the utter and absurd feebleness of his manly effort.

I've known people who visit as many national parks as they can partially to lug a stone away from each one. When their back yard rock piles are large enough they seem prone to build fireplaces with them. Almost without exception their handiwork ends up as a gaudy and mismatched eyesore. And yet Jackson Hole, built much the same way, is a marvel.

*when an indan lookes in to my eye he
drops his eyes oh i wosh i could give
to the world my experance in indan
life . . .*

DIARY OF "BEAVER DICK" LEIGH

3 / The Snake Country

The great, geologic cataclysms have at least paused in Jackson Hole. It takes some imagination now to visualize the dim past when men may have squatted at the base of the Tetons and stared stupidly at the slowly retreating glaciers. Even the recent past, when travelers had to plan their tours with deference to hostile or mischievous Indians, is all but forgotten.

Now, in the summertime, in the commercial city of Idaho Falls, Idaho, you can see members of the Shoshone–Bannock tribe lying inert upon the park grass overlooking the Snake River. Lying beside them are equally inert wine bottles, partially concealed in brown-paper bags. Less than a hundred years ago the ancestors of these benighted people might have been found along a stream in Jackson Hole, leading very different lives. Indians are not particularly welcome there today. And no one, save the political candidates who pass routinely through the reservations once every four years, wonders much about the modern Indians' whopping suicide rate.

The recriminations and guilt pangs some white Americans are currently experiencing about our treatment of the Indians are not new. Some nineteenth-century Americans felt them even while the pogroms were going on. As a boy I saw the romantic and inaccurate painting of *The End of the Trail* on many living room walls. Even more homes displayed the Santa Fe Railroad's calendars, which featured noble portraits of Indians. We felt bad then, too. But in many respects what has been done to the Indians was simply a proof of a biological fact. A strong species is fated to destroy the weaker or less adaptable one almost in spite of itself.

The Indians' culture did not meet the norm expected by most whites coming to the frontier. Given flour to make into bread the ignorant Indians threw it into the air and watched delightedly as the white powder was carried off by the wind. When a frame house was built for the Shoshone chief, Washakie, he stabled his horse inside it and lived outside in a tipi.

Such behavior was incomprehensible to whites, who often acted with equal ignorance toward the Indians. Some bored pioneers shot the dirty, begging Shoshones from their covered wagons much as latter-day westerners blast highway signs as they pass them in cars. In the Jackson Hole country you occasionally still hear an old-timer revile some family by calling them, "that tribe." Younger people have no idea of the depths of loathing the epithet reaches in the mind of the speaker.

But given some time in the wilderness, many whites could at least temporarily adopt savage ways. While in Yellowstone Park prior to exploring in Jackson Hole in 1873, Capt. William A. Jones wrote, "Thursday, August 28th. At night the Indians in camp up the valley had a scalp dance over two Sioux scalps that had been given by the Crows to two of the Indians. . . . They invited everybody to join, which invitation was eagerly accepted by the young men of my party, the guides, packers, and soldiers. This dance gives everyone a chance to sing and yell with all his might and they literally made the welkin howl. There was considerable lung power in action. The waves of sound were echoed back and forth from the woods and hills on either side of the narrow, grassy valley and came billowing to the lake with a tremendous effect which was heightened by the lurid glare from the numerous campfires standing out in the darkness against the mass of black forest behind. The West Pointers in the party called it our '28th Hop.' "

Even the Mormons, who as a group treated the Indians a trifle more charitably than most other whites, discriminated against the savages, whom they called "Lamanites." The Saints taught that Indians were a degenerate remnant of the House of Israel, destined, at some future and unspecified date, to be lifted up from their fallen condition. And at such time as they are lifted up the Indians will become "a white and delightsome people."

While awaiting this elevation the Indians of the early West lived as they had always done. For recreation they broke all four of a dog's legs and then watched delightedly as he writhed in agony. They gambled endlessly, sold their women into whoredom, and made economic idols of their horses just as we do of our cars today. The Indians made warfare a way of life, sometimes counting coup, sometimes killing. When they killed their enemies, white and red, they mutilated the corpses; sometimes hacking out the genitals and stuffing them into their victims' mouths. This was often a calculated show of hatred, for the Indians believed that a person entered and resided in the next world in the condition in which he left this one. If this is so, the streets of Paradise have some very unusual-looking pedestrians walking along them.

The ferocious Blackfeet jabbed holes in their captives' wrists, shoved notched sticks tightly into the wounds and then sent these miserables stumbling into the wilderness with their hands fastened behind them. As a variation, the Blackfeet sometimes just hacked off a prisoner's hands and turned him loose.

The Indians killed their game any way they could, and the millennia of pain and dumb terror they perpetrated has scarcely been equaled by white North Americans. When game was plentiful the Indians slaughtered and wasted it just as whites later did. A Shoshone would kill a buffalo and trade its hide for three rifle cartridges—presumably using them to kill three more buffalo.

They ate liver raw and hot from a carcass, and, going one step further, Washakie, the remarkable leader of the Wind River Shoshones, is probably best known for killing a Crow enemy and then cutting out his heart to eat it raw. In later years Washakie would neither admit nor deny this story, but he never missed an opportunity to brag about the number of enemies he had killed. After he became too old to go to the wars himself, Washakie could generally be counted on to send his young bucks along with the cavalry when there was a chance of their participating in a genocidal campaign against old foes. The chief was also a polygamist, and probably a slaveholder, but he was also a realist of sorts, and this, plus his desire to get some of the things white men had, helped him to become a friend of the whites.

Washakie was born of mixed blood, Shoshone and Flathead, about 1802. Several people who saw him felt he also had some white forebears. His features did resemble the Anglo-Saxon, and in the surviving old group photographs Washakie stands out remarkably from his fellows. In one portrait, taken when he was quite old, the chief is a handsome, noble man.

As a youth, Washakie worked for both the Northwest and the American Fur Companies. He knew Jim Bridger and the other mountain men who were to become legendary. The Stone Age became the age of the Iron Horse all in his exceptional lifetime. Caught up in the great change, he was a man who could treat skillfully with the whites in councils and then trot pathetically behind their wagons begging for whiskey.

"Uncle Nick" Wilson, for whom the town of Wilson is named, was cajoled away from his pioneer home in Utah and lived for two years as a member of Washakie's band. According to Nick, the Indians treated him with great kindness, and Washakie became something of a mentor to the boy, one day crippling an elk and according young Nick the honor of finishing it off with his bow and arrows. Despite his powerful friend, there were members of the band, possibly Pocatello and his followers, who didn't like the white boy. It was only the watchfulness of Washakie and Nick's beloved "Indian mother" that kept him from being murdered.

During the time he lived with the Shoshones, Nick remembered hunting within sight of the "Hoary-Headed Fathers," the Indian name for the three majestic Teton peaks, and years later he returned to settle in Jackson Hole at the foot of Teton Pass.

Shortly after Nick left Washakie's band, the Indians met government officials at Fort Bridger, Utah Territory, to conclude a treaty. (Actually the Indians came to get "presents," for few of them understood much English, and treaties to them were nebulous things at best.)

But this treaty, made on July 2, 1863, was to have a vast effect on the Shoshone people—even to this day. For it made official record of what the Shoshones considered to be their land. Article IV of the treaty states: "It is understood the boundary of the Sho-Sho-nee country as defined and discribed [*sic*] by said nation is as follows [:] On the North by the Mountains on the north side of the Valley of Sho-Sho-nee or Snake River [,] On the East by the Wind River Mountains Punahpah the north fork of Platte or Koo chin a gah and the north Park or Buffalo House and on the south by the Yampah River and the Uintah Mountains [;] the Western boundary is left undefined there being no Sho-Sho-nee from that district of Country present but the Bands now present claim that their country is bounded on the West by Salt Lake."

This area comprised about twenty-nine thousand square miles in the Intermountain West. It took in varying amounts of what were to be the four states of Wyoming, Idaho, Utah, and Colorado. Jackson Hole was only a small part of the total, and, like other parts of the area defined by the Shoshones, it was not theirs exclusively. Jackson Hole was an unbelievably rich summer and fall hunting ground, and it attracted Blackfeet, Crows, Bannocks, Gros Ventres, and undoubtedly others during the hunting time.

Considering the Shoshones' mode of life, the huge area claimed by them in the treaty was not so ridiculously large. The Indians were hunters and root gatherers, and it took the produce of many square miles of mountain wilderness to feed and clothe just one of them. Basically they followed the game, but these wanderings were also governed by the dictates of warfare, superstition, mosquitoes, and the desire for trade.

The window by which I sit writing looks out upon an old Indian hunting ground. Some of my neighbors still remember when Shoshones or their allies came here to camp by the streams every summer. Most of the large game had been exterminated or driven into the mountains by that time, so the Indians were often reduced to eating the abundant Uinta ground squirrels. In earlier times Indian boys had learned to use their bows and arrows by hunting these cute little animals. Today they are often poisoned as pests.

The Indian people who came here traveled as families, not members of a tribe. Families banded together and often looked to men like Washakie for a kind of leadership, but there was no civic organization as we know it. The Shoshones were a people in the course of change. They sprang from the desert-dwelling "Digger" Indians, whose tribal organization never developed beyond the family level. Around 1700 some of these Indians started moving eastward from their ancestral Great Basin. Soon afterward they began to acquire horses, acquisitions that immediately opened up tremendous new opportunities and ways of life.

The Shoshones rode their horses north into Blackfoot country only to learn, to their sorrow, that, while the Blackfeet lacked horses, they had guns. For their lack of firepower the Shoshones were forced south, into the apparently inhospitable mountains where the first whites met them.

It was these same whites who first called them the Snake Indians. And the river that bears the name probably was named for the Indian tribe rather than for its sinuous route. The name, Snake, has several possible derivations. It may come from the tribe's fame as expert basket weavers, or it may have derived from the weaving motion of the hand, which identified the basket makers in sign language. Some Snakes identified themselves with a sinuous mark painted on their lodges. And, many years ago, when Blackfoot hunters found a group of their fellows massacred they knew instantly who the killers were because each corpse was marked with a snake's head.

The Blackfeet, incidentally, may have drawn their name from a time when their people were forced to march west over miles of burned prairie to their new base in the Northwest. It has also been suggested that they wore black moccasins.

The name "Shoshone" may refer to the Indians' place of abode in the high mountains. It has also been suggested that "Shoshone," the exact meaning of which has been lost, is a name of contempt given them by the hated Sioux. The Sioux were lords of the plains, and their ferociousness encouraged the weaker Shoshones to keep to their mountains.

Groups of Gros Ventre Indians, often allies of the Blackfeet, used to travel through Jackson Hole on their way to trade. Many of them probably traveled up the river that now bears their name. It is of French origin, and translates as "big bellies" or "big guts." Since it's unlikely that these active hunters and fighters all had big stomachs, the name probably has a different origin. It may have come from sign language, since the sign for the Gros Ventres was a gesture in front of the stomach—which may itself have derived from the Gros Ventre reputation of being "always hungry." The Gros Ventres are also said to have painted their stomachs, thereby emphasizing this portion of their anatomy. The big-bellied Indian of today's West is the product of brewers and the poor diet associated with reservation life.

While a few individuals like W. C. "Slim" Lawrence have made extensive collections of Indian artifacts found in Jackson Hole, no real effort has yet been made by universities or the government to study Indian life there. While we were on a summer trail ride in the Gros Ventre Mountains, guide and dude-wrangler Bruce Johnson found a very curious "arrowhead." It was short, and lacked an arrowhead's characteristic long, tapering shape. Although this point was chipped from obsidian, it markedly resembles flint points characteristic of northern Africa and it also has characteristics of an atlatl point. This primitive weapon, known to have been used in prehistoric Wyoming, predates the bow and arrow by thousands of years.

Finds like Bruce's and some curious rock structures high in the mountains around Jackson Hole have made some people reconsider the Indian history of Jackson Hole. Until recently it had been assumed that no Indians lived there year round. But now it has been theorized that Sheep Eaters, shy and very primitive relatives of the Shoshones, may have lived year round near Jackson Hole. They did live in Yellowstone Park, often in squat, little conical huts concealed in the most remote areas. These Indians depended heavily on bighorn sheep, which at one time were abundant in the Jackson–Yellowstone area. As a defense against their enemies, the Yellowstone Sheep Eaters would sometimes cringe beside boiling, spouting hot springs in the hope the phenomenon would frighten away the attackers.

When Capt. William Jones led the army exploration party through the northern reaches of Jackson Hole in 1873 his only competent guide was a Sheep Eater. This Indian knew the way from the upper Yellowstone River, down Pacific, then Lava, creeks to the present vicinity of Moran Junction. Moreover, he knew that the rest of the party did not know the route and tried to make the most of it. One morning, when the somewhat bewildered expedition was ready for the day's march, they found their guide had gone off to trap beaver. Before he got the Indian's cooperation Jones had to threaten to put him in the Camp Brown jail.

Richard "Beaver Dick" Leigh was one of the last whites to live among "wild" Indians and to make a record of their actions and his reactions. His diary, "dyra" as he spelled it, was started at the suggestion of some of the explorers and prominent men he had guided in the Tetons and Jackson Hole. The diary's chronology is a bit hazy, but seems to cover some of the time between 1873 and 1879. The spelling is fun to read, but I have added some punctuation.

At the time of his first entries Dick was living with his Shoshone wife, Jenny, and six children in Teton Basin on the west side of the Teton range. Dick's wife, Jenny, or "Jinny" as he wrote it, followed many of her native ways. On August 27, Dick wrote, "when i returned to camp Jinny and the childrn ad thare horses sadled ready to cros the river to dig yamp." Yampa was one of the several plants whose roots the Indians dug and cooked. When whites drove cattle onto the Indians' root-digging grounds it was yet another step toward the Indians' starvation. One day, after Dick had passed his children at work, he wrote, "they wer digging away like good fellows." He was a hunter and trapper, never deigning to pitch in and help dig roots.

Shortly thereafter Dick went on another hunt and wrote, "the indans cam a longe. i talked with them. they ware sho-shones [h]unting elk and deer but was making very poor work of it. thay ad Killed 2 deer and no elk and ad beene out 6 weeks. i set 3 traps hear and 3 more at camp. the indans went on below."

On June 8 of the following year Dick was on an extended hunt with his son, Dick, Jr. They had visited two camps of Indians on Strawberry Creek to get information about trapping. Dick noted, "the indans ad run the elk and scaterd them . . ." In early days elk were sometimes run on horseback much the way buffalo were run. Often, too, just the elks' hide was sought.

Later in the summer Dick came down from the mountains to a cabin he had previously built on a bend of the Teton River. On August 17 he wrote, "2 lodges of Banock indans, the hunfry famlys, came and camped with me. thay were weeping and waling the los of humpys Brother that the white men ad Killed wile in the act of steeling horses on the other side of the range 12 days ago."

This "range" could mean the Teton Range, but, considering the date of settlement in Jackson Hole, it was more likely north, in Montana.

Two days later, "Dick Juner traded his Black Pilley [filley] to humpry for a large rone mare and cot [colt] that ad belonged to his Brother that was Killed. i crosed the indans the river with the Boat. thay are on thare wa[y] to Boysa [Boise] river. the father and mother say thay will not stop in this cuntry eny longer [——] supershishon [superstition]."

More Indians wanted Dick to ferry them across the river on August 24. "thare was allso 4 indans at my cabing wanting me to cros them in my boat. the indans that was out hunting the teton range as got a big scair. and thay say thare is war parteys of suex indans in the range and it is making these indans go for the reserve in duble quick. . . ."

At this time the Sioux were indeed on the warpath. They either had just, or were about to, annihilate Custer and his command at the Little Big Horn. Dick's Indian visitors were almost certainly correct about Sioux war parties being in the Tetons.

On October 2 Dick noted, "some indans came hear. thay had shot a Boflo Bull, Braking his hind leg . . . he came down hear and crosed to the west side of the river; the indan hunters crosed this eavening to hunt him up. this is the first Buflo that as been seene since the spring of 1871."

In the fall Indians who had been hunting in the Jackson Hole country began passing by Dick's cabin headed for the "resirve" and anticipated government handouts. Since the extirpation of the buffalo, this was becoming an increasingly familiar trek throughout the Indians' West. Dick noted, "the indans left hear for the resirve. i caught 2 Beaver."

With the approach of winter Dick moved his family to an old cabin of his near the mouth of the Teton River. Jenny was pregnant, and her time was not far off. While the family was moving, the Indian wife of the Bannock, Humpy, came to them begging food for herself and her three-year-old daughter. The Leighs gave her some food and blankets. The woman later told Jenny that "Humpy's father had died and his mother ad broke out in the face with little bumps."

The miserable woman was sent away, but again returned. Dick told her, "to go away. she sade she was heavy with child and could not wak so i tol my wife to gie hur our lodge [tipi] and some provishons and let hur camp in the bushis."

Since Humpy's wife had not been around her family for several days, Dick assumed her illness was only a part of her pregnancy. Nevertheless he told Jenny and his children to stay out of the sick woman's lodge. Then, after a day's hunt, "we mey [met] my wife and the rest of my famley coming to meat us. i knew what was the mater as soone as i saw them—the indan womon was dead.

"i asked my wife to take the little indan girle to the house and wash and clene it. she sade not do [to] do it, something told hur the child wold die. but at my request she took it to the house and clened it up. it played with my childron for 4 days as lively as could be and that night it broke out all over with little red spots . . ."

The little red spots were the scourge of the Indians, smallpox. Dick's whole family died of it during his sorrowful Christmas of 1876.

Dick did not completely escape himself. He was heartsick and ill for some time and finally wrote, "if i get no better i shall start downe to black foot crk. on the 30th if i am able. then i will knowe what the indans are doing and what i can depend on. [The Bannock Indian War was brewing.] i ave sene no indans since i was downe las Jenury. thay are not coming up this way to hun[t] as usual—not yet."

At this period in the West many Indians seemed to rely on white charity during the winter in order to fight it all summer. It kept the army busy, as Dick noted on June 16th; "Johnson told me thare ad [been?] thre compneys of cavelry gon to be statoned at the lerri [Lemhi?] resoure [reserve] on salmon river and he tels me thare is no indans around this year at all. but plenty as pased on by, going to salmon rever. he also say thay are ver sulon [sullen]. thay ave got no trade this year and the store keepers can not help but notice this fact. the troops going to Salmon may put a stop for the presant to thare intencons [intentions] for thare intencons are hostile. i am surtin of this from former experince that i ave.

"but thare is plenty others tht trustes they [them] yet and will not be made to think thay do eny damage. it is this class of whites that does the most damage amongst the indans and when and out brake comes thay are the one that genrly gets worst of the out brake. i am well prepard ever since thae first brake las year. i keep my 2 guns in good order and 2 hundred rounds of amuniton alwise in resirve . . .''

The Bannock War did not touch Dick; as he says early in July of 1878, "the hostile indans are doing thare fighteng from 3 to 4 hundred miles west of us but the las new[s] was thay were turning north. we may ave to take the field yet."

Despite a hint of gleeful anticipation of an Indian battle Dick did not have to take the field except to hunt. On August 8 he wrote, "i saw a big smoke 7 to 8 miles north of me at the mouth of the midle fork. the snk [smoke?] is about half way north to were the nispercys [Nez Percés] went last year." Dick refers to the year 1877, when Looking Glass, White Bird, and Chief Joseph made their fighting retreat toward Canada.

Dick found that the fire had been carelessly set by whites. It burned over a hundred miles "of cuntry . . . and still a burn-ing. . . ."

The Indians often set such fires both to burn off old grass and to force game out of the timber and into the open. In 1879 a huge fire burned all summer in the Jackson Hole area, shrouding the valley in smoke. The Indians were roundly damned for burning the forests, but it has been shown recently that forest fires can be beneficial, even necessary, to the life of forest land. To this end a controlled burning program has been recommended for certain forest areas in Grand Teton National Park.

Dick's diary returns to the subject of Indians on August 25: "wile fixeing up some fur to take to the sand Hole store my old Banock frend came to my lodge. he was the 2nd big dog in the out brake this year with the indans. he had got enugh fighting and came here until the tribe suranderd or got away. i made him leave his bow and arows 300 yards from my lodge. we had a big talk. i got all the news of the war and were the banocks was and what thair intencons were witch was not very flatering for me. we wnt back to the camp that he had left his wife and daughter at; goshas's camp, 8 women and 2 men had a pass from the agent at Salmon river—not right. [Apparently Dick felt the Indians should not have been allowed to leave their reservation.] he told me i most [must] not go to the mountins; where i should ave beene in 2 days mor if i had not seen him."

The next day Dick wrote, "went up to the camp to be shure that i was not being deceved. PPAMA and famly came and campd with me."

On August 28 Dick noted, "drove up to the house, aveing the indons drive all my horses up." The next day he "sent them to the head of canon crk to camp and to spye for me."

Dick's selection of a recently hostile Indian as his sentinel seems odd, but his trust was apparently well placed. He wrote on September 4, "i went to John Adms to post a letter to the agency. the indans ar steeling horses on the road from Bannock cy, Montana to the sand hole staton. 1 cayale troop went up the rod [road] on the 2nd. they alwis go the rong way to catch them much. it apers thay alwis ame to get in rear of the indans."

The contemporary explanation the army gave for the way its troops were moved was, according to the explorer, Capt. William Jones, "The obvious mode of getting at these Indians after their presence has been made known in the usual manner by some depredations is to move the troops with the utmost celerity to some point near the junction or convergence of these lines . . . and there throw out an efficient line of signal pickets. By this means if they do not reach their objective point in advance of the escaping Indians they would not be unlikely to stumble over them on the way. Indians travel over the country guiding themselves by prominent or noticeable landmarks, and when these are not sufficient they build piles of stones on a hill or in a doubtful pass. As a consequence their trails of general travel almost of necessity must converge or diverge near these points. . . . These are really strategic points in Indian warfare because the most difficult part is to get at the Indian. . ."

All this could more usefully have been shortened to "They went thataway," and "Cut 'em off at the pass."

On September 5, 1878 Dick wrote, "came to camp and found a Mr Watson thare with a lettr from Major Donlson, the agent. i was to go north on the midle and north fork to examin the rivers and timber with watson. the indans is scatrd thrue the timber hunting elk, so i signald for my spy and he told me it was not safe to go. i sent him back to his post and made my mind up to go with mr watson as he was so onsus [anxious]. so i moved everything [a cache of belongings] back to the house on the 11th and wrote to Mager donlson . . . explaining the danger we were going into."

As Dick crossed the river, he "saw an indan coming up the river. i aproched him until our horses nec[k]s loped [lapped] then questioned him. i saw what he was, but i did not let him see it by word or acton. wile i was talking i saw a long string of others coming ½ mile off. the indan turned back to his party. we cept [kept] the trale when to within a quarter [mile] of them thay turned out of the trale to the river bank, when we got opesite them i told watson at go slowly untill he got over the rase of ground out of sight, then to go as fast as the horse wold cary him to adoms.

"when we parted i road toward the indans; 9 of the Bucks dismounted and wolked about 200 yards towrds me. i knew what that ment. there was other warers [warriors] seting on thare horses with the woman that did not want me to see thare fases. i set on my horse and talked a wille. . . . when i was satisfide that watson was out of reach . . . i bid them goodby. . . ."

A lone white man meeting a band of Indians at that time was very fortunate to get away without at least being robbed. Dick must have had a considerable standing among the Indians. Nevertheless, his Indian worries continued, for he wrote, "old bending bow [a rifle whose barrel had been bent over the head of an obstreperous horse] and 80 rounds of cartriges as been my Bed fellow for the last 2 months; acompanys [accompanied] with my old hunting Knife. but wether it will aveale me anyting remanes to be seene. my being all alone makes it hard on me somtimes for want of sleep . . . living in advance of settlements and avend [having] to watch and protect the covering to my head. but i have the pleshur of knowing that i ave led the setlements on snake river."

Dick wrote on the twelfth, "my spy as not made his aperince yet, the hostile i met yesterday crossed the for[d] and pitched camp close to ware i had left my lodge pitched. i was on my look out at day light but saw nothing. it was very smoky. after brexvast i went up agane. i saw 4 indans coming a mile of[f]. i walked sesurly [leisurely] to the house and put myself in readyness. thay came withen 200 yards then caled my name. i sined for them to come up within a hundred yards. they dismounted, left ther horses and 3 of them le[f]t thare guns; only one of them armed came to the house i watched every move thay made. . . . we exhange news or strategam. . . . thay left for thare camp after 3 hours stay. for the first hour or so my mond [mind] was not as easy as it might ave beene but i did not allw them to see it.

"mr Watson got back a 12 Oclock from posting letters and fetched me word the indans atached [attacked] a stage staton at birch crk wonding the driver and stock tender and steeling the horses. thay split them in small band[s] and are gathring in my vercinaty. this indans that was here today are a part of them. . . . wither we will get cler or loose our hair remanes to be seene in the next 3 days. i ave to depend on my farmer [former] experience nie [now]. i ave not beene in as tight a place since 1863."

Dick's unexplained reference to 1863 may mean the Battle of Bear River. It was the only major action against the Indians that year in which Dick might logically have participated. General Conner, with superior forces, made an early morning, surprise attack on a mixed band of Piutes, Shoshones, and Bannocks in their winter camp on Bear River. Many of the band of three hundred Indians were killed. The soldiers burned seventy lodges and destroyed or confiscated the Indians' food and tools. One of the Indians who escaped was said to be Pocatello. He, remember, was the dissident Shoshone who had wanted to kill Nick Wilson when Nick lived with Washakie's band.

Beaver Dick took good care of his hair for many more years. He remarried, choosing another Indian girl, who bore him four more children before he died in bed in 1899. One daughter, Rose Koops, is still living (1971) in Idaho.

Aside from occasional lapses, the Shoshones have a long record of nonviolence toward whites. Partly because of Chief Washakie, and partly because of their lack of tribal organization, they bent rather easily to white wishes. They moved onto their Wind River Reservation soon after making the treaty of 1868. But since they had been given the right to hunt and fish on "unoccupied government lands," they continued to travel into Jackson Hole.

But the people who believed that the world had been discovered by a chickadee were no longer free, not even in spiritual things. By presidential edict all the western tribes were assigned to one or another of the Christian churches. This is how the Shoshones awoke one morning to find themselves Episcopalians.

Then an Indian agent on the Shoshone reservation decided he had a problem because his charges lacked surnames. He reported, "I took a census of over two thousand names and had them all changed, though it took over two years." We had their land, we subverted their culture—I think the chickadee story of creation is as good as the Bible's—and then we systematically destroyed the Indian identity of every Shoshone.

In 1878 whites again betrayed the Shoshones when landless Arapahos were summarily moved onto the Shoshone reservation. The Shoshones protested bitterly, since the Arapahos were legendary enemies. But the government was adamant, promising that the Arapahos were only there temporarily until suitable lands could be found for them. The Arapahos are still on the Wind River Reservation, and the tribes still live apart from one another.

Recently the federal government settled about fifteen million dollars on the Shoshone tribe as restitution for past wrongs. Some of this money was paid in cash to tribal members. It undoubtedly became a boon to white merchants, who were shown on local television doing great business with the newly rich Indians. The money may do certain Indians some lasting good, although we are still failing to remember that the Indians never accused us of taking their money. We took their land, and to an Indian that is a very different matter.

A highway over Togwotee Pass was completed in the summer of 1921 connecting Jackson Hole with Lander, Wyoming. As a gesture, the white dedication committee got old Dick Washakie, a Shoshone, to say a few words. These are the words: "In my early manhood many years ago I escorted some of your people, the white people, through this very pass, and at that time I felt a great honor in doing it. Remember, my friends, prior to this time, my people hunted and roamed free from one hunting ground to another without even being molested by your people. But since I escorted the Great White Father [President Chester A. Arthur] and all his officials from Washington many years ago, through this very pass,* my heart has grown sad. I have been told by your people that I must cease hunting. If I continue to hunt as I have in the past, I shall be put in jail. My people now at this time are hemmed in a small corral called a reservation and prohibited at almost every turn. My good heart feels sad if this may be the appreciation which my white brothers have bestowed upon my people. Upon the departure of the great government officials from Washington and my friends they said, 'Mr. Washakie, we thank you for what you have done for us' and I said, 'You are welcome.' "

* The old man seems to be confusing Union Pass, over which the Arthur party passed, with Togwotee Pass. He undoubtedly traveled both of them many times during his long life.

These were circumstances under which almost any man but an American hunter would have despaired.

JOHN BRADBURY,
Travels in the Interior of America,
1817

4 / John Colter

The Blackfeet were the only Indians who never rested in their violent efforts to stop American entry into the northern Rockies. From the time of Lewis and Clark to the end of the beaver boom, about thirty-five years, these people never missed an opportunity to kill Americans. Their ferocity probably was not based so much on a remarkable foresight as to their eventual fate as it was on simple savagery. The Blackfeet didn't like anyone, except the Gros Ventres, who were allies. And they only tolerated British fur traders, who weren't especially fond of Americans themselves. Between them the two tribes successfully thwarted American exploitation of their domain for many years. And it was not force of arms or diplomacy that eventually subdued the Blackfeet. It was smallpox.

The disease was spread to the Indians by traders for the British-owned fur companies. Lacking any clear idea of how the decimating disease reached them, the Blackfeet continued to trade with British firms. This fostered American complaints that it was the English who promoted Blackfoot hostility toward the Americans, complaints that probably had a basis in fact, for the English were naturally interested in holding and enlarging the lucrative markets they had developed among the northwestern tribes. The British, in the form of Peter

Skene Ogden, complained about the Snakes, and each side tended to ignore the other's laments. The British government was unmoved by it all, for England had a rich stake in the Northwest it did not want to lose. And, if the breaks of history had been slightly different, this book might have been entitled *McKenzie's Hole*.

The English traders undoubtedly took pains to point out to their Blackfoot customers that the Americans were busily arming the tribe's enemies—just about every Indian who wasn't a Blackfoot. It made the Blackfeet more unhappy, for what side has not historically needed this "just cause" to promote its wars?

The vicious Blackfeet hardly needed such an excuse. Lewis and Clark had been warned of this tribe's hostility, and, although they tried hard to avoid trouble, the only Indians they had to kill were Blackfeet. For a time these killings were blamed for all the Indian hostility that followed. Then, when it was discovered that John Colter, a former Lewis and Clark man, had helped the Crows in an 1808 battle against the Blackfeet, the blame was shifted to Colter. He did not deserve all of it, either.

John Colter may not deserve many of the things that have been credited to him. In Jackson's town square the citizens have placed a stone memorial to Colter for being the first white man to have entered their valley. A bay on Jackson Lake has been named for him, as has a canyon in the Teton Range. Colter has even been accorded the ultimate twentieth-century accolade of having a trailer park named for him. But what is known of John Colter must be weighed against the sources of this knowledge—the fragile and sometimes dubious chronicles of a very young country.

In 1806, while the Lewis and Clark expedition was making its rapid return to the United States, it met two beaver trappers on the headwaters of the Missouri. The men, Dixon and Hancock, were up from Illinois, and they quickly talked Colter into getting his discharge from the expedition in order to hunt beaver with them. (Apparently the members of the expedition were doing considerable trapping for themselves during this stage of their journey.)

Lewis and Clark gave Colter his release, along with enough supplies to equip him for a prolonged stay in the wilderness. Although from the *Journals* it is clear that Colter had proven a valuable crew member, from my own experience in the back-country manner of doing things I doubt that the expedition was releasing its very best man. In the scant retellings of his activities there is little evidence that Colter was a particularly wise man, though he must have possessed some native shrewdness. Going hunting with two total strangers in a wilderness is not an act of wisdom even today.

Apparently Colter found this out, for his partnership did not last very long. He soon went to work for Manuel Lisa, a speculating trader who, if alive today, would probably be subdividing wild lands and selling them by mail for low down payments.

In October of 1807 Lisa established a post he called Fort Raymond at the place where the Big Horn River enters the Yellowstone. Lisa then talked Colter into making a winter's goodwill junket to the Crows, who were believed to be in winter camps somewhere south of the new fort, in order to acquaint them with the new trading facility. This remarkable trip of Colter's has been food and drink to historians ever since. It is the trip on which he is said to have discovered Jackson Hole and Yellowstone Park.

Colter left no diary of this trip, but he apparently did describe it to his old boss, William Clark. When Colter returned to the States in 1810 he found Clark in Saint Louis, serving as the government's superintendent of Indian affairs. Clark kept a map in his office, and whenever someone like Colter returned from the mysterious West he was questioned in the hope that his answers could be used to improve the map.

This map, while never perfect, was made even more inaccurate by the cartographer, Samuel Lewis, before it was published in 1814. Nevertheless it purports to show Colter's 1807 route, and has been used as a major point of evidence in the claim that Colter saw Jackson Hole first.

This trip, remarkable regardless of its actual route, began when Colter left Fort Raymond in early November of 1807. He traveled in a southerly direction past the future site of Cody, Wyoming, to the head of Wind River. The consensus now is that he crossed the Gros Ventre Range by way of Union Pass and followed the main drainage down into Jackson Hole. Colter, traveling all the way on foot, crossed the valley to the ford near the present site of Wilson. He then crossed the Snake River, climbed Teton Pass, and went down into Pierre's Hole—today's Teton Basin. The next leg of his march led north through Teton Basin to a point somewhere east of present-day Ashton, Idaho, from where he recrossed the Teton Mountains. He came down Berry Creek on the eastern slope of the Tetons and then turned north toward Yellowstone Lake.

Colter is then supposed to have circuited the western side of Yellowstone Lake, forded the Yellowstone River below the falls, and gone on northeast, eventually returning to Fort Raymond. As described, this was a journey of over five hundred miles, and would have required many weeks or months to complete. Much of it was through country not usually frequented by friendly Indians, especially in the winter. Colter's exact route will never be known, but most of those who claim that he made the trip at all base their theories on three main bits of evidence.

The first bit is Clark's map. Then there is the Colter Stone, which was found in Teton Basin, and finally, a tree blaze supposed to have been discovered partway between Jackson and Yellowstone lakes.

The Colter Stone is a four-inch slab of rhyolite about thirteen inches high, resembling, from the side, a human face in profile. On one side is the date, *1808*, and on the other the name *John Colter* has been scratched. The stone was plowed out by a farmer breaking ground east of Tetonia, Idaho, in 1931. This farmer had never heard of John Colter but he kept the curious rock until a neighbor traded him a pair of old boots for it. This neighbor subsequently delivered the stone to employees at Grand Teton National Park. Fritiof Fryxell, a geologist with an excellent reputation, examined the stone in his capacity as a seasonal Park Service ranger. Fryxell decided the stone was authentic, basing his decision mainly on the weathering that had occurred on the worked parts of the stone but also upon the fact that a ledge of similar rhyolite existed near the site of the stone's discovery.

Historians have assumed that Colter had been forced to seek shelter, either from a storm or hostile Indians, and passed the time by embellishing the rock, which already bore a resemblance to a human profile.

The next piece of evidence of Colter's journey was the blazed pine tree found in the late 1880s by the historian, Phillip Ashton Rollins. Rollins was on a guided hunting trip at the time and found the blaze, as he claimed, "on the left side of Coulter Creek, some fifty feet from the water and about three quarters of a mile above the creek's mouth . . ."

Rollins had his guides clean away the accumulated pitch and dead bark from the blaze. Under it all they found a large X just above the initials *JC*. According to the story the two guides both thought the blaze was about eighty years old. And they further decided it would be unwise to cut the tree down in order to count its annual rings. The tree was supposed to have been cut down later by Yellowstone Park employees, who removed the section containing the blaze. This section was to be delivered to a museum in the park, but it never arrived and no record of its actual fate has ever been found.

The story of the blazed tree has always seemed pretty doubtful to me. Aubrey Haines has pointed out that cutting the tree down in order to preserve its blaze in a museum is an unlikely story, since no museum was even planned, let alone existed in Yellowstone at this time. Then, hiking and riding horseback over parts of Colter's purported routes has made me wonder if he had been in Jackson Hole at all.

The seeds of my doubts were planted one day when I

dropped into the Jackson Hole Museum. The museum is owned by W. C. "Slim" Lawrence, a long-time resident of the valley and an accepted authority on its history. He led me through his large collection, which contains everything from an outlaw's death mask to prehistoric stone cooking vessels.

Lawrence is especially fond of the fur trade and its history. "Have you seen Lewis's map of 1814?" he asked. We had stopped beside a set of hanging panels that display old photographs and documents. Lawrence quickly turned through them until he found the one containing a copy of the old map. I had seen it before, but it still left me with as confused an idea of Colter's true route as the map's makers must have had.

"Do you know," Lawrence asked me, "about the theory that John Colter never came to Jackson's Hole? That Brooks Lake over by Dubois has been mistaken for Jackson Lake?" I did not.

He went on to explain that Jackson Lake had been called Lake Biddle on the old map and also that it had been shown as draining east into the system of the Big Horn. Since Brooks Lake does drain to the east, it has been theorized that the two lakes have been confused. By using Brooks Lake as the western limit of Colter's trek, Slim Lawrence then traced a very plausible route for Colter through the area east of Jackson Hole.

Colter is supposed to have begun his journey alone, and with only a light pack on his back. Several accounts say the pack weighed thirty pounds, though none say who weighed it. In addition to items necessary to the barest sort of survival, Colter's pack must also have contained such small trade goods as awls, beads, vermilion, and fire steels. Small looking glasses were the fur trade's equivalent of our TV sets; the bucks gazed into them by the hour, and Colter probably carried a few. He would have needed such items both to impress the Indians and to trade to them for food.

It seems probable that Colter found the Indians' winter camps. Shoshones as well as Crows are known to have camped in the general area he set out to reach. Why, then, did these Indians, who knew Jackson Hole, not tell him that he would find no camps there in the winter? The Indians would have had to aim Colter, if not actually guide him, across the several mountain passes that lay ahead along his purported route. It is difficult to imagine why the Indians would have helped him on such a route when they knew there would be no trade, or food, along much of it. And since they would certainly have coveted his small store of trade goods, it seems doubtful that they would have let Colter go until they had it all.

The weather would have been another obstacle. In Teton County, which includes Jackson Hole and the western side of the Teton Range overlooking Teton Basin, the average December temperature is less than twenty degrees. The mean precipitation, which nearly always falls as snow in November and December, exceeds three and one half inches. This could easily amount to sixteen inches of snow, and while Colter might not have found this much on the valley floor in December he may well have found more than sixteen inches on the high passes. The Indians would have mentioned the potentially killing weather, and since Colter had already experienced a Rocky Mountain winter he is unlikely to have ignored the danger by taking only a light pack. December snow is often very different from the kind found later in the winter. It is a feathery fluff, and a man on snowshoes is only a little better off as he wallows through it than a man without the webs. I have spent two hours floundering, in Wyoming's downy December snow, in a meadow that I could have crossed in minutes on firmer January or February snow. To fight his way day after day in similar stuff would have exhausted even a John Colter. Combine this with the unrelenting savagery of a Jackson Hole winter, in which men still occasionally perish and are not found until spring, and you have an excellent case for keeping Colter out of the valley.

But there have been mild winters in Jackson Hole, so let's give the Colter legend the benefit of the doubt it merits and put him on the banks of the Snake River ready to climb

Teton Pass. The ford near Wilson has always been dangerous, even to men on horseback. And Colter was on foot. He would either have had to build a bullboat of hides, if elk or buffalo could be found to provide them, or he would have had to wade the stream. It does not freeze over. But even if it had been frozen it seems that a man whose life in the mountains depended upon following streams would remember that he had crossed a hell of a big river. There is no evidence on the old Lewis map to indicate such a recollection. Remember, Colter is thought to be the source of the information the map-makers used in showing the drainage of Lake Biddle.

Crossing the Tetons at Teton Pass, which is the historic route, is another memorable experience, particularly in winter. Colter seems to have been unimpressed by it, too.

Even if Colter did get across Teton Pass and down into the basin below there is increasing doubt that he carved on a stone while he was there. Colter was supposed to be traveling light, and for him to have risked his precious knife or hatchet by chipping with it against a rock is absurd. And only a fool would pound on a rock while hiding from Indians. Having been briefly snowed into a couple of modern wilderness camps, I spent some of my time cutting enough wood to stay warm and the rest of it relaxing after cutting that wood. I have never seen a competent outdoorsman pass the time by whittling on a rock.

With all respect to Dr. Fryxell, I don't think he or any other geologist can precisely date chipping on a rock. Although the finders of the stone were unaware of John Colter, there were many others passing through the area who were not. Several stones bearing the names of very early travelers, including William Clark's, have lately been turned up in the same general area where the Colter Stone was found. Clark was certainly never in the area, but, as Aubrey Haines points out, members of the Hayden Survey of 1872 were there. And some of these survey members were frolicsome young men who, wanting a lark, got on the expedition through political influence.

By itself the stone is a curiosity, for it is the only known item of this form of purported mountain-man art. Other stones have been found, perhaps genuine, bearing the names of early trappers, but none shows attempts at sculpture. For the present, at least, the Colter Stone is on display at the Park Service's Museum of the Fur Trade at Moose. The service does not insist upon the stone's authenticity, although the implication is there.

The blazed tree mentioned earlier is even flimsier evidence than the stone. Coulter Creek, named for the Hayden Survey's botanist J. M. Coulter, has undergone some cartographic revision since the Hayden Survey first mapped it. The mouth had been shown as emptying directly into the Snake River some distance below Heart Lake. More recently it has been shown to empty into Wolverine Creek, which, in turn, flows into the Snake. But Rollins probably is referring to a point three-quarters of a mile up the creek from Snake River. The terrain that far up Coulter Creek from Wolverine Creek is too rough for either idle tree blazing or idle blaze finding.

Had Colter been in the area it is conceivable that he might have traveled up the Snake River. But why he might have turned south, directly away from his supposed route, to carve his X on a tree is an unanswerable question. The trails in this area are sometimes just simple improvements on routes the Indians used. They generally follow the streams, especially when there are open meadows adjacent to the streams. It doesn't make sense that Colter would have darted off into the timber in the dead of winter to carve his initials.

During the late summer of 1971 my neighbor, Mike Hanson, who is a forest ranger, and I hiked along Coulter Creek from its mouth on Wolverine Creek to the lonely headwater area. It is a confusing, heavily timbered area, where map and compass are essential. In my notes for that day I wrote: "Up Coulter Creek to the mouth of Rodent Ck. then S.E. over ridge to Coulter Ck. again. Then up Coulter Ck. to a huge meadow near the head of the creek. If Mike hadn't been a veteran map reader I'd have had to walk much farther to get out, for the trail forks are obscure and unmarked. On some stretches there hasn't been any maintenance for years.

"As I wrote this a doe and her fawn came out of the timber across the meadow. Much of the route was through timber and uninteresting, although the meadow on Wolverine, beyond the bad section of trail, was beautiful and Coulter Ck. is a pretty stream, too, although we had to wade across it so many times my appreciation palled."

In Lieutenant Doane's journal of 1876 he describes the tremendous difficulty he and his men had traveling down Heart River to this Coulter Creek–Snake River area from Heart Lake. It is the sort of country in which a man given to wandering up lonely little creeks might lose himself forever. It is also the sort of place you travel through as quickly as possible without stopping to carve your name on the trees.

This portion of the Colter evidence grows even softer when you go into the area, much the same now as it was in 1807–1808, and look at the trees. It is lodgepole pine country, and, while the trees there today are probably not the ones Colter would have seen, the extent of the stands probably hasn't changed much. A striking thing about these trees is the multiplicity of old blazes throughout the stands. Very often the blazes are actually scars left by gnawing porcupines or even scratching bears, although they could just as easily be the scuffs caused by one tree falling against another. That Rollins could pick out an eighty-year-old blaze from all these other marks is, at least, remarkable. It becomes even more remarkable if you consider that blazes cut on trees by CCC boys thirty-five years ago are barely discernible today.

Rollins probably found the blaze, but in his enthusiasm to spread the Colter legend he conveniently neglected to consider that the botanist, John Merle Coulter, had collected in the area the summer of 1872. Botanists have more time for such handiwork than mountain men half lost in a snowy wilderness.

The Colter itinerary has been worked on and added to by many helpful tinkerers sitting comfortably in cavernous libraries and going over old maps. Many of them have never seen the country they've set Colter snowshoeing over, and they never seem to realize how easy it is to miss a mountain pass or to follow the wrong trail.

For example, here are some of my experiences while walking in a few of John Colter's purported footsteps on the eastern slope of the Tetons: "Got up before six. There was frost on my tent and it was chilly. Ate and packed up. Lady [my pack mare] began rearing, and I hobbled and snubbed her close to a tree. With some reassurance she calmed and I was able to pack her.

"Left the campsite about 8:25. It was a lovely cool, clear morning with heavy dew on the thick grass overgrowing the trail.

"Found an old, cut-off trail that shortened the distance to the Grassy Lake Trail. I made good time until shortly after leaving the Park Boundary. On the Forest Service section of the trail I took a wrong fork and was soon in a web of game trails that were thoroughly confusing. In one spot we struck a bad bog, and I went halfway to my knees in it. Lady lunged across, knocking me down and giving my right leg and foot a banging that I momentarily feared might have broken a bone.

"Presently I found a trail that had been blazed. I followed the blazes because, according to my compass, they tended north, but the trail eventually ended in the bottom of a boggy ravine. We struggled along the steep hillside parallel to it until we emerged and came upon what I concluded was Game Creek. . . . I followed the creek and in about ¾ths mile found the correct trail."

If he made his great trek across the northern end of Jackson Hole and into the Yellowstone, Colter was in this sort of country most of the way. Even with Indian guides it would have been a questionable trip.

Discounting the Colter legend makes the first white men likely to have entered Jackson Hole members of Andrew Henry's trapping expedition. Henry was a Missourian who in 1810 built a crude fort on what has become Henry's Fork of the Snake River. A beaver pelt was considerably more valuable in 1810 than it is in 1972, and the West's bountiful supply of these furbearers was a constant lure to an infinite number of poor Americans willing to risk their lives for. them. But, as Henry soon learned at his ill-fated post, beaver weren't all that easy to get. His trappers were so violently besieged by Blackfeet, grizzly bears, and horrible winter weather that the post had to be abandoned.

At least three of the defeated Henry men, John Hoback, Jacob Reznor, and Edward Robinson, made their way east through Jackson Hole in the spring of 1811. When they reached the Missouri River, a major artery of the fur trade, the men built a dugout canoe and began paddling downriver. Near the mouth of the Niobrara, by the present border of Nebraska and South Dakota, the trappers met a westbound party led by Wilson Price Hunt.

Hunt was traveling overland with a group that was to become famous as the Astorians. His destination was the fur-trading post John Jacob Astor was trying to establish on the mouth of the Columbia. While passing through Missouri, Hunt had met John Colter, whom he tried to enlist. Colter refused, but is supposed to have told Hunt something of what lay ahead. Nevertheless, it was on the advice and with the guidance of the three former Henry men that Hunt chose the overland route that was to lead him through Jackson Hole.

The Hunt party came down the Hoback River, as it was later named, and camped near its mouth on the Snake River. Here some members of the party suggested that they abandon their horses and float on down to Oregon in dugout canoes, but, fortunately for the party, their new guides talked them out of such a potentially disastrous float trip. After some rest and reconnoitering from their Hoback camp the party turned north, following the Snake into South Park. They crossed the meadows and eventually forded the Snake at the foot of Teton Pass. Some horrible miles and days lay ahead, because the Astorians eventually did try floating down the Snake to Oregon.

Their historic camp at the mouth of the Hoback has since

been subdivided, and a community has sprung up there. Some of the attractive ranch-type homes of which have been hidden by less handsome roadside businesses. The place itself is officially known as Hoback Junction, but the subdivider, W. P. Rogers, has also allowed it to be called Rogers' Point.

In keeping with the new conditions at Hunt's old camp, the trail signs have changed, too:

RIVERSIDE CABIN   BAR V

Fish, Hunt, Hike, Rest

VACANCY   MASTER CHARGE

FOUR AND ONE-HALF ACRE LOTS FOR SALE

W. P. ROGERS

WELCOME TO JACKSON HOLE—THE TETON MYSTERY

Bring your camera

Entertainment for young and old   one mile

TEXACO, BLOCK ICE 25 lbs. 75 Cents

Nearby is the

BALSAM ROOT GENERAL STORE

General Store   Fishing Licenses   Souvenirs

Picnic supplies   Fishing tackle   Ice—blocks/cubes

Bread   Milk   Meat and Fruit

Across the highway at the "POINT BAR" you are offered

Firecrackers, Fruit   Welcome as You Are   Amusement

Cherries, Peaches

Beside the Point Bar, like the second of a pair of buttocks, is the

LAZY S CORRAL   TRAVEL TRAILER PARK

Now Open

Welcome Overnighters

You can't miss it—even if you try.

Before he left Jackson Hole, Wilson Price Hunt detached four of his men to trap there that winter. They were Carson, St. Michel, Detaye, and Delaunay. These are the first whites known to have spent a winter in Jackson Hole. They might also be considered its first explorers, since they hunted along the streams. They made a good catch of beaver and left the valley via Teton Pass in the spring of 1812.

The four had hardly gone when another Astorian, Robert Stuart, entered Jackson Hole en route to Saint Louis from Astoria. The new post had been unsuccessful for a number of reasons, and Stuart was traveling east with a party of six in search of help. It was a journey, documented by the intelligent and well-educated Stuart, that more than matches the Colter legends. The party, trekking east over unknown territory, was alternately plagued by Indians, illness, starvation, and dissension. By the time they had left Jackson Hole via the Hoback route the men were ready to eat the first thing they saw. But they were not able to kill any game until they reached the Green, where they killed an old buffalo. Along much of their route the men saw numbers of antelope, but, although these diminutive animals were as much a staff of life in certain areas as were the buffalo, Stuart and his men didn't know how to hunt them. Time and again the fleet pronghorns skipped away like wind-blown snowflakes when the starving men tried to stalk them.

Stuart is credited with making the first overland trip to Saint Louis traveling from west to east and also with discovering South Pass. His journal is a classic, as fresh today as it was a hundred and sixty years ago.

Wilson Price Hunt's journal came into the possession of the writer Washington Irving, and was the basis for his *Astoria*. Irving's classic, if somewhat florid, account credits Hunt with naming the Tetons the Pilot Knobs. Pilots the peaks certainly were, but they are not knobs. And if that name choice is indicative of Hunt's imagination, it may be just as well that the more imaginative Irving wrote the explorer's books.

By the time (1819) that Donald McKenzie explored the Jackson Hole country for the Northwest Company, the prosaic Britons were calling the majestic peaks The Three Paps. Perhaps there is a genetic weakness in the Anglo-Saxon character that has doomed us to originating horrible place names. Even "Rogers' Point" isn't as ridiculously bad as "The Three Paps."

The British name for the great peaks must have repelled even the common trappers, for it did not prevail. To see the Tetons shining in the distance is thrilling even today, but, for the trappers who first saw them and realized that they had at long last reached their Golconda at the headwaters of the Snake, the sight must have verged upon the sublime.

I recall a day in late September when I was guiding an elk hunter southeast of Yellowstone Park in an area that is a two-day horseback ride from Jackson Hole. At the end of that day I noted, "Clear, cold morning. Ice crystals in the air were very beautiful as we rode down toward the bottom of the horse meadow.

"Hunter and I went up on saddle overlooking a great canyon. Began seeing elk on ridge across. Saw about 24 over there, 2 fair to good bulls. . . . Sun bright and warm in afternoon. From the ridge top I could see the Grand Teton."

By line of sight I was more than forty miles from the great mountain. Between us lay the Continental Divide, the wellspring for a thousand streams. My sense of awe has not diminished from that day. It has made me hope that, somewhere along his winter's march from Fort Raymond, John Colter had a chance to see the Tetons, too.

5 / *The Fur Hunters*

Very early in our history we Americans developed an attitude that fast became a habit. When we thought about the mountain West at all, we considered it as a place to get something to take back home. Today that something might range anywhere from a cheap souvenir to an elk's carcass or even a township strip-mined for its coal. All this taking began with the beaver.

Beaver are stupid animals, and easy to trap. Indirectly, this vulnerability explained much of nineteenth-century America's interest in the Rocky Mountains, because the sought-after beaver were already dwindling in the more accessible parts of the country. Trapping, almost to this day, has meant a second income or even a last-ditch way of making a living in the mountain West. With a little help anyone can learn to trap beaver. And so it was in earlier days, when the men who often became beaver trappers were those who could do nothing else.

Trapping was also a calling that once held out rich rewards —although it rarely paid them. To win these rewards, and also to emerge from the wilderness alive, the beaver hunters had to be ruthless. They made the West the cradle for a technique of "search and destroy." It worked so well in our own country that many of us were surprised recently when the same technique failed in Asia.

The beaver had no ability to resist. Nor did they have any sympathy from groups that today deplore killing animals for their pelts. Actually, the majority of Rocky Mountain beaver were killed for far less than their hides. The fur houses were not interested in beaver pelts so much as they were in the soft underfur that grew on the hide. Although it amounted to scant ounces on each animal, this fine fur was the material hatters needed for the felt to make their famous hats. The rest of the pelt was a by-product. The skin went to the gluemakers, and the outer fur was used to stuff upholstery.

Since there was no satisfactory method of removing and shipping the underfur alone, the whole pelt had to be sent east. This quest for underfur explains why trappers could keep working into the summer when fur was poor and also why the stretched and dried pelts retained their value after the rough handling they received in shipment.

The relative scarcity of beaver underfur, plus the time and skill necessary to form it into a hat, made the price of those hats historically high. Samuel Pepys paid over four pounds sterling for a beaver hat when they were the fashion in seventeenth-century London, and today a Stetson made of genuine beaver felt sells for a hundred dollars. Most fur-felt hats of beaver *quality* are actually made from rabbit fur. The beaver fur used now in hats comes from otherwise valueless kit pelts. For the pelts of these immature beaver the lowly trapper of today is paid a dollar or two.

Like his modern counterpart, the early beaver hunter customarily skinned his catch where he trapped it. Before he began that he would be careful to squeeze the few drops of beaver castor from glands near the anus. This was collected in a wooden bottle carried on a thong around the trapper's neck. Castor was smeared near future sets in hopes of luring other beaver into the waiting traps. There was also a small amount of trade in beaver castor, which was limited mostly by the tiny supply.

Beaver Dick Leigh wrote about enjoying a supper of the beaver he caught. Most of the earlier trappers, however, seemed to prefer the flesh from any of the larger game animals. Jedediah Smith left the impression that he enjoyed a nice young dog as much as anything. Beaver Dick also mentioned eating the legendary mountain man's delicacy, beaver tail. The only person I knew who tried eating one said it was a horrible, gluey mess. I have trapped a few beaver, but thought the tails looked too much like steamrollered snakes to be appetizing.

I admit to owning a pampered, twentieth-century appetite. Few of us have ever experienced the kind of bleak privation that once forced young men to join the fur brigades and enjoy such bizarre food. For many young men on the American frontiers, the unknown wilderness offered more than they had at home. Jim Bridger joined Ashley's brigade rather than be sentenced to a life of impoverished apprenticeship. Others who signed up were boozy bums and the diseased dregs of an uncharitable society. A few joined the brigades because they were adventurous romantics who eagerly responded to thrilling broadside advertisements headed, *For the Rocky Mountains!*

The realities they found were not always so exciting. After the failure of Henry's Fort on the Snake and the loss of Astoria to the British, the American fur trade in the northern Rockies fell into a slump that lasted ten years. A few fur traders like Manuel Lisa and the Chouteaus beat away at it, but the trade was moribund until the early 1820s.

It was at this time that William Ashley joined Andrew Henry in a fur-trading venture to the headwaters of the Missouri. Ashley was a different sort of man from most of his American predecessors. His successful approach was a mixture of shrewdness, sufficient capital, and hard work. Many of his competitors had hung on in the fur business by using cunning, greed, and someone else to do the hard work.

At one time or another Ashley had commanded militia, been a surveyor, a mine owner, and a manufacturer of gun powder. He had been the lieutenant governor of Missouri, and when he became less active in the fur trade he was elected to Congress. Ashley operated on the old American premise that what was good for Ashley would also be good for the country. He was a remarkable man—able and more honorable than most, but not altogether admirable.

His new partner, Andrew Henry, had seconded Ashley in the militia. His previous experience in the west dictated that he go first to the mountains while Ashley handled the firm's affairs in Saint Louis. But it was not long before Ashley followed Henry upriver in a keel boat—where his party of greenhorns was promptly given an almost decisive beating by the Arikara Indians. Ashley had the capital and credit to refit, and soon developed to perfection the techniques that were to make him rich.

He gave up trying to establish trading posts along the rivers and began instead to conduct his business in the mountains at what became known as "rendezvous." Goods were carried into the wilderness by pack string, later in wagons, and sold or traded at predetermined locations. None of these wild sprees was ever held in Jackson Hole, although the trappers did meet several times on either side of it—both on the Green and in Pierre's Hole.

One of the many interesting things about the fur trade as Ashley developed it was its dubious legality. The business grew up in an era that was often as confused as our own. Jackson Hole was probably included in the Louisiana Purchase, but when the sale was made the French were uncertain of the western boundary. Actually, the conditions under which France had acquired the vast area from Spain specified that the French were to retain it. But this provision was brushed aside, and the western boundary was placed at the Rocky Mountains—a decision that led to immediate problems with the English because such an indefinite boundary could be argued over for hundreds of miles. In 1819, however, the United States reached an amicable settlement with Great Britain concerning the line. American traders were permitted to cross over it, and they did so repeatedly, with little concern as to whose land produced the beaver. What mattered to both sides was who got to the beaver first.

To its credit, the American government had, since the administration of Washington, tried to regulate the fur trade in order to stop the exploitation of the Indians by unscrupulous traders. Government trading houses were established on the early frontier in an effort to open equitable trade with the tribes. Goods at these houses were exchanged for Indian fur at cost. Private fur traders were permitted to continue operations, but under government regulation. Like many other attempts at reform, however, this one didn't work very well. Great competition came from British firms. And because of their close ties to the manufactories of Europe, they were able to offer the Indians better goods at lower prices than could the Americans.

By the early 1820s, however, the various problems the United States had affecting the western fur trade were near enough solution that American traders could go out with a reasonable chance of success. Congress passed a law specifying that licenses to trade with the western Indians were henceforth to be issued only to American citizens. Coincidentally, the government's fur houses were allowed to collapse. This helped the private businessmen, even though the houses had already proved impractical for trading with the far-flung western tribes. When William Ashley, with his valuable political connections, applied for a government license of trade with the Indians, it was promptly granted.

Ashley never intended to rely on the Indian trade, however. Even though the government hoped to keep the Indians employed and usefully occupied providing the traders with fur, Ashley knew he would have to catch most of his own beaver; the western Indians had no conception of the technique of trapping. To get a beaver they built little catch pens in beaver runs or just tore open a lodge. They did not have spring traps, and without them there was no way they could supply the whites' demand for pelts. Also, the western tribes had never become particularly dependent on trade goods, so there was no overriding pressure on them to hunt for beaver. And rather than teach and encourage the Indians to trap, as the British sometimes did, the Americans did it themselves. Their supply of labor was not, as it was in the British case, the Indians, but the lower-class American.

Ashley's green crews had gone west, ostensibly to trade but actually to trap. Undoubtedly the men had lots of "wring-offs," and populated the streams with many three-legged and wiser beaver. But in the beginning such mishaps scarcely mattered, for the animals were abundant, and Ashley prospered from the first. And this prosperity gave him valuable time to learn and develop his business.

Today, as much as in 1822, the wilderness outfitter who does not perfect his equipment and the techniques for using it efficiently will fail in competition with the man who does. Ashley described his "outfit" in a letter written in 1829: ". . . mules are much the best animals for packing heavy burthens, each man has charge of two of them for that purpose, and one horse to ride. The equipage of such horse or mule consists of two halters, one saddle, one saddle blankett, one bear skin for covering the pack or saddle, and one pack-strap for the purpose of binding on the pack, and a bridle for the riding horse—one of the halters should be made light for common use, of beef hide, dressed soft—The other should be made of hide dressed in the same way—or tared rope, sufficiently strong to hold the horse under any circumstances, & so constructed as to give pain to the Jaws when drawn verry tight. The reign of each holter should not be less than sixteen feet long—A stake made of tough hard wood, about two inches in diameter & two feet long . . . should be provided . . ." This stake was used to picket the animals.

Pack outfits in the Jackson Hole country still use essentially the same equipment that Ashley recommended. Good mules are much in demand for both riding and packing. Today's guide or packer can consider himself very lucky, though, if he has only two pack animals to lead. More likely he will have five, even seven strung out behind him. Leading these long pack strings through rough, timbered country can be a minor art in itself. But a man could never escape from Indians while tied to such a long string, which is one reason Ashley's men only led two animals.

The personal outfit has not changed too much, either. In his classic *Journal of a Trapper,* Osborne Russell listed the things in a trapper's outfit: "one or two Epishemores [robes used as saddle blankets and bedding] a riding Saddle and bridle a sack containing six Beaver traps a blanket with an extra pair of Mocasins his powder horn and bullet pouch with a belt to which is attached a butcher Knife a small wooden box containing bait for Beaver [castoreum] a Tobacco sack with a pipe and implements for making fire with sometimes a hatchet fastened to the Pommel of his saddle . . ."

The early beaver traps were handmade of iron, and each weighed about five pounds. Each one cost the trapper between nine and twenty dollars. By comparison, a modern machine-made steel beaver trap weighs little more than half what the old one did, and costs about three dollars.

On the day Slim Lawrence guided me through his museum he mentioned that early trappers in the area used to bury their traps in caches after a season rather than pack them out to rendezvous or winter quarters. A few of these old traps have been found, and some are displayed in Lawrence's museum. Their owner guesses that many more still lie hidden in the mountains.

They lie there because trapping was a risky business, and there were literally dozens of ways to lose traps. There were also many ways for a trapper's plans to go awry and force him to abandon his traps in the wilderness.

Only by careful organization could a trapping party hope to operate with both success and safety. Ashley wrote about his method: "In the organization of a party of, say 60 or 80 men, four of the most confidential and experienced, of the number, are selected to aid in the command—The rest are divided in Messes of Eight or ten, a suitable man is also appointed at the head of each mess, whose duty it is to make known the wants of his mess, receive supplies . . . make distributions, watch over their conduct enforce order . . ."

Ashley clearly considered his brigades as well-disciplined crews who operated on a strictly business basis. A record of each article in the many packs was kept, along with the name of the man responsible for it. A man who carelessly lost something of Ashley's probably had its cost deducted from his wages.

The wages these men earned were hardly sumptuous. When Osborne Russell signed up as an engagé with Nathaniel Wyeth he was to be paid two hundred fifty dollars for eighteen months of work. Experienced trappers were paid more, but not a great deal more. Some engagés undertook their lowly chores as camp flunkies for even smaller wages than Russell was paid. Many of the trappers preferred a piecework arrangement with their employers. The fur company provided them with basic necessities and in return took half the men's catch. Since a beaver pelt was worth about three dollars in the mountains, a man might earn more under this system. This was especially true in places like the headwaters of the Snake, where parties were said to have taken fifty and more beaver in a single morning's "lift."

Still other mountain men operated independently as "free trappers." While they might travel with a company party for mutual safety, their operations in beaver country were independent. But the fur companies got their cut from these men, too—because, like everyone else, they came to rendezvous and paid the traders' prices. Sugar was sold there at two dollars a pint. Coffee was also two dollars. Watered liquor cost four dollars a pint, and lead for bullets a dollar and twenty-five cents a pound. Tobacco, more a staple than a luxury in the mountains, cost two dollars a pound. Cotton shirts were five dollars each, while a woolen blanket cost twenty. The little brass nails with which the trappers and Indians often decorated their gun stocks cost fifty cents a dozen. The trappers who kept squaws frequently spent hundreds of dollars decking them out in hawk's bells, ribbons, and fancy riding tack.

The beaver was such a common medium of exchange that it often took the place of dollars in mountain commerce. The short lines or "points" on Hudson Bay blankets today are holdovers from the fur trade, when each point equaled a beaver. Some firms worked out rate tables whereby the pelts of other animals were equated with and converted to beaver, so an otter might be the equivalent of two beaver, while a marten equaled a third as much.

What with the risks of the hunt and the high cost of mountain living it is little wonder that many trappers left a rendezvous with hardly more than hangovers. They were lucky, for many of the Indian squaws who flocked to the rendezvous were great, flowing springs of venereal disease, and they passed it around freely. The more experienced trappers also tried to leave rendezvous with a good personal outfit for the coming season. This was meager enough, as Osborne Russell described it: "His personal dress is a flannel or cotton shirt (if he is fortunate enough to obtain one if not Antelope skin answers the purpose of over- and undershirt) a pair of leather breeches with Blanket or smoked Buffaloe skin, leggins, a coat made of Blanket or Buffaloe robe a hat or Cap of Wool, Buffaloe or Otter skin, his hose are pieces of Blanket lapped round his feet which are covered with a pair of Moccasins made of Dressed Deer Elk or Buffaloe skins . . ."

It is little wonder that men living under such conditions in the mountains usually got out as soon as they could afford to. Andrew Henry ended his partnership with Ashley soon after his return from the Yellowstone in 1824. Ashley, though heavily in debt at the outset of their partnership, hung on alone. The pelts from his first hunt earned enough to pay off all his debts. And the Saint Louis papers in the next few years were to repeatedly announce the general's latest return from the Rocky Mountains with yet another rich haul of furs.

In 1826 Ashley attended the rendezvous in Cache Valley with an eye toward selling his business. And, before the gathering had ended, he succeeded. Three of his best men, Jedediah Smith, William Sublette, and David E. Jackson, agreed to buy

Ashley out. This didn't mean that Ashley was quitting the beaver business. In his agreement with the new partnership Ashley undertook to supply and deliver to them the trade goods necessary for the next rendezvous. By this device he kept the most lucrative part of his business and, on top of that, secured the right to go into competition with his former employees if he wished.

None of the new partners had either Ashley's acumen or his luck in being in the trade at precisely the right time. But they were hard, industrious men possessed of the knowledge and ability they needed to succeed.

Jedediah Smith was an educated and intelligent, if peculiar, man. There was virtually no humor in him. He was deeply religious, although the latter attribute never seemed to stand in the way of his business or to imbue him with any significant amount of Christian feeling for his fellow men.

Smith was the explorer of the new firm. In his lifetime he made some of the most extensive western explorations of the period. There is evidence that he crossed the southern end of Jackson Hole in 1824. If he did, he was the first American to visit the valley since the Astorians were there in 1812. He would have been among the second group of white men since Finan McDonald trapped there for the Hudson's Bay Company in 1819. This first visit of Smith's was only one in a series of journeys that were to take him to the Pacific Ocean and back again.

The sort of man he was comes through in Jim Clyman's eyewitness account of an attack upon Smith by a grizzly bear. Smith had accidentally surprised the animal at close range when it emerged from a thicket. As Clyman described it, "Grissly did not hesitate a moment but sprang on the capt taking him by the head first pitc[h]ing sprawling on the earth he gave him a grab by the middle . . . breaking several of his ribs and cutting his head badly."

By "cutting his head badly" Clyman meant that the bear had ripped off one of Smith's eyebrows and nearly scalped him. When the bear left, Smith's scalp was hanging and one

ear was almost torn off. Remaining conscious, Smith immediately realized that he had to be sewn up. And despite the
qualms of his men, who had never done such a job, Smith was
able to tell Clyman how to do it using an ordinary needle
and thread. Considering the conditions, the operation was a
success, but for the rest of his life Smith wore his hair long
to hide his disfiguring scars.

Of his trapper's life Smith wrote to his brother, ". . . I go
for days without eating, & am pretty well satisfied if I can
gather a few roots, a few Snails, or much better Satisfied if we
can affo[r]d our selves a piece of Horse Flesh, or a fine Roasted
Dog. . . ." Smith may have exaggerated a bit in order to dis-
suade his brother from entering the fur trade, as some of Bill
Sublette's relatives had done. Nevertheless, there was also truth
in what he had written.

Bill Sublette lacked his partner's asceticism. He liked a
drink, probably dallied with squaws, and ignored the law that
prohibited bringing liquor into the Indian country. As anyone
had to who hoped to survive in the mountains, Sublette developed a hard self-sufficiency. He is supposed to be the one who
abandoned an ailing Hiram Scott to eventual starvation at
the place in Nebraska that became Scott's Bluff. But it was
also Sublette who, near the end of an incredibly hard winter's
walk out of the mountains, traded his pistol for an Indian
pony so that his sole companion, Moses Harris, might ride.
Harris was a Negro.

Several months after this trek, in 1829, Sublette met his
partner, David E. Jackson, on the headwaters of the Snake. It
is at this meeting that Sublette is supposed to have named the
valley Jackson's Hole. Sometimes it was referred to as Jackson's Big Hole, since the area now known as Hoback Basin
was once called Jackson's Little Hole. The Hoback River was
sometimes known as Jackson's Fork. It is strange that Jackson
Hole, which by 1829 had been crossed and recrossed by hundreds of beaver hunters, had no name until that time. It seems
to have been referred to mostly as the "Snake country" until
it became Jackson's Hole. Many people have lamented the
pseudo-fastidiousness that led to dropping the final " 's" many

years ago. My feelings on the matter are mixed, although from a historical standpoint it should be called Jackson's Hole.

David E. Jackson is thought to have been one of the original Ashley men, and is also believed to have been present during Ashley's defeat by the Arikaras. But until he emerged as a partner in Smith, Jackson, & Sublette he was historically invisible. I have read opinions that Jackson was a little older than his partners, who were quite young. But this is only a guess, since no one today even knows what he looked like.

But, despite Jackson's historical anonymity, the affairs of the new firm prove him to have been a very able man. His hunts for beaver were consistently successful. These catches were an integral part of the new firm's success, for Jedediah Smith, for all his great explorations, added little to the firm's profits.

Just how much time Jackson actually spent in Jackson Hole is unknown. He may have reached there as early as 1824, and historians think he spent the winter of 1828–1829 in the valley. Whatever the actual length of time, it must have been considered enough by the trappers to justify applying Jackson's name to the valley.

The new partnership prospered so that by 1830 Jedediah Smith could afford to leave it and return to Saint Louis. Jackson and Bill Sublette remained partners, but, with Smith, they sold out their fur business, and Smith, Jackson, & Sublette now became the Rocky Mountain Fur Company.

Once back in Saint Louis, the three old partners launched upon a trading mission to Santa Fe. En route Smith was killed by Indians, but David Jackson went on, eventually reaching the Pacific Coast in California. He appears to have been buying mules, and he followed this business as far north as San Francisco. While he was in California a former employee of the original firm, a man named Wilson, brought suit against Jackson for back wages. His claim must have been convincing, for Jackson settled it for one hundred dollars.

During his California career, Jackson entered into a new partnership, Jackson, Waldo, and Young. According to one story Jackson absconded with this firm's funds. And when his partner, Young, went into Oregon, he took with him the reputation of being a rustler. It is difficult to believe that the persevering Jackson, who had been such a rock to his first partners, should suddenly become an absconder. But stranger things have happened, and at best Jackson's reputation on his return to Saint Louis carried a new thread of doubt with it. According to historian Dale Morgan, Jackson returned to Saint Louis in the early 1830s, blew his money in the best traditions of the mountain men, and then died in bed in the presence of friends.

The Rocky Mountain Fur Company, which bought out the previous firm, had five partners, the most famous of whom was Jim Bridger. But the others, Thomas Fitzpatrick, Milton Sublette, Henry Fraeb, and Baptiste Gervais, are also well-remembered mountain men.

Bridger had come west as a green kid. He was with some of the Ashley men who trapped Jackson Hole in 1825, and was to be in and around the area for thirty-five more years. Unlike many of his counterparts, Bridger stuck it out in the West and did not return to the East until age and increasing blindness forced him to.

He adapted perfectly to the mountain wilderness. He adopted Indian ways, took their women for his wives, and followed their superstitions like a religion. These were the very acts that, in the opinions of more "civilized" Americans, turned mountain men into animals.

But Bridger has come down to us as a man of more parts than many of his sophisticated contemporaries. It is doubtful that he could even write his name, yet he made up some delightful tales about regions of the West he had seen. Very few men of Bridger's background ever rise to the levels of leadership that he reached. And when the great era of the beaver hunter ended, Bridger, unlike many others, accepted it and made the best of the new conditions. He acted with somewhat more sympathy and generosity toward the first pioneers than did many other mountain men. How the pioneers repaid Bridger is another, shabbier story.

One of the stories about Bridger that had enough witnesses to assure its truth happened at the 1835 rendezvous on Green River. Three years earlier Bridger had been shot in the back with an iron-tipped arrow, and its point was still lodged there. Since the missionary doctor Marcus Whitman was at the rendezvous, Bridger decided to have him remove the arrowhead. The operation was successfully performed in the open before an awed audience of mountain men, and when it was over one of them wanted to know how Bridger had suffered through it for so long.

"Meat don't spoil in the mountains," said Bridger.

The annual rendezvous was generally held during the Fourth of July, although many of the participants would begin arriving at the site long before that time. Once things started, a rendezvous could last for two weeks. In all, five rendezvous were held at various sites along the Green River. It was a popular area because of the abundance of game, grass, and fine camp sites. And while it was accessible to the friendlier Indians, the area was still a safe distance from the dangerous Blackfeet. It was also accessible by wagon from Saint Louis, an asset that Jackson Hole could not claim.

Today the Sublette County Historical Society sponsors an annual reenactment of the rendezvous on the second Sunday of July. Sublette County borders Teton, and this proximity encourages many Jackson Holers to attend the festivities. In a sense it is still a rendezvous, because residents from all over the vast area converge on Pinedale for some fun and to play parts in the show. It takes the form of a historical pageant, but it is saved from the mawkishness and amateurism of many such events by the skills and exuberance of the cast—upwards of two hundred of them—and almost that many horses and donkeys. The people in the cast provide their own costumes, and since the major characters are ordinarily played by the same persons each year the costumes develop a bit each summer. Many of the outfits worn now are as wildly imaginative as the gaudy dress of the original fur trader.

To start things the "trappers" gallop into the simple arena

in the best traditions of the old Wild West shows. But the really exciting part of the show for me is when the big trade wagons come rumbling in. They come with a pounding rush—a dozen heavy, canvas-topped wagons drawn by big, powerful draft horses. Their drivers gallop them in, then bow their horses' thick necks with deftly handled reins to slow the teams and then stop them abreast in the middle of the arena. One after another the big wagons roll in with a rattling, thunderous boom. Chains clink, axles squeal, and nostalgia reigns.

As they drive by the stands the teamsters hoist earthenware jugs and bay at the crowd. And those are real bays, for many of the jugs hold just what they are supposed to hold, and some of the boys have been getting ready for rendezvous since the night before.

Costarring with the big teams and wagons in 1971 was a slender boy of about fourteen. Made up like an Indian, with swabbed-on Man-Tan and a slightly askew, coal-black wig, the boy sat his dark bay horse like a Sioux. He rode bareback and with an Indian-style bit of rawhide thong. And did he ride! There is a certain time in his life when a boy, who rides beautifully anyway, reaches a peak of graceful, native form. It was that time for this boy, and watching him on that brilliant July afternoon was alone worth driving a hundred miles to see.

The price of the show includes a barbecue dinner of beef furnished by local ranches. But after the show my wife and I decided the line to the cook shack was just too long. So we skipped dinner and started home. West of Pinedale a rustic wooden sign reads *Trapper's Point*. It is only a short drive over the dirt road that leads to the "point," which is actually just a barren knoll overlooking the Green. But coming fresh from the rendezvous I could look down on the silent verdure of the river meadows and imagine what Osborne Russell had seen there in 1837.

"Here we found the hunting Parties all assembled waiting for the arrival of Supplies from the States. Here presented what might be termed a mixed multitude. The whites were chiefly Americans, and Canadian French with some Dutch,

Scotch, Irish, English, halfbreed, and full blood Indians of nearly every tribe in the Rocky Mountains. Some were gambling at Cards some playing the Indian game of hand and others horse racing while here and there could be seen small groups collected under shady trees relating the events of the past year all in good Spirits. . . . Sheep Elk Deer Buffaloe and Bear Skins mostly supply the Mountaineers with clothing . . ."

Once the rendezvous was over and the trappers began lining out over the hills for the fall hunt, much of whatever comradery had existed in the encampment left, too. Competition for beaver and trade had grown furiously. Bill Sublette outraced the inexperienced Nathaniel Wyeth to the rendezvous of 1834, and by so doing virtually destroyed Wyeth's chances of success in the trade. Only the prevailing threat of the Blackfeet and Gros Ventres held many of the competing parties together.

So it had been after the rendezvous in Pierre's Hole. This valley, which had been named for a well-known old Iroquois trapper, Pierre Tivanitagon, was a favorite of the trappers. After the rendezvous a small group of them were precipitously attacked by Gros Ventres on July 18. Help soon came from the much larger band of trappers nearby who drove the Indians into a thicket. The trappers riddled the thicket with rifle balls, and, though many of the Indians were killed or wounded, the trappers didn't follow up their advantage. This permitted the surviving Indians to escape, some going over Teton Pass into Jackson Hole.

A week after the fight a group of seven ailing and dissident trappers left the Wyeth and Sublette party in Pierre's Hole and struck out for Saint Louis. Somewhere near the mouth of the Hoback River the men were attacked by about twenty Gros Ventres. Trappers More and Foy were killed on the spot, and their leader, Alfred Stephens, badly wounded in the thigh. The four surviving men were able to escape, taking Stephens with them. They headed for Sublette in Pierre's Hole, leaving More and Foy where they fell. Stephens disproved Bridger's remark about meat spoilage and died.

Just where the two trappers were killed and where they

were eventually buried has resulted in some minor controversy. The location of the graves, if they were ever dug, is
unknown. About a hundred years after the fight the skull of a
supposed white man was found in an excavation near the town
of Jackson. At the time it was speculated that it might be
More's.

Washington Irving, who became Captain Bonneville's aman-
uensis, wrote that the captain buried the men. But, since
his party probably came into Jackson Hole via the Gros Ventre
route, the story is doubtful. Perhaps Irving simply used it to
enliven the captain's otherwise uneventful journey through
Jackson Hole.

There is an old, but unconfirmed, story about eight trappers'
graves being in the area of Moran Bay, now under the waters
of Jackson Lake. It was told both by historian Grace R.
Hebard and pioneer–attorney William Simpson. Since no
proof for this story exists, the killing of More and Foy must
stand as the only known Indian–trapper battle in Jackson Hole.

By the time of Bonneville, knowledge of western routes
was widespread. Men who knew the trails could travel from
the head of the Green, cross Jackson Hole, and be in Pierre's
Hole in just four days. The important trapper routes in and
out of Jackson Hole probably began as Indian trails.

There were seven major routes. First, there were Teton
Pass, Togwotee Pass (which some say is Indian for "You
can go any way from here"), and Union Pass. All of these
were heavily used. Many trappers, including the rough-
tough Joe Walker and Kit Carson, used the Upper Snake
River–Pacific Creek trail to reach the Yellowstone. The Grassy
Lake route connects northern Jackson Hole with upper Pierre's
Hole, as does the Conant Trail beginning on Berry Creek in
northern Teton Park. The Grand Canyon of the Snake was
not heavily traveled until well into the twentieth century.
Even after World War II I remember the highway as a narrow,
tree-crowded ribbon that would have appalled many of today's
high-speed tourists.

Osborne Russell provided in his *Journal* some of the very

few descriptions of Jackson Hole as it looked to the early trappers. Having come down the Gros Ventre, Russell and his companions crossed the valley to the Snake River and then followed it north to the outlet of Jackson Lake. "This lake is . . . bordered on the east by pine swamps and marshes extending from 1 to 2 Mls from the Lake to the spurs of the Mountain. On the SW. stand the 3 Tetons whose dark frightful forms rising abruptly from the Lake and towering above the clouds casts a gloomy shade upon the waters beneath. . . . The high range of Mountains on the west after leaving the Tetons slope gradually to the Nth and spread into low piney mountains. This place like all other marshes and swamps among the mountains is infested with innumerable swarms of horse flies and musketoes to the great annoyance of man and beast during the day. . . . Game is plenty and the river and lake abounds with fish."

A few years later, in 1839, Russell was attacked by Blackfeet while camped in the Yellowstone. Though wounded, he made a harrowing escape south into Jackson Hole and then across the Tetons into Pierre's Hole via the Conant Trail. This trail passes through country as pristine now as it was a hundred fifty years ago. The trail parallels Berry Creek through a long, grassy valley that rises almost to the crest of the northern Tetons. The abundant grass and wood make clear why the trail was so popular with both Indians and trappers. There is big game in the meadow and trout and beaver in the stream.

The Park Service has purposely left the area undeveloped. There are almost no improved camp sites, and the not inconsiderable streams usually lack footbridges at the crossings. To see this area I hiked into it leading a pack mare in August of 1971. Here are some of my field notes: "The trail to the lower Berry Ck. meadow is fine and I have encamped on a wooded knoll near the stream. The knoll is surrounded by wet meadows and willows but doesn't seem too boggy. Lady is tied in the shade and for once quiet.

"I can readily see why the Indians and trappers used this route. It has such abundant forage.

"It sure felt good to flop here in the shade and eat pilot biscuit and cheese and to drink the good water. Also to remove my wet boots and put on a pair of dry socks. So many small things bring such sensual delight after a few days in the mountains."

After a dinner of fried Spam, potatoes, and coffee, I munched on a slab of milk chocolate—with almonds—and then went down to look at the stream and get a pail of water. "I saw a small trout in the stream. It looks like it might be good fishing. There is very little sign of anyone. This spot of timber has been camped in before but my predecessors were very neat. The meadow is surrounded by heavily timbered, unspectacular hills. Still, it's lovely.

"The meadow is crosscut by beaver channels and I fell in one—nearly to my waist—earlier this evening.

"8/17/71 Awoke about 6:30 and surprised to find it cloudy; the sky had been clear when I went to bed. Because it looked like rain I got things under cover in the tent and cooked breakfast there, fried Spam, potatoes, and eggs.

"About 10:20 I took the camera bag and raincoat and started up the trail. It was sunny and warm for a time, but now it is cloudy and raining slightly. I'm sitting in a patch of timber below the R.S. [Park Service Patrol Cabin at the upper end of Berry Creek] waiting for the rain to stop. Looking up the canyon it is very gray and I'm afraid it will be wetter here before it gets drier.

"My heel is still sore [from where the mare had stepped on it] and my legs are, too. Can't understand the latter. My legs should be used to walking by now.

"This is a big, lush meadow all the way, with game tracks common and several signs of beaver activity. As noted before most of the slopes are heavily timbered—mostly lodgepole but some alpine fir and even a few patches of aspen.

"I heard a beaver or two splash and flap their tails in the water last night."

Early the next morning I got up and packed out to the Grassy Lake Road, where I'd left my car and horse trailer.

Previously an old trail, the road had been developed as a freight road. If anything, the ascent of the Tetons via this road is more gradual than on Berry Creek. There are not many fine meadows along this route, however, and much of it passes through seemingly unending lodgepole pine. It struck me as a route the trappers might have chosen to avoid Indians using the Berry Creek region.

Once he had crossed the Berry Creek Divide, in 1839, Osborne Russell never returned to Jackson Hole. There were still a few beaver on the Snake's headwaters, but the demand for them was dwindling. Jedediah Smith and David Jackson were dead. Bill Sublette had taken up land in Missouri. The only man to have made a substantial fortune in the Rocky Mountains, William Ashley, was dead of pneumonia. In a few years some of the old beaver hunters would be eking out a living ferrying emigrants across the Green. The heyday of the fur brigades was ending, not with a bang or even a whimper, but with a sigh of resignation.

I told you, you could not get through.
A bird could not fly over that without
taking a supply of grub along.

JIM BRIDGER,
quoted by Captain Raynolds

6 / The Explorers

The last great rendezvous of the fur trade was held on
the upper Green River in 1840. It was not a success. One of the
participants, Robert Newell, described it: "I went to the
American rendezvous, Mr. Drips, Fraeb and Bridger from St.
Louis with goods, but times were certainly hard, no beever and
everything dull. Some missionaries came along with them for
the Columbia . . ."

The silken hat has often been blamed for the decline of
the fur trade, but the blame also lies with the fur brigades.
They had trapped themselves out of business. The northern
Rockies were especially hard hit, since the Hudson's Bay Company was there in direct competition with the Americans. In
league with the British government this venerable company had
entered that portion of the mountains to destroy the beaver.
By so doing they hoped to discourage American trappers, who
would in turn discourage the American homesteaders and
missionaries who were sure to follow and claim the land. However, as it turned out, the beaver were gone but the Americans
were not.

Some of the trappers, like Joe Meek and Osborne Russell,
moved on to Oregon, where they took up land. Bill Sublette
went back to Missouri to live in comfortable circumstances to

the end of his life. Jim Bridger and Tom Fitzpatrick became guides for emigrants and later explorers. Bridger also built a trading post at Black's Fork in southwestern Wyoming. Some of the mountain men lounged around there and operated ferries across the Green River. A few of the other trappers turned renegade and existed for a while by robbing the Indians. And others who could not, or would not, adapt to the changing times continued roaming the mountains as solitary trappers.

One afternoon last fall I was lying by the fire another hunting guide and I had built in the open timber just north of Bridger Lake. It was a raw day, mostly overcast. There were six inches of snow on the ground, and the nearby Yellowstone River was completely frozen over. The other guide had unrolled the waterproof pack cover he carried tied behind his saddle, then spread it and a GI raincoat under a tree. Then he lay down on them and took a nap. I was lying propped against another tree. I had taken off my leather batwing chaps and was using them as a waterproof groundsheet. My legs were propped up, one across the other, to keep them out of the snow. Periodically I reached in my coat pocket for a caramel, which I unwrapped and ate.

Finished with his nap, the other guide came over to the fire with a sandwich in his hand—a hand, incidentally, that in places was still caked with the blood of an elk he had dressed earlier that day. In his other hand the young man had a slender, forked stick about two feet long. He placed his cold sandwich on the forked end of the stick and began toasting it over the fire. It was the last half of the last day of the hunting season.

"Think you'll be back again next fall?" he asked me.

"I always say I won't, but here I am again," I said.

"My wife says all they have to do is drive a truckload of horses by the house in September an' I'll follow it." The guide had eaten his sandwich, which had smelled pretty good while he toasted it, and now he filled a pipe that had a little round bowl and a yellowish stem. He lit the tobacco with a brand from the fire. Puffing, "If we didn't have to put up with these hunters, I'd like it a whole lot better."

"Your two guys seem pretty good this time," I said, reaching inside my heavy coat and pulling out a plug of chewing tobacco wrapped in a small plastic bag. Holding it in one hand I reached with the other into my pants pocket and took out a jackknife. I cut off a chip of tobacco and nuzzled it off the knife blade into my mouth. Then flipping the knife shut with my thumb, I put it back into my pocket and stuffed the plug back under the layers of heavy clothing into my shirt pocket.

"I like to be out," I said.

"So do I," said the other guide. "I like to hunt by myself."

"Me too."

Just then one of our hunters walked up to the fire, turned his back to it, and broke wind.

We looked up at him but did not move.

"Sounds better since you had it fixed."

The hunter ignored the remark, and the other guide began telling us about the "dago hunter" who had once threatened to kill him.

Why any man would enjoy lying in snow beside a frozen meadow and indulging himself in base talk and crude habits is virtually inexplicable to one who has never done it. After a time in the outdoors a man learns to accept the weather and make a truce with it. When he has done this and knows he and his hunters are as well off lying beside the fire as they would be anywhere else, he can be at peace.

Perhaps this is why some of the mountain men never left the mountains after the collapse of the fur trade. They had found a kind of peace. And despite lives of cruel privation, from our point of view, these men were better off than many of their compatriots who abandoned the mountains and then spent the rest of their lives reminiscing about their days in the wilderness.

Beaver Dick Leigh came to the Rockies many years after the last rendezvous. The son of a British seaman, he had been brought to the United States as a boy. He served in the American Army during the Mexican War, and then seems to have spent the rest of his life as a trapper and guide. Leigh was a remarkable man, who, to me anyway, serves as a link between the last days of the dying fur trade and the first days of permanent settlement. There were many men like Dick, ignorant but nevertheless shrewd and resourceful, wandering in the Jackson Hole country during the historically clouded years after 1840. One was the trapper Bill Craig, who is generally credited with the carving, *E.W.C. 1850*, on a tree near the head of Jackson Lake and was known as far south as the Uinta Mountains. Working alone or with a partner, these men more often tended to stay in one general area and eke out a living from it.

According to a letter he wrote to an editor, Beaver Dick had explored the Teton Range with John Lumphara in 1858. They were looking for a central route across the mountains. They did not find one, and with that brief mention John Lumphara disappeared. In the "jurnall" Dick kept in the mid-1870s he mentions at least five other men who trapped the Tetons, Jackson Hole, or both. One, John Pierce, is known to have spent the winter of 1876–1877 alone in a Jackson Hole cabin. Pierce did all his traveling on foot and had to carry his outfit and furs on his back. Other white men like Beaver Dick who married or, as was more usual, lived with Indian women were often scorned by white society. This ostracism must have added to the men's desire for solitary lives. The people who came to Pierre's Hole in the late 1800s to settle and then lived to be feted as pioneers hardly mention men like Beaver Dick in their reminiscences. The same thing is true in Jackson Hole, where the wife of John Carnes, the first settler, was a Shoshone Indian. Virtually nothing was recorded about this human being except to note that there was a half-breed kid in the valley's first school. The first white woman, in many western communities has, however, become a royal being. And from reading some accounts you'd think there was a whopping, big star shining above the cabins where the first white children were born.

In recounting the bitter days when his first family was dying of smallpox, Beaver Dick mentions the white man, immune from the disease himself, who refused to come to Dick's aid unless a subscription was taken up in his favor. Dick called the fellow a "brute." From my point of view it was an ironic choice of words, because the life Dick and his "comarade trappers" lived was as brutish as any aborigine's. Dick's diary covers part, or all, of eighteen months in the mid-1870s. A good third of it was written after the death of his first family when Dick had only himself to feed. Because meeting this basic necessity occupied many of his waking hours, Dick's notes are laden with reports of trapping success. I made a quick tally of the big game Dick and his son, Dick, Jr., reported killing and wounding in their quest for food. Perhaps it is because I'm a former game warden and also a hunter who grew up observing limits of one deer a year, but I was appalled by Dick's kills.

In the eighteen months of record the family took forty-seven deer and wounded ten others, which escaped. They killed fifty-eight antelope and lost four more. Dick killed one elk and another was badly wounded but escaped. A moose and bear were also wounded and lost. The trout, waterfowl, grouse, and small animals such as rock chucks and ground squirrels the family killed were almost without number and, to them, hardly worth mentioning, except in happiness and glee at killing them. There was no selectivity in their killing; anything that jumped up was shot or shot at. One day Dick wrote, "I Kiled 2 fawn deer this evening. the skins were so prity i streched and saved them."

Dick was feeding four growing children, plus his wife and himself. Living vigorously as they did required more high-protein food than today's sedentary family needs, but it still appears that they abused seeming abundance—just as we abuse it today. With modern meat-preservation methods, and a little wifely imagination, my wife and I can subsist very well for a year on a deer, an antelope, and an elk. We have done it often, never buying more than an occasional pound of bacon and a few chickens from one fall to the next.

But depending upon wildlife for food is also a reiteration of the saying, "Poor folks have poor ways." And the trapper-settler turned ever more to other resources for his living. Dick guided prospectors into the Tetons and apparently helped ferry the DeLacy party across the Snake River when they were bound for Jackson to look, unsuccessfully, for gold in the summer of 1863.

As America grew in size, and especially in population, the decisions were made, or solutions were forced upon the decision makers, that included opening the West. It was the era of Manifest Destiny, and new lands had to be found for settlers. Minerals were increasingly needed for the country's burgeoning industry. To get these things the Indians had to be forced into an ever-narrowing ribbon of the less desirable land between the Pacific coast and the Midwest. Just as they do today, the government bureaucracies jockeyed for positions of authority to administer the dwindling frontier, and for a time the army prevailed. It was in the West in undisputed force, and had been since the time of Lewis and Clark. It had given Captain Bonneville's fur-trading venture the secondary mission of gathering intelligence. And, while Bonneville had returned late and under a dark cloud, he was soon back in the army's esteem; presumably because he fulfilled his secondary mission.

Beaver Dick remarked about the first, after Bonneville's military reconnaissance into Jackson Hole; he wrote that the "winter of 58 and 59 was the winter that Leutenant Renolds winterd in Jackson Hole with two compy of US Cavely near the Govanment Butt[e] James Bridger was the Guide on a two years exploring trip. F V Hadon [Hayden] was geoligist and J H Stevenson was Botinast with the party."

How Dick got this information is unknown. The man he referred to was probably Captain James Raynolds of the Topographical Engineers, who led a party of thirty picked dragoons through Jackson Hole in June of 1860. The expedition had wintered at Deer Creek, site of the Upper Platte Indian Agency in 1859–1860—which is nowhere near Jackson Hole. However, Jim Bridger was the guide, and Hayden and Stevenson were there in their scientific capacities.

It was a sort of vacuum-cleaner operation. The participants

were to explore the upper Yellowstone and en route check out the Indians, minerals, and agricultural possibilities, as well as prospects for rail and freight roads. They were also to hurry north from Jackson Hole in order to observe an eclipse. Bridger led the party across Union Pass and onto the head-waters of the Gros Ventre. From here they entered the heavily timbered Mount Leidy highlands, where they wallowed in deep snow and began having doubts about Bridger's sense of direction. There is no explanation, save perhaps Raynolds's impatience, for Bridger's failure to take the party north through Jackson Hole to the Pacific Creek trail and from there to its assigned destination on the upper Yellowstone. He had not been in the area for over twenty years, but it is hard to believe that a man of his abilities would suddenly get lost in an area he'd once traveled with ease.

I suspect that Bridger, then in his early fifties, was apprehensive of an early June trip to the upper Yellowstone River. At this season there is still plenty of snow in that area, although enough has melted that the streams are in flood and the meadows through which they flow are often inundated. Eileen Johnson, who works in a fishing and hunting camp on the upper Yellowstone, told me of seeing trout swim ahead of her in the trail when she rode into the camp one July day. Since Bridger was paid by the day, it probably didn't matter greatly to him if he got to the upper Yellowstone.

After the travails in the highlands he brought the party into Jackson Hole and to the ford near Teton Pass. A trooper was drowned here attempting to swim his horse across the Snake River. This accident and another with a raft prompted Bridger to make a bullboat of hides. Using this vessel to transport its valuable equipment, the party found a usable ford and crossed over Teton Pass into Pierre's Hole. As far as its exploration of Jackson Hole was concerned, the party's visit there was hardly worth the effort.

The next expedition to the area was guided by Beaver Dick Leigh. Popularly called the Hayden Survey of 1872, it was actually under the supervision of James Stevenson. Beaver Dick called it "the grand geologacil survy of 1872." And guiding it was a high point in his life.

Ferdinand Vandeveer Hayden was an energetic man of diverse talents. He served as a medical doctor in the Civil War but made himself famous afterward as a geologist. One historian has aptly called him "the businessman's geologist." Hayden was constantly on the lookout for minerals in commercial amounts. Indians were reputed to have given him a name that meant "man who runs bent over picking up stones." But above all Hayden was a collector of data. Under the auspices of the Interior Department he published voluminous annual reports concerning his western ventures. The reports were illustrated by such artists as Thomas Moran and contained photographs by William Henry Jackson. They were lavish documents designed as much to ensure continued congressional appropriations for the expeditions as to advance science; they were successful on both counts.

Yellowstone, not Jackson Hole, was the region that early caught the explorers' imaginations. For a time all trails seemed to lead there, and Jackson Hole was ignored by the explorers. Anyone who has visited Yellowstone Park recently might wonder why the explorers bothered. The magic is gone, and as a friend remarked, "All it is now is a chance to smell some fat lady's armpit." Even the early explorers found tourists there ahead of them, "taking the waters" at some of the hot springs.

But the Snake River division of Hayden's 1872 expedition was concerned primarily with the area south of Yellowstone Park. From the railhead at Ogden, Utah, they traveled by wagon to Pierre's Hole, now being called Teton Basin. Beaver Dick Leigh was hired to guide the party, and one of their first excursions was up Teton Creek on the west slope of the Teton Range. Dick described the route in a letter: "the Best and easeyist is to travel up the ridge and mountin on the south side of the West teton river. by making these acencons all the buty and Grandur of the teton and the range of mountins can be seene to the best adventge."

It was on this trip that James Stevenson and Nathaniel Langford claimed to have climbed the Grand Teton—they named it Mount Hayden. While this was going on an event far more important was occurring on the flat top of Table Mountain, just west of the Grand Teton. William Jackson was taking the first photographs of the Tetons. Working with big wet plates and cumbersome, primitive equipment packed in on a mule, Jackson took photographs that are seldom equaled today.

The area is now accessible by good Park and Forest Service trails, but to look at Table Mountain is still to wonder how Jackson ever got up there with a pack mule. Mike Hanson and I camped in the canyon below this mountain one summer night, and I noted, "Our camp is directly under Table Mt. It looks so high and is so straight above camp that it gives a perspective of leaning out over us."

I also noted, "This is a canyon of towering, gray-tan peaks rising above a green but generally rough canyon bottom. Above camp to the west is a huge peak that seems to reach near the parabola of the sky. Our elevation here is about 9,500'."

Later we hiked on up to Hurricane Pass, where we must have been close to the area Beaver Dick described. I wrote, "Just below the Pass—a lowering of the ridge—we encountered a large, hard snowdrift that was too steep to cross safely. We rattled through the talus going around it and finally reached the top. 'Jesus Christ!' I said."

It wasn't up to Washington Irving's description of the Tetons through the eyes of the beaver men, but Irving had neither been out of breath nor there. I tried, sitting on the pass, 10,372 feet above sea level, to write down what I saw: "to the west, but close by, is a gray-green, semicircular basin that gives into a deep, timbered canyon. The canyon spreads down to eventually open out on a 30-mile vista of Teton Basin. This nearer basin is in itself a phenomenon; it must be three miles across from the long wall that runs a mile west before dropping into the aforementioned canyon. To the east the view is even more spectacular, with the three Tetons dominating a glacial cirque below which are green, alpine meadows with irregularly shaped tarns scattered on the left-facing slope. The Tetons are pristine and unchallenged in their majesty. The Wall, which faces east, goes up from the basin and cirque in one gigantic step. It is probably 400′ high and a mile long, with snowdrifts on the talus below. This is all above timberline, the last trees are about ⅓ mile back down trail.

"I have seen swallows and a butterfly at this spot while making these notes."

After their exploration in the mountains the climbers of 1872 rejoined the main party in Teton Basin. They continued north along the west slope of the Teton Range, eventually crossing into the Yellowstone region for a rendezvous with the expedition suppliers. They had left Beaver Dick in Teton Basin, and he and his family later crossed over the Conant Trail and rejoined the party in the northern end of Jackson Hole. While the party moved south from campsite to campsite, survey teams spread out, mapping the area and collecting all sorts of data on rocks, weather, animals, and flowers. As they traveled they named Leigh Lake, Jenny Lake, and Leigh Canyon for their guide and his family.

William Jackson made a photograph of the family beside their tipi, or "lodge." Technically it isn't one of Jackson's better pictures, although it is certainly one of the best known in the Jackson Hole country. Dick, who was forty-one at the time, appears as a man in peak condition. He has a good brow and thick hair cut fairly short and parted on the left. His square shoulders are covered by a heavy, if nondescript, shirt— he may actually be wearing two shirts. His beard is full but not weedy or long. In his hands is the long barrel of a rifle, whose butt rests on the ground beside his left foot. Dick's hands are square but without beefy fullness. They seem to be very large, with long heavy fingers that easily encircle the rifle's stout barrel. His body is bent slightly at the hips and his legs are spread, putting more of his weight on the right leg. It is uncertain, but under magnification Dick's hands resemble those of a man who has recently dressed a big game animal.

To Dick's left, sitting on their legs Indian fashion, are his children, John and Ann Jane. John is wearing a queer little cap with a short but wide bill. His small, plump face wears an expression of wistful curiosity. This expression is repeated in Ann Jane's face. Both children appear to be wearing shapeless cotton clothing. Beside and just behind them sits Jenny, her thick, black hair parted in the middle. Her face is wide, and she gives the appearance of heaviness of body. It is not possible to say this for certain, because she is holding in front of her a small boy, William, whose slightly tousled head hides his mother's mouth and jaw. William was between two and three years old, and Jenny appears to be hiding behind him. Her arms are around the little boy, but the hands do not grasp him. Rather, they hang at his waist like limp paws. I have never seen any other woman hold her child quite like this.

To Jenny's left are two sleepy-eyed donkeys standing beside one another, their heads together. On the back of the donkey in the foreground sits Dick, Jr. He is wearing a floppy coat and baggy trousers. Like the other children's, his hair is long, to his collar, but not Indian straight. He is wearing moccasins with high tops and the same kind of queer little cap that John has. His face is in shadow, but he has the look of a small boy who very much wants to be thought the man.

In the old photograph it is only Beaver Dick who cuts a romantic figure. The others appear timid and strangely deprived. Looking at the children, I find it a rather sad picture.

After completing their work in Jackson Hole the Stevenson party divided, some crossing into Teton Basin while a survey party went on down the Snake River. In contrast to other opinions of the steep-walled canyon, this latter group reported that it had little trouble making the trip. In about a week's time they traversed the entire canyon and rejoined the main party at the northern end of the Snake River Range, near a place they named Camp Reunion. The Hayden Survey for the year of 1872 was over. The explorers headed for civilization and Beaver Dick for his home in Teton Basin.

The rivalry between civilian and military explorers continued the very next year, when Capt. William A. Jones led still another expedition into the Yellowstone. Billed as a military reconnaissance of northwestern Wyoming, the junket's chief result was the siting of a military road from the Point of Rocks on the Union Pacific Railroad past Yellowstone Lake and ending at Fort Ellis, Montana. Such a road was entirely feasible, but it would have eviscerated the brand-new (1872) Yellowstone Park and also what was to become the Teton Wilderness in northern Jackson Hole. Fortunately, Lt. Gen. Phil Sheridan sent a covering letter with the captain's report, which read in part, "I in no manner can endorse the contemplated road from the Point of Rocks . . . to Fort Ellis via Yellowstone Lake as a military necessity. . . . I am not prepared to give even a shadow of support to anything so absurd as the military necessity for such a road."

Captain Jones deviated from what had become the almost stock exploration of the new Yellowstone Park by entering it from the rugged east side. In doing so he crossed the formidable Absaroka Range, which he named the Sierra Shoshone. His name didn't catch, and it's just as well—the range's accepted name, Absaroka, is supposed to mean "home of the Crows." After the usual visits to Yellowstone Lake and the geysers the Jones expedition headed south toward the lake's inlet.

I have never visited this area, but those who have tell me it is a dreary and monotonous trip. Jones wrote of the area around the outlet: "The valley about the mouth is very marshy with numerous small ponds and sloughs. There is also a great deal of timber on the low ground on the west side but from its proximity to water there must be in it a great deal of fallen timber. . . ."

Osborne Russell, the trapper-journalist, had visited the Yellowstone meadows nearly forty years before. He described the valley as "lying Nth and South about 15Ms. long and 3 wide thro. which it [the upper Yellowstone River] winds its way slowly to the Nth. thro swamps and marshes and calmly reposes in the bosom of the Yellow Stone Lake. The South extremity of this valley is smooth and thickly clothed with high meadow grass surrounded by high craggy mountains topped with snow."

The trails have been improved, and the Forest Service has built a substantial horse bridge across the Yellowstone River at the foot of Hawk's Rest Mountain, not too far from where Jones must have camped, but other than that the area has changed hardly at all in the intervening years. The great meadow in September is a golden meld of the placid and the spectacular. It is a long day's ride from anywhere, and virtually no one who has seen it for the first time has not felt some semblance of weary relief. It is a great river of grass in which huge moose become easily overlooked specks in the distance. When I asked Mont Harmon, who has guided in the area for almost twenty years, how far the meadow extended, he said, "All the way to Yellowstone Lake." It is actually longer by a few miles than Osborne Russell said it was.

Captain Jones did not linger in the area that had been so well used by the earlier trappers that it became known as the Thorofare. Instead, he turned west into the timbered canyon across from the Hawk's Rest ford and continued up Atlantic Creek. When he emerged from the canyon it was to find another large meadow, equally as marshy as the Yellowstone meadows. But, as he wrote, there was something here of "remarkable interest."

Jones described it: "A small stream coming down the mountains to our left I found separating its waters in the meadow where we stood, sending one portion into the stream ahead of us and the others into the one behind us. The one following its destiny to the Snake and Columbia Rivers back to its home in the Pacific. The other to the Yellowstone and Missouri seeking the foreign water of the Atlantic by one of the longest voyages known to running water."

Osborne Russell wrote that "here a trout of 12 inches in length may cross the mountains in safety." This place of "remarkable interest" is, of course, Two-Ocean Pass. What is unusual about the captain's and the trapper's descriptions is that they both described South Two-Ocean Creek. I've brought a lot of casual observers across this stream and not one remarked about it being on the Continental Divide. The parting of the waters is far more apparent across the meadow on North Two-Ocean Creek.

Numerous visitors there have played God, diverting the creek waters, first east and then west, by moving a few stones. It is possible that Jones had had a little coaching regarding the stream he found so remarkable. But what is truly remarkable about the area is the grasp the ignorant trappers had of western geography. They were able to recognize the "Dividing Spring" as being on the Continental Divide.

Only one of Jones's Indian guides claimed to have any idea of where they were, and, as previously mentioned, he obviously rejoiced at holding this advantage. Jones noted that "when all ready to start it was discovered that he was enjoying all the comforts of home in the bosom of his family and taking a quiet smoke after having been told to get ready an hour before." Jones hesitated to reprimand the Indian, since he realized that if the man got in a huff he would likely abandon the party and take all "his dusky brethren" with him.

The Indian, an unnamed Sheep Eater from Washakie's band, seems a rather delightful fellow in retrospect. After another day's journey Jones noted, "The Indian difficulty came up early. The fellow after being told to get ready in time to start with us went off up the stream to trap for beaver."

The party was low on rations, and at least the white segment of it was anxious to return to civilization. It didn't matter to the Indian that his trapping venture would cost the party a day's delay. He apparently didn't even consider it. Unfortunately for the enterprising Indian, Jones threatened to have him thrown in jail on their return to Camp Brown if he failed them now as a guide. Two of the other Indian guides, assuming that they would also be put into jail, went out and retrieved the erstwhile beaver hunter. Jones reports that "without a word he took his place at the head of the column and soon appeared perfectly cheerful and contented."

The Indian led the party down Lava Creek to its junction with the Buffalo Fork River. From here the party turned east and crossed over Togwotee Pass, to be eventually disbanded at

Camp Brown. Jones seemed to think that his Indian guide had been chastened, but his selection of a route down Lava Creek is certainly not one that would have been made today. I suspect the routes I have used to reach Two-Ocean Pass are better ones. This leads me to the additional suspicion that the nameless Shoshone had his way after all.

*. . . with a Stage rout the way i ave
menchond tourists and sight seers
could take in all the sights and hunting grounds from the Lake north to
the head of the Grand canon of Snake
river. . . . this will take them thrue
the butifull vally of Jacksons Hole . . .*

LETTER OF "BEAVER DICK" LEIGH

7 / *Gustavus Cheney Doane*

Just as many Indians and mountain men knew the big
game of the West would be virtually destroyed long before it
actually was, others anticipated settlement long before that
was a fact. When the Washburn–Langford–Doane party explored Yellowstone in 1870 many in the party saw a chance to
exploit the area. Nathaniel Langford noted in his diary entry
of September 20, 1870:

"Last night and also this morning in camp, the entire party
had a rather unusual discussion. The proposition was made by
some member that we utilize the results of our exploration by
taking up quarter sections of land at the most prominent points
of interest. . . . One member . . . suggested that if there could
be secured by pre-emption a good title to two or three quarter
sections of land opposite the lower fall of the Yellowstone and
extending down the canyon, they would eventually become a
source of great profit. . . . Another thought that it would be
more desirable to take up a quarter section of land at the
Upper Geyser Basin. . . . A third suggestion was that each
member of the party pre-empt a claim, and in order that no
one should have an advantage over the other, the whole should
be thrown into a common pool for the benefit of the entire
party."

A hundred years later I have heard from various men how wonderful it would be (for them) if the Yellowstone meadows could be turned into a great stock ranch. What is really so depressing and exasperating about this sort of destructive greed is that the ones who profess it do not recognize their desires for what they are.

One day I had an eastern hunter high on a snowy ridge overlooking the vast country called the Thorofare. Looking out over the ridges and canyons beyond us, the hunter asked, "Is this open range?"

"In a way I guess it is. It's in the public domain."

"Public land?" asked the hunter.

"Yeah. But it's wilderness, no logging or livestock allowed."

The hunter thought for a moment. "Too bad they can't do something with it."

The last significant exploration, if it can be called that, of the Jackson Hole area seems to have lacked even the justification of mercenary practicality. The Doane expedition of 1876 had the fuzzy mission of making a *winter* exploration of "Snake River from Yellowstone Lake to Columbia River." This was a military expedition, and, unlike other earlier ones through the area, did not in its makeup even nod to the sciences. Lt. Gustavus Cheney Doane was the leader, and behind-the-scenes proponent, of this wretched but also heroic trip.

The best source for information about Doane is the Bonneys' *Battle Drums and Geysers,* a work I have relied on frequently.

Lieutenant Doane had been born May 29, 1840, in Galesburg, Illinois. While he was still a small boy, Doane's family moved to California, where he later attended the University of the Pacific, graduating from there with honors in 1861. Soon after the Civil War began Doane enlisted in the Union Army. He saw considerable, if not particularly significant, action, and was commissioned a lieutenant.

Owing to enlistment procedures peculiar to the times, Doane was discharged some months before the war was over. He soon became a front runner in what a southern historian labeled "the vandal horde"—Doane was a carpetbagger. But evidently he was not a successful one, for in 1868 he requested reinstatement in the army. He was accepted and commissioned a second lieutenant of cavalry.

Doane was immediately sent to the West, serving in Nebraska, Wyoming, and then at Fort Ellis in Montana. While at Fort Ellis Doane participated in a winter attack on an encampment of Piegan Indians. Later he boasted that he had been the "first and last man in Piegan camp," and called it "the greatest slaughter of Indians ever made by U.S. troops."

In his official report Doane described the action: "Not an Indian got through several were followed high up on the slope of the opposite Bad Lands, and killed with revolvers. . . . Corporal Etheridge distinguished himself in killing Indians, taking great risks by standing in front of the lodges and firing into the doors. I saw him three times drop Indians who had bows presented . . . with the arrow drawn to an aim. . . . He was a splendid shot, and killed several. Sergeant Howell displayed good judgment in destroying the lodges and in caring for the *wounded squaws and children*." (Italics mine.)

Others were not so delighted by the outcome of the daybreak attack. The army tried to cover it up, but a young officer, Lt. William Pease, submitted the facts to U.S. Commissioner of Indian Affairs Ely Parker. In the first place, the attack had not been justified. Some said it was mounted because an American Fur Company trader had been killed the *previous summer*. As it turned out, the victim, a squaw man, had been killed in a family feud.

Despite its provocation, the army's attack had been merciless. The Indian camp had not been defended. The few men there were old, and several of the others were sick with smallpox. There had been 219 people in the camp when Lieutenant Doane burst in upon it. He and his men killed 173 Indians—33 men, 90 women, and 50 children. The troopers lost one man killed and one injured.

Doane was responsible for destroying the Indians' lodges and all their winter provisions. And when it was discovered that some of the captive women and children had smallpox they were turned loose to fend for themselves. At the time the United States government had been seeking some sort of rapprochement with the western Indians, and this incident, naturally, touched off a series of incidents and further damaged already bad relations. Doane's pride at his part in this bloody debacle never seemed to wane—because, nineteen years later, he used it as a testimonial to his fitness for the post of superintendent of Yellowstone Park.

The ambitious lieutenant never got the job, although his experience with the Yellowstone country had begun in 1870. Doane was an officer "with his finger on his number," and, when he learned of the Washburn–Langford excursion into the area in 1870, he wangled himself the command of its military escort. It turned out to be a valuable assignment, for, despite the greediness of some of the party, it inspired reports that led to the establishment of Yellowstone as the first national park.

In the summer of 1871 Doane again led a military escort into the Yellowstone. This time it was a civilian expedition under the direction of the indefatigable F. V. Hayden. Somewhere Doane had developed what was at the least disgust, and at the worst hatred, for the civilian explorers. He wrote that they were lacking in practical knowledge and relied too much upon classroom theory. He even took a peevish whack at Dr. Hayden, saying that he, Doane, had shown him Bridger Lake and that Hayden still denied its existence. This criticism, coming as it did years after the purported incident, hardly seems mature.

Indeed, Doane wasn't a mature man. In old photos he obviously loved to strike heroic poses. He fancied himself an explorer, and he was one of sorts, but he lacked the knowledge and the wisdom to be a very good one. He also probably resented the civilian preemption of western explorations, since many in the army considered themselves the ones for the job. A prideful man, Doane must have been jealous of the attention and subsidies bestowed upon civilians like Hayden.

Whatever the cause of Doane's exploratory frustrations, they at one time reduced him to megalomania. It was the time in 1874 when he wrote to the Smithsonian "Institute" [sic] proposing that it send him on a trip to the headwaters of the Nile. If it were not so sad, Doane's letter would be funny—no, it is funny. Doane claimed he had a rare qualification that enabled him to "travel without difficulty not only in known, but also in unknown districts."

He further claimed he could "follow a true course under all circumstances, Without Guide, Map or Compass. . . ." He partially explained his wonderful facility by explaining that "water always runs downhill." And while it was on record that, as any mortal might, he had become lost in the Yellowstone, Doane exclaimed, "I have repeatedly traversed the dense forests of the National Park in the darkest of nights, to reach camps at locations where I have never been, and which I did not know, with the same unerring certainty." His letter continues full of bombast and pretentious generalities. At one point he writes regarding Sir Henry Stanley, of Stanley–Livingstone fame, "The expedition of Stanley, its object being to hunt a man, and not to explore a Country, was a success, both as to means, and results, but Stanley lacks calibre. He does well what he is sent to do, but does not rise to the Conception of Great Achievements."

Doane asked the Smithsonian for ten thousand dollars in expenses, plus six thousand more to cover the salaries of himself and a junior officer for two years. "I would hire but two white men, a Photographer and an Engineer, and would qualify myself to dispense with both if necessary." Since Hayden was getting as much as forty thousand for a season's work in the Yellowstone, Doane was offering himself at a bargain. And eventually he found someone willing to send him off as leader of an expedition.

It was not to Africa's Nile but to the Snake River, which he was supposed to explore "from Yellowstone Lake to Columbia River." To perform this jaunt Doane was authorized a sergeant and five privates, rations for sixty days, pack animals, camp gear, and a small boat, the latter to be built under the lieutenant's direction.

This boat, which was to play such an important part in the

trip, was a double-ended affair. Built of inch planking, it was twenty-two feet long, forty-six inches wide, and twenty-six inches deep. Doane figured that it could float two tons. The boat was a takedown affair, held together by screws, and when disassembled it made a load for two pack mules. This was the craft that Doane would be taking down the section of Snake River the trappers had called Mad River. Some of them had dissuaded Hunt from trying such a voyage in 1811, but there were no trappers who could have swayed the determined Doane.

He apparently concocted and promoted his exploration during the summer of 1876 while campaigning in Montana with Gen. A. H. Terry. Terry went over the head of Doane's commanding officer to authorize the exploration in a letter written on October 4, 1876. Since he was not working through regular channels, Doane knew in advance that his scheme was going to be approved. He also knew it was going to be a winter trip over much the same ground that Hayden had covered earlier in the decade.

Doane's men were certainly competent, even outstanding, soldiers, but they had no qualifications as explorers. Doane's scientific instruments consisted of a compass, a barometer, maximum and minimum thermometers, and a long tape measure. With these things, plus plenty of guns and ammunition and sixty day's rations, the party left Fort Ellis on October 11, 1876.

It took them about three weeks to march across Yellowstone Park to Heart Lake on the headwaters of the Snake River. The party had already experienced some severe winter weather and plenty of snow. At Heart Lake they found that the boat's planking had shrunk, and they were forced to recalk the seams, using pitch from the nearby trees. This was only the beginning, for when the boat was launched in the Heart River, preparatory to the party's descent to the Snake, it would not float. The stream was only about six inches deep, and it grew even shallower downstream from the lake. The already worn pack animals had to be reloaded with the boat's cargo and the boat hauled by hand down the waterway. On this first disappointing day the party, by Doane's estimate, made three miles, and the next day was no better. The men hauled the boat over the rocky stream bed in twenty-three-degree weather, and still could not make more than another three miles. They had to abandon one of their unfortunate horses.

For days on end the boat was a terrible burden to the tiring men. Because of the shallowness of the stream, it would not float and had to be dragged down canyons and around boulders and lowered over waterfalls. It was so cold that the leaky boat could be calked simply by tossing a cup of water, which immediately froze, over the offending crack. This method worked until the party approached the southern boundary of Yellowstone Park, where a number of hot springs entered the river and warmed it to the extent that the ice "calking" melted and the boat again leaked. It had to be hauled out and repaired once more.

The unexpected scarcity of game, which Doane had counted on for food, added to the men's distress. When one of them, Private Warren, proved himself a skillful angler and fed the crew with his catches of trout, Doane mentioned it, calling him "invaluable."

The journey so far had been too laborious to permit Doane to make any but the most superficial observations about the region through which he was passing. And, indeed, some of these observations concerning distances, minerals seen, and the sources of streams were inaccurate. Considering the hardships the party was encountering, it is remarkable that observations were made at all.

Once the men had reached the Snake River and could see the Teton Range, Doane noted, "There are beds of strange limestones very ancient and signs of coal, in regular carbon- iferous beds. These show grandly among the Tetons below." There is no coal in the Tetons. The lieutenant may have confused the black, diabase dike in Mount Moran for coal, although he could not have seen this dike from where he sup- posedly made his notes.

A little farther on Doane noticed an ousel alight on a rock near the camp, and it "sang for an hour." He compared the bird's song to that of a canary, and then remarked that these birds "do not sing in the summertime," an attempt at natural history that was inaccurate. The bird, however, proved a good omen, for the boating improved somewhat and the party was able to make faster progress. One evening, as the boaters were encamping, Doane reported that "an old moose screamed at us during the darkness just after nightfall, but ran off before the moon arose so we failed to get a shot at him"—another bit of inaccuracy, since moose are not noted for screaming.

As the party neared the inlet of Jackson Lake they saw "hundreds" of otter. These delightful animals still exist in the Snake River in Jackson Hole. Unfortunately, their numbers today don't approach those reported by Doane; indeed, today professional float-trip guides may spend weeks on the river without seeing an otter. The decline of these animals is probably tied to the decline of fish in the river, plus the fact that they have always worn a good price on their backs.

The Snake River between the south entrance of Yellowstone Park and the inlet of Jackson Lake is about five miles shorter today due to the enlargement of the lake by the dam at its outlet. The character of the land and waterscape today is, however, about as Doane described it in 1876. The trail running north and south through Jackson Hole lay east on the lake, and has now been superseded by a highway. Its location is a natural choice, leading through open and relatively flat countryside. For some unspecified reason Doane chose to lead his men down the west bank of the river and lake. Doane wrote, "An hour after we ran out into Jackson's Lake we passed the train just as a mule fell under a log across the trail, struggled a moment, and died." This ominous event might have served as a warning to the men of what lay ahead of them on the west side of the lake. It did not, and they struggled on.

When the expedition reached Jackson Lake it was forty-five days out of Fort Ellis. The men assigned to the boat were at last making reasonable progress, but those with the pack animals were only being drawn deeper into hell. Doane noted, ". . . terrible, severe traveling for the train, climbing over rocks and through tangled forests of pine, aspen and other varieties of timber. Passed the termini of several avalanche channels. Abandoned one horse."

A worn-out horse or mule abandoned in the Jackson Hole country is one of the saddest sights a man can see. Two years ago we picked up a young mare that had been abandoned on the Thorofare. The animal had been used up by an ignorant wrangler, and when we found it pecking around for survival on the snowy meadow it was a rack of bones. We caught the miserable creature and then half led and half dragged it into our camp. It stayed there for ten days while we tried to restore its strength with grain and abundant grass. The mare began a feeble recovery, but it wasn't enough—the emaciated creature collapsed on the snowy trail to Jackson Hole. The camp boss shot her.

The route along the western shore of Jackson Lake was not only rough but lacking in game. The men tried to eat some of the otter they had killed, but it had a fishy taste that caused all but one of them to vomit. They had run out of flour, and were depending upon trout as their only source of meat. But even in their semistarved condition the men were awed by the great range towering above them. And when they encamped on Moran Bay, at the foot of Mount Moran, their luck seemed to change. A deer was spotted swimming in the lake, and, when it reached the shore, Doane shot it.

The report of the rifle produced an astounding echo, which resounded far up into the canyon above. The men were intrigued by this phenomenon, and repeated the shooting experiment, which came back to them like "the rattle of musketry." Then they tried yelling, and eventually decided that the words "Oh Joe!" produced the grandest echo. What such a tumult would never produce was the game the party so badly needed. But Doane apparently never realized that his relatively worthless experiments with an echo would be sure to frighten off any game in the area.

Today, with Jackson Lake secure inside the boundaries of

the Grand Teton National Park, there is no chance to hear a gunshot echoing into the Tetons. But in the fall, after the tourists and pleasure-boaters have gone, migrating waterfowl rest on the lake in vast numbers. When they rise in flight, or simply patter excitedly to a new resting spot on the lake, the roar produced is stupendous. It races across the still waters like the musketry Doane mentioned, and often travels so far that the birds causing it are invisible.

After seven weeks of tremendous, painful effort, the party had still to reach the outlet of Jackson Lake. The hundreds of miles of Snake River, which they were to explore still lay before them. The men had all been sick: the deer that Doane had shot, which had seemed like manna from above, had given them diarrhea. Doane's horse had to be abandoned. And it was so cold that the vapor rising from the streams and lakes froze, then fell to earth again in a sort of automatic snow-storm. Today, people in the area call this "frost," and I have seen it fall in accumulations of an inch or more. On one oc-casion I was in a heavy fall of frost that seemed to precipitate a snowstorm from the queerly pinkish overcast.

Once the men reached the outlet of Jackson Lake, both the stream and the terrain improved and made easier traveling. Near Pacific Creek, which empties into the Snake, and which was also singled out by Beaver Dick as one of the great "hunt-ing tribriterys," they saw a herd of elk. Had they been healthier and riding sounder horses, and above all had they had more time, the men might have found even more members of the huge Jackson Hole elk herd. But they had none of these things, and were forced to toil through one of the last great game ranges in the West on the verge of starvation.

The shoreline that the Doane party followed around Jack-son Lake is no more. The lake's impounded waters have long covered it, and such a trek today, over steeper hillsides and through even thicker timber, is not pleasant to contemplate. But the shoreline of Leigh Lake, immediately south of Jackson Lake, is still natural, and certainly very much like the terrain Doane's men fought their way across. To get an inkling of what it must have been like, I hiked around Leigh Lake one summer day. There had been a trail, but it has been abandoned for years, and the Park Service discourages travel there.

I went to little Bear Paw Lake, which lies between Jackson Lake's Moran Bay and Leigh Lake. From there I struck out on a good trail that apparently led to the western shore of Leigh Lake. In my notes for the day I wrote: ". . . the trail began deteriorating. Parts of it were obscured under the increasingly heavy vegetation and other sections were gone, fallen down the steep slope into the lake. Some predecessor on the trail—moose and at least one hiker—had beaten down the vegetation well enough to make a path I could follow.

"Then I came on a large rock slide. I could hear water running underneath and looking up the steep gulch [above] saw a good advertisement for not lingering there too long. It was full of rocks, big ones, that seemed poised to come crashing down. Getting across wasn't difficult, and once across the old trail was visible again.

"The trail led along the beach here . . . then into some timber. I could hear a stream roaring ahead and presently was walking over cobbles on the bank of a fast, clear stream. From a small waterfall about 75 yards above, it swept down over the rocks, following a couple of channels. I walked downstream, looking for a crossing. There was none, so I sat down by the best-looking ford and removed my boots and socks. I pulled my pants up to my calves, gathered trash bag, boots, and raincoat and picked up a stout stick. The water was deceptively deep, and I was soon in to my knees. If I hadn't been able to feel my way with my toes and the help of the stick I probably would have been knocked down. I had only a few feet to wade across, but they were exciting feet."

On the far bank I put on my boots again, noting that the going was becoming "progressively worse."

"Many trees had fallen across the trail, and there were numerous boggy spots. I got completely off the trail for a time but found it again just before reaching another rushing stream—there were two good-sized ones and several rills. The first had debris across it and I forded easily, but the second was a roaring gush of water that I crossed by sitting on a convenient log and hunching myself across.

"The next couple of miles were almost a wilderness. The trail was distinct, but so crossed with downed timber and mired-in little bogs that I made poor progress. . . . At one point I carelessly stepped on the slanting face of a smooth wet rock and went down rather heavily. It would have been a bad place to be hurt, but I was not and went on, depending upon use to loosen up my slightly twisted ankle and throbbing knee.

"When I reached a clearing on the lake I was able to look back and see that the big rock slide I had crossed was below Falling Ice Glacier on Mt. Moran. It was truly a place to hasten by."

What had been a difficult few hours for me were terrible days for the Doane party. It is probably a tribute to the lieutenant's ability to lead, and perhaps to his men's practicality as well as their sense of duty, that the officer wasn't "fragged." Surely lieutenants serving in Viet Nam have been killed by their own troops with much less justification.

On December 1, 1876, their fifty-second day out of Fort Ellis, the party encamped along the river opposite Blacktail Butte, which had been named Gros Ventre Butte by the Hayden team. Doane still had diarrhea and was very weak. Another herd of elk was seen, but the famished men were unable to kill one. Their remaining animals were now too weak to carry any loads at all. The stream was, and still is, broken by many channels that confused the boaters. A wrong guess and their course led them onto shallow shoals and bars, where they had to get out and haul the boat over.

The men were subsisting on trout and finding them not enough. Doane noted, "We now have no coffee, tea, sugar, bacon, and worst of all, no tobacco. Nothing but a few beans left. The game is scarce and shy. I cannot hunt and keep the observations at the same time."

Within hours of writing the last sentence, Doane and his men ate their last beans, and with them gone there was no food in camp. They spent another day hunting, but could not reach the game, which was high up in the Gros Ventre. Only Private Warren, the party's inveterate angler, was able to bring any food to camp. He caught sixteen trout, which were eaten at a sitting. It was not enough, and Private Warren's horse was shot.

One quarter of the animal was prepared and put on the fire to boil. In addition, the bones were cracked for marrow and the bullets were drawn from a packet of cartridges so that the powder could be used for seasoning. The men had high hopes for a fine gravy, but it all came to nothing. They could not make gravy, and the boiled horse was tough and tasted like its sweat had smelled. But it was food, and the men worked at chewing and swallowing it. They had already been reusing their tea and coffee grounds for two weeks, so there was nothing to drink but water. They tried smoking the bark of red willow and "larb," which is bearberry and also the "kinnikinnick" of the Indians, who used to mix it with their tobacco.

As they floated and led their stock south from the locale of present-day Moose, they had sunny weather and made good time. But it was cold, and shelves of ice had begun building up along the stream banks. The boat leaked water, which then froze and had to be chopped out. Below the mouth of the Gros Ventre the diversity of river channels again caused them difficulty. They had no food save horse meat and the trout Private Warren was able to catch.

When they got downstream and in the vicinity of present-day Wilson, they were still toiling through long shallows. They could not find any game, and one of the men became very ill from struggling in the water for so many hours. It must have seemed a miracle then when Doane's sergeant found a trapper's cabin at the base of the mountains. It was John Pierce, a man Beaver Dick had befriended and camped with in Pierre's Hole.

Pierce was a loner. He had entered into a brief trapping partnership with one of Beaver Dick's friends, but seems to have spent most of his time alone. In the few accounts of him, he appears to have had the peculiar shyness of the solitary backwoodsman. Beaver Dick first met him in mid-September on the lower reaches of the south fork of Snake River. The year is uncertain, since the chronology of Beaver Dick's journal is unclear. But it was probably 1873 or 1874. Pierce told Dick that he was from the Yellowstone country. He also said that he hadn't caught much and was then on his way to Eagle Rock (Idaho Falls) to outfit for the fall season. A week later Dick ran into Pierce again, several miles north of Eagle Rock. Pierce had fallen sick and Dick took him home with him. In a few days the man recovered and started for Montana.

A year later Dick returned home to find Pierce and his friend Tom Lavering. The two had entered into a fall's trapping partnership and hired Dick to pack their outfit north into the Henry's Lake area. The men did not reach their cabin on Buffalo Creek until nearly November. As they were unpacking, Dick records, Pierce shot a wolverine. Later they attempted to cut wild hay, but the snow was already too deep. Dick then bid his friends good-bye and took all the horses back to the Teton Basin. John Pierce does not reappear until Doane's sergeant found him in 1876.

The old man gave the sergeant a good meal and sent back some salt, which made their horse meat more palatable. On the morning of December 8 the trapper paid the explorers a visit. He brought with him a quarter of elk and some flour. The soldiers immediately began cooking the meat and soon had eaten it all. When they finished, Pierce gave Doane detailed information about the mining camps of the Caribou district, which lay just beyond the mouth of Mad River Canyon. Pierce had been unable to believe that anyone would try to boat down the Snake River in the wintertime. And he seems to have had to see the boat before believing the sergeant's story. He was all by himself, although when Beaver Dick knew him Pierce had owned a dog, and also without horses. Lacking them for transport, he told Doane he was bypassing beaver and only trapping "fine furs"—mink, marten, fisher, and otter.

Doane wrote that throughout Pierce's visit the trapper had been "completely puzzled as to what motives could have induced us to attempt such a trip in such a way and at such a season."

In their book, *Battle Drums and Geysers,* Orrin and Lorraine Bonney mention an early settler's report that Pierce was still living in Jackson Hole in the late 1880s, taking up land north of the town of Jackson about 1887. He is little remembered today, although the Doane party owed a great deal to the old trapper's generosity.

After the trapper went home, the party continued down the river and camped at the head of Snake River Canyon, where the river, between sheer rock walls, narrows. The water is a swirling green and, in the many great pools, very deep. Nevertheless, it is a stretch that can be navigated with ordinary boats. But once these relatively placid waters are passed over, the river becomes a treacherous burst of rapids, whirling eddies, and gigantic boulders. The men had to handline their boat through these while the horses were brought along game trails on the canyon walls.

On their first night in the canyon a big ice floe ground its way down the stream, keeping the men awake with its sounds. The winds that customarily wash down this canyon have convinced me that it is one of the coldest places in Wyoming. Even in summer it is seldom hot along the river. I remember leaving home one morning in early December when the temperature was thirty below zero. Compared with the temperatures I experienced a few minutes later in the canyon, we'd been having a heat wave.

As the men worked the boat farther down the canyon it had to be slithered across blocks of floating ice. More ice piled into the eddies, making the passage even more difficult. Doane's observations at this point in his journal become somewhat inaccurate. His reports of the distances traveled are exaggerated, and physical features of the canyon are a little out of place.

But such lapses are understandable, because the men were now dragging the boat over ice shelves and then going back to drag the cargo in a painful series of relays. They were again out of food except for a bit of flour. Private White's horse was shot for food. This left them with two horses and one mule. Sergeant Server and Private Warren, "whose stomach had begun to give way," were detailed to go ahead with the stock and the party's pooled funds. Doane guessed that they were forty miles from the settlements, where he hoped the two could buy supplies and return.

After the pair had gotten packed they followed along beside the boaters. Doane and two others got into the boat. The other two privates walked along the frozen shore, holding ropes attached to the boat. At one point the boat suddenly swung to the bank and lurched onto a rock where it filled with water. The men sprang ashore and barely succeeded in saving the boat from swamping. All their gear was soaked and had to be unloaded. Then the empty boat was lowered by hand down the rapids.

The same method had to be used on two more sections, and then the lieutenant was able to note that the river was improving. Doane wrote, "We let the towline go while we held her following along the ice afoot. The river was becoming better, the ice foot more uniform and the channel free from frozen pools, when all of a sudden the boat touched the margin, turned under, and the next instant was dancing end over end in the swift current. All of the horse meat, all the property, arms, instruments, and note books were in the roaring stream."

By great luck the men were able to recover their clothing, bedding, and the tent. The men also saved a hind quarter of the horse. They were able to dry their gear, but at last Doane seemed to completely grasp the gravity of their situation and sent the sergeant and Private Warren ahead for help. The party was without food, save horse meat, and they had lost all their guns, plus Doane's notebooks and instruments. (Doane later compiled his journal from a duplicate notebook kept by the invaluable Sergeant Server.)

The river did not improve for long. The famished men were again compelled to do the exhausting work of lowering and dragging the boat down the unrelenting river. They had matches and sheath knives and so were able to roast the remaining horse meat. But when it had been eaten they were again out of food and without the means to get more. The boat slowly filled with ice, and since their axes and hatchets were lost they could not chop it out. The boat became ever more difficult to handle. On December 15, the sixty-sixth day, the men cached their bedding and, leaving the boat, started on foot in search of help in the Caribou mining district. The party had nothing to eat but a few rose hips. In his weariness Doane tended to overestimate his progress through the canyon of the Snake. He noted that he and his men had to keep going just to keep from freezing, but that the snow and their exhaustion prevented them from making more than a mile an hour.

Below the mouth of the cruel canyon the party found a frozen creek that showed evidences of placer mining. They followed a fork of the stream until they came to a huge beaver dam. Here they were forced to spend still another agonizing night in the open and without food. On December 17, the sixty-eighth day of the march, Private Davis began acting strangely. While the other party members were building a fire, Davis began frantically climbing the adjacent hillsides. He had to be called back several times.

As they were building the fire and warming themselves, Doane found a timber he identified as coming from a miner's flume. With this and a few other signs of human activity to guide them, the men labored on up the creek. Doane wrote, ". . . Applegate declared he smelled the smoke of burning pine. In half an hour we reached a miner's cabin and were safe."

Soon after, Sergeant Server and Private Warren, who had been detailed to leave the boat and go ahead with the horses, also arrived at the cabin. It was a remarkable journey both in the imbecility that inspired it and the heroism with which it had been accomplished.

To my knowledge no one has ever tried to duplicate the Doane party's winter expedition of 1876. There were no significant discoveries. A surveying team from the Hayden expedition of 1872 had already covered most of the Doane Route four years earlier. The only unknown parts of the Snake River still lay far beyond the little mining camp of Keenan City, where the party was recuperating. Doane had endangered the lives of his men, subjected his horses and mules to the most pitiless toil, and wasted government money. When he reached the miner's cabin he weighed one hundred twenty-six pounds, which was sixty-four pounds below normal.

While he was resting, Doane sent messages to Fort Hall and Fort Ellis reporting his expedition safe. He had small sleds built, to be drawn by his three remaining animals, on which he planned to carry provisions and the party's bedding. After only five days' rest Doane, his men, and the horse-drawn sleds started for Fort Hall. He said that his men were in good spirits but that they were "not very strong." The sleds did not work properly and had to be rebuilt.

In his journal covering this part of the trip, Doane is very matter of fact. Once he and his men had walked through the snow to Fort Hall, he was making plans to refit, send for his boat, and "resume the survey."

Before they had walked far, a small relief party met Doane on the Snake. He thereupon sent the redoubtable sergeant and four men back upstream after the boat. When the sergeant returned it was to report that the boat had been smashed to bits by a passing gorge of ice. Doane never questioned whether or not the sergeant had wisely assisted the ice in its work. Instead he made fresh plans to retrace his steps and to then rebuild the infamous boat at the spot where it had been broken up. From there, he decreed the party would resume navigating the Snake River.

Doane's plan, in his own words, was to ". . . make all possible speed to Fort Hall, there refit and returning bring lumber to rebuild the boat on the ground where it had been lost, and to continue on to Eagle Rock Bridge on the Snake River, *previously going back far enough beyond Jackson's Lake to take a renewal of the system of triangulations and notes lost in the river* when the boat capsized." (Italics mine.)

Providentially, Doane's commanding officer at Fort Ellis stopped this insanity by ordering Doane and his men to return to post. They did, and so ended this, and all other, military surveys of the Snake River in winter.

In 1880 the vainglorious Doane again went off on an exploration. This time it was to the Arctic, and this time it was an even greater failure. The ship in which the explorers embarked proved unseaworthy and was barely able to return to its port, let alone reach Arctic waters. Once again Doane's ambitions were wrecked, but he was undaunted. He now applied for the superintendency of Yellowstone National Park—and his application was passed over.

He might have expected it, for after the pretentious trip into the Yellowstone in 1870 Doane's ambitions were star-crossed. His army career was not particularly distinguished, and he only made his promotion to captain by outliving those officers on the list ahead of him.

There is a peak in Yellowstone Park named for Gustavus Cheney Doane. Another one, in the Tetons, is called Doane Peak. It is 11,354 feet tall. It rises in the northern part of the range, but, like its namesake, does not loom large on the horizon.

This country beyond the Tetons is a wild and beautiful district and a valuable one. . . . At this time it was a favorite rendezvous for bands of desperadoes and thieves.

LIEUTENANT DOANE'S 1876 JOURNAL

8 / The Outlaws

It is a peculiar ritual every summer evening in Jackson, Wyoming, to cordon off certain streets in the center of town. As the automobile traffic stops, the shops empty and a crowd begins forming on the sidewalks. Newcomers, unaware of the customs of Jackson, may be startled over their dinners to hear a guest at an adjoining table ask the waitress, "What time is the hanging?"

The answer appears at approximately 7:00 P.M., when a procession of mounted men rides into view, escorting a horse-drawn buggy abloom with young actresses in 1890 costumes. As the cavalcade passes, appreciative murmurs rise from the crowd, and, before the procession has reached the thronged intersection where action seems imminent, people are six deep along the curbings. Every tourist seems to be carrying either a small child on his shoulders or a camera in his hands.

Soon a stagecoach comes rattling up to the intersection, and as it arrives young men in cowboy suits suddenly appear on the low tops of adjacent buildings with guns in their hands. A pistol shot is fired, and a man slumps. Before he can quiver his last, the square is spattered with gunshots and littered with bodies. The crowd murmers and titters. No one in the melee in the street seems to mind the titters, especially the horse that languidly raises his tail and defecates.

The cue to cease firing does not come until all the blank cartridges have been fired. Then the bandit leader surrenders and a posse member quickly steps forward and slips a formidable noose around the "outlaw's" neck. The crowd is asked whether or not the lynching shall proceed. My vote, like most others that night, is affirmative. But, despite a vote that seems overwhelmingly to favor it, the hanging is postponed. Then, for reasons unclear, its potential victim addresses a mawkish lecture to the children in the crowd. Not many of them listen, although their parents do, and some applaud heartily when the speech ends.

This nightly ritual, with a debatable kind of good triumphing over evil, is part of what the big tourist crowds come thousands of miles to see. And while I object to the patent falsity of the show's premise I remember, too, that the staged evil rises like the phoenix every night all summer in Jackson; that nightly resurrection, unintentionally, seems to give evil the importance it deserves.

The western story with its essential bad man ranks high among America's best-loved entertainments, and one of its birthplaces was Jackson Hole. Furthermore, the valley and the stories told about it were a source of inspiration to Owen Wister when he wrote *The Virginian*.

In the seventy years since it was first published, that book has sold over two million copies and has been filmed four times. A television series using the novel's title and some of its characters ran interminably. Wister was a fairly well-to-do eastern dude who had an unabashed love affair with the West. He traveled widely, when he could afford to, and later intertwined what he saw in the West with the romantic things he imagined about it. What Wister did to make his novel so popular was to take some already stock ingredients, add some experience, and then turn it all out in a new blend. His cowboy was a knight of the rangeland who, under his deep tan, epitomized the white Anglo-Saxon Protestant. And, for his proper point of view, Wister let his cowboy fall in love.

The Virginian set the standard for modern western novels, and Jack Sheaffer's *Shane* followed that standard so well that it has been called the perfect western. *Shane* was filmed in Jackson Hole, and by all measures is the best of the many pictures made there. The film is still shown in Jackson Hole during most summers. And so great was its initial popularity that a whole generation of young men named for its hero can now be found in the audiences, watching it.

It has never really mattered, even to the people who live in Jackson Hole and who know better, that the picture is full of incongruities and factual errors. What matters is that *Shane* showed us exactly what we wanted to see and did it in one of the most beautiful settings in America.

The outlaw, Matt Warner, who claimed to have gone to Jackson Hole after a bank robbery, said it was a great country long before films proved it to us. In June of 1889 Warner, Butch Cassidy, and their poisonous mentor, Tom McCarty, robbed a bank in Telluride, Colorado, of some ten thousand dollars. After a nerve-wracking summer on the dodge, Cassidy finally went to ground near Lander, Wyoming, while Warner and McCarty spent their winter in Star Valley, just south of Jackson Hole. At this time and for many years thereafter Star Valley's deep snows left it virtually isolated all winter. The two outlaws rode in and told the gullible Mormon pioneers that they were ranchers who had just sold out and wanted to share their good fortune by setting up a free bar in their cabin.

Because many of the residents of Star Valley were polygamists and not fond of lawmen themselves, they hastened to accept the outlaws' story. Besides dispensing free drinks, the pair furthered their popularity by holding up a profiteering storekeeper and forcing him to provide staples to pioneers impoverished by a particularly bitter winter. Warner said he later paid the storekeeper eleven hundred dollars for the goods the people took. The outlaws both capped their winter sojourn in Star Valley by marrying local girls. Matt's bride was fourteen years old.

There men's wedded bliss was interrupted by a pair of deputies. In the early spring, as soon as a trail opened, they had ridden into the valley looking for the outlaws. When they came to the outlaws' cabin, however, McCarty got the drop on them. Then, with Warner's help, McCarty ran the two officers out of Star Valley. But the outlaws realized that the respite they had won was only temporary, and so they made immediate plans for a fast trip to Jackson Hole.

They acquired a wagon, and with Tom on its box and Matt on horseback and driving a small bunch of horses, the two couples started for Jackson Hole via the Stump Creek Trail, which was a segment of the historic Lander Cutoff to Oregon. Parts of the trail and the names pioneers carved on the aspen trees are still visible—not that the outlaws would have noticed them, for they were traveling mostly at night, and even forbidding their wondering brides warming fires after dark. To explain this secrecy the men told the girls it was all part of their grand honeymoon adventure.

Years later Warner described the outlaw trail more realistically to Charles Kelley: ". . . No sleep! Even when you know you're perfectly safe you can't sleep. Every pissant under your pillow sounds like a posse coming to get you."

After checking to make sure no ambush awaited them at the Eagle Rock Bridge, near present day Idaho Falls, Matt said the quartet went on to Jackson Hole. He also wrote that they stayed there a month, fishing, hunting, and keeping to themselves. After this idyllic life palled Warner wrote that they went on to Butte via Yellowstone Park. In Butte their money ran out, so the men sent their brides home, then robbed a gambling game.

Matt Warner wrote his story almost fifty years after the fact, and there are some doubts in my mind about his visit to Jackson Hole. Even after so long a time it seems strange that he would not mention what was then a very rugged route over Teton Pass. The trip would have been especially difficult since, according to Warner, they seem to have taken the same wagon all the way to Butte. Such a trip through Jackson Hole to Butte via Yellowstone Park would have been extremely difficult because no road existed through the Park's south entrance at that time. Furthermore, the men would have been taking a great risk by traveling through the park at a time when it was sternly patrolled by U.S. cavalry. My own guess is that, while Matt Warner probably did pass through Jackson Hole at some time, he confused it with Teton Basin while writing his memoirs.

Matt Warner's young wife died of cancer a few years after her strange honeymoon. Warner later settled in Price, Utah, where he was alternately a marshal, a justice of the peace, and a bootlegger. He died in 1938, revered by a few, a town curiosity to most.

One historian of outlaw days said that Jackson Hole was the special province of "Teton" Jackson, who did not welcome strangers in the valley. This outlaw has become one of the best-known, and in some minds the king, of Jackson Hole's wild bunch.

In the Park Service Museum at Moose there is an old photograph of Teton Jackson. He is mounted on horseback with a cased rifle under his leg, his rough clothes and heavy moustache all contributing to a fierce appearance. Jackson is supposed to have been a packer in General Crook's command during the Sioux campaign of the late 1870s. After that he is reputed to have been a denizen of the infamous Hole-in-the-Wall hideout near Buffalo, Wyoming. Jackson was next reported in the Teton Basin during the summer of 1882. According to lawyer-historian Ben Driggs, Jackson, in partnership with Harry Thompson and Robert Cooper, built a cabin and horse corral on Badger Creek and claimed to be prospecting in the area. The following January Cooper foolishly boasted to a neighboring settler of the trio's real business by announcing that he and his partners had some stolen horses in their corral.

After Cooper went to bed that night one of his partners shot him in the forehead. Jackson and Thompson then rode down to Rexburg, Idaho, and turned themselves in, claiming they had killed Cooper in self-defense. Two officers were sent back to the Badger Creek cabin, where they found Cooper. His corpse had frozen solid, and, having no means of transportation other than their saddle horses, the two got an ax and chopped off Cooper's head. It was then stuffed into a gunny sack and returned to the court at Malad.

Despite this startling evidence, there was no real proof against the pair, and they were acquitted of the killing. According to Drigg's *History of Teton Valley* new charges of horse stealing were immediately placed against them. But before their trial could begin, it first had to be established where the theft had occurred and whether the case was under Idaho or Wyoming jurisdiction. Jackson was subsequently convicted of horse stealing, but, contrary to some reports, his partner, Thompson, was not sent to prison. It is probable that Thompson came to Jackson Hole after the Cooper acquittal. There is also reason to believe that Jackson was out of custody between the Cooper hearings and his later conviction for horse stealing.

Teton Jackson was sentenced to fourteen years for grand larceny, and was received at the Boise City Penitentiary on November 5, 1885. At the time he gave his name as William J. Jackson and his birthplace as Rhode Island. He was thirty years old, five feet nine and three-quarter inches tall, and had red hair and brown eyes. His occupation was listed as shoemaker. This may have been a trade assigned him in prison, since there is no other record of his following it either before or after his prison years. A few months after entering the prison, on August 26, 1886, Jackson and a companion escaped by tunneling under a wall.

After his escape Jackson returned to the Teton Basin–Jackson Hole area, and was soon accused of reviving the local crime wave. During this period, as well as throughout his criminal career, it seems that the actual amount of time Jackson spent in Jackson Hole was relatively short.

Despite a meager record of him there is some basis for thinking that Jackson went to Jackson Hole after the Sioux War of the late 1870s and before he appeared in Teton Basin during the summer of 1882. Although he apparently headquartered in the Badger Creek cabin after that time, it is reasonable to believe that his horse-stealing forays occasionally brought him into Jackson Hole. There are a few contemporary reports that say that Jackson was in Jackson Hole after his escape from prison.

The outlaw's retreat in Jackson Hole was said to be in the

marsh, now included in the National Elk Refuge, just north of the present site of the town of Jackson. This cabin had been built in the "morass" to help make it and its inhabitants safe from attack. Robert E. Miller, who settled in Jackson Hole in 1885, claimed to have bought Jackson's cabin from either Jackson or one of his men. Miller was later said to have torn down the bandits' cabin and used the logs to construct other buildings on his ranch.

A news article written years later fantasized Teton Jackson as "a gentleman rancher in Teton Park with a fine home, ample ranch buildings [and] hay aplenty." The article further alleged that unsuspecting cowpunchers would be hired to gather cattle "belonging to some English syndicate . . ." and "in the course of a few weeks the herd would be in Teton Park near Jackson." Then Jackson would rework the stolen cattle's brands, and when the signs of meddling had healed he would have the animals driven west for sale.

Rustling was a way of life among a large segment of the population in late nineteenth-century Wyoming. But it never afforded Teton Jackson a rich living. He is remembered for specializing in horses. And, as an early settler, Lee Lucas, wrote, "The days of the rustlers were over before the cattle industry [in Jackson Hole] started. They never rustled cattle anyway. Their operations were confined to horse stealing. Cattle were too slow moving to be brought in and out of this kind of country."

To balance Lucas's opinion, however, it is fair to mention old-time stock detective and marshal Joe Lefors's belief. He wrote that a herd of steers could actually be moved over a long distance faster than could a herd of horses. Also, there are a few eyewitness accounts of some rustled cattle being in, or sought in, Jackson Hole during its earliest days. Still, there is even more evidence of the valley being used as a hiding place for stolen horses.

William L. Simpson, whose family was one of the first to settle in Jackson Hole, wrote this reminiscence in his later years: "I came into the Jackson Hole country during the

Thomas Moran
in Yellowstone country, 1871.

The first wheeled vehicle in Jackson Hole.
This cart was handmade by pioneer John Carnes.

LEFT ABOVE
An early-day pack trip guided by S. N. Leek in the wilderness
country of Jackson Hole.

LEFT BELOW
Owen Wister (facing camera) helping his guides extricate a
bogged-down horse in the Jackson Hole country.

*Teton Jackson. Photo taken after the outlaw
had settled down on his ranch.*

RIGHT ABOVE
*Teton Jackson astride a horse he surely would not have
stolen during his outlaw days.*

RIGHT BELOW
*Buffalo roaming in Jackson Hole. These animals are not
presently afforded protection in Wyoming, and when they
venture outside the boundaries of Grand Teton Park
they are often killed.*

Rose Koops in August of 1970—the only surviving child of Beaver Dick Leigh.

LEFT ABOVE

Thomas Moran, the artist who helped spread the fame of Jackson Hole.

LEFT BELOW

Owen Wister's home near Moose. It is now owned by the National Park Service.

*Horse and rider descending the switchbacks
of Cascade Canyon in the Teton Range.*

The Tetons as seen from the Deadman's Bar area on the Snake River.

Bull and cow elk on winter range
in Jackson Hole.

RIGHT ABOVE

A Wyoming or Shiras moose photographed
in Jackson Hole.

RIGHT BELOW

A hiker's view of the Cathedral Group
in the Teton Mountains.

*Coyote. These animals are plentiful
in Jackson Hole, where they grow so large
that they are frequently mistaken for wolves.*

RIGHT ABOVE

*An early photograph of R. E. Miller's homestead in
Jackson Hole. Miller was one of the first settlers in the valley
and the only one to become wealthy.*

RIGHT BELOW

*A first harvest of oats in early-day Jackson Hole. The abundance
of the first crops misled many settlers, who in later years either
failed and moved on or stayed and eked out a meager existence.*

*Hidden Falls. This lovely waterfall issues
from Cascade Canyon and flows into Jenny Lake.*

RIGHT ABOVE

*Male sage grouse displaying in early spring. These native
birds still survive in Jackson Hole.*

RIGHT BELOW

Winter near Jenny Lake. The snow is about four feet deep.

Buffalo eating new shoots of grass.
Teton background.

Bar BC, the old Struthers Burt Guest
and Cattle Ranch.

Month of October 1885. I was with a posse of Stock Association Men, Sheriffs, and Deputies who had information that a large band of steers had been stolen from the head of Wind River. The party was under the command of Pap Conant; there were fourteen men and myself in the party; I was seventeen years of age. I was brought along solely to take care of the horses, and not to do any fighting.

"We camped at the old Indian Trail on the Grosventre 5 miles north of Jackson. There were only two cabins—which belonged to a man by the name of Tommy [*sic*] Carnes, and John Holland, his partner, was trapping in the Jackson Hole country that fall. We found a few steers on the head of Spread Creek, the snow was about fifteen inches deep on the divide; and all cattle trails had been obliterated. As we came in the valley we noticed that there were a great many horse signs, but no horses in sight. The reason being that the person engaged in horse stealing at that time had information that we were coming into the valley, and placed one band of horses on the Flat Creek Meadows; the other band was corraled on the head of what is known as the Leek's Draw. We were not looking for horse thieves or horses and made no particular inquiry."

Simpson, who later became a frontier prosecutor and was the only man ever to send Butch Cassidy to jail, also included in his papers a "Memorandum and Statement of William Arms, Malad, Idaho." In it "Arms," whose correct name was Arnn, stated that he had come into Jackson Hole in June of 1885. During the following winter he counted six men besides himself in the valley. They were John Holland, Robert E. Miller, Ed Thompson and a partner named Hilderbrand, Locke Beye (or Behy), and Ed Harrington. Three of these men, Thompson —who was probably the "Harry" Thompson implicated in the Cooper killing—Hilderbrand, and Ed Harrington were known outlaws. John Holland has been accused of horse stealing and also, with his partner Carnes, of providing supplies to rustlers using the valley. Whatever the individual degree of guilt, it was a rough crew that first settled in Jackson Hole.

Teton Jackson has been reported to have associated with

Harrington as well as Thompson in the Teton Basin. Simpson claimed that Teton was working with Harrington at the time of the Cooper killing.

For reasons I have not been able to learn, William L. Simpson had a fierce dislike for Teton Jackson. Simpson has been reliably reported to have been a good friend and an implacable enemy, and this latter characteristic should be remembered when reading Simpson's accounts of Teton Jackson. Simpson once wrote, "Teton Jackson did have a reputation as being a small time horse thief but he was not in the same class as Ed Thompson, [or] Red Campbell. . . ." It is worth noting that Jackson was thought to have ridden with both Thompson and Red Campbell.

Recalling Teton Jackson in his autobiography, Frank Canton, another frontier sheriff, stated that Jackson was a multiple murderer and a member of the notorious Mormon Destroying Angels, and that the Territory of Utah had offered thirty-five hundred dollars for him dead or alive. He also claimed that Jackson was a nephew of the convicted murderer, John D. Lee, and that he, Jackson, used his Mormon religion to get protection from Mormon families while he dodged the law in outlying areas.

The Utah Historical Society carefully helped me to check all of Canton's claims, and we found that none of them was proven. Juanita Brooks, who is *the* expert on Utah's notorious John D. Lee, wrote me to say that since Lee had no brothers or sisters it would have been difficult for him to have been Teton Jackson's uncle. Apparently there was no relationship of any kind, and there is no record that Jackson ever belonged to the Mormon church in his outlaw days.

Despite his supporters, Frank Canton is being shown by most historians as a very dubious character. I don't think he was above making up the stories about Jackson in order to enhance his claim of having captured Teton Jackson. This arrest, in the Big Horn Basin, would seem to have been the one for horse stealing following the shooting of Cooper. According to Ben Driggs, when Jackson was arrested and returned to prison in 1888 he had been in the vicinity of Henry's Lake.

Jackson remained in prison until 1892, when he was pardoned. Afterward he went to the Wind River country, where he ran afoul of William Simpson, who wrote, ". . . the next incident of his [Jackson's] life occurred in Fremont and Sweetwater counties on the West side of the range. That was in 1894." Simpson tells how a hundred sacks of gold ore from an Atlantic City, Wyoming, mine had disappeared. Because Simpson was Fremont County attorney, the suspected ore theft was brought to his attention. Investigating, he found that four or five heavy boxes had been shipped from Green River, Wyoming, to Salt Lake City. On the suspicion that these boxes contained the missing ore, Simpson went to Salt Lake, where he was unsuccessful in locating them.

He wrote, "I returned to Green River and got a tip that Jackson and a young man by the name of Howard had shipped the boxes to Salt Lake City. I returned there . . . and found the boxes intact in the basement of the Templeton Hotel and instead of containing gold ore they contained dried deer, antelope and elk meat. I returned to Green River, filed a complaint . . . against the two parties Jackson and Howard, under the theory that the asportation of the wild meat was in and through Sweetwater County."

Simpson's case, as he described it, was very weak, and the charges were properly dismissed. It seemed to mark Teton Jackson's last brush with the law. Shortly after his release from prison he took a Shoshone wife and began operating a ranch near Crowheart, Wyoming. He is also said to have done some guiding—and he'd have been a good one, considering his knowledge of back-country trails.

Slim Lawrence has a picture of the mellowing bad man taken around the turn of the century. It shows Jackson, hard-faced as ever and wearing a big hat, sitting outdoors on a plain wooden chair with his legs crossed. He is wearing leather puttees and on his knee is a baby, dressed in white. Standing behind Jackson and slightly to his right is his expressionless Indian wife, wearing a black dress. As a family portrait it is unique.

Years ago Slim Lawrence visited Jackson on his ranch, and

recently told me that the old outlaw appeared to have earned a comfortable and honest living in his last years. An article in the *Wyoming State Tribune,* however, paints an unhappier picture. It states that the aging bandit died in 1927 as a public charge in the county home. According to the article he was "cared for by Mrs. James Fyfe who found him an interesting character."

Ed Thompson, who was described as a lieutenant of Jackson's when the men were in Jackson Hole, disappeared soon after the valley began to be settled. But he left behind a legend, the setting of which is the low butte that rises on the eastern edge of the elk refuge marsh and is now called Miller Butte.

On the east side of this butte, until a road construction crew blasted it away, there was a ledge locally known as Fort Standoff. It was from this ledge that Ed Thompson is supposed to have stood off three peace officers. According to the story, Thompson met the officers while he was en route to John Carnes's cabin to check the front sight he'd just replaced on a rifle. Shooting started, and, though Thompson's buckskin shirt was riddled with bullet holes, the outlaw was not hit and he eventually drove off the lawmen. An article in the October 12, 1886, edition of the *Cheyenne Daily Leader* states, "A posse started out for Jackson's hole. They got there and encountered a portion of 'Teton's' band under the efficient conduct of Bill Thompson, Teton's lieutenant, a fearless desperado and the best rifle shot of the border. After a sharp fight in the open ground, the robbers retreated to their log castle in the morass, and the posse let them stay there."

Owen Wister apparently used this same ledge as the site of an incident in *The Virginian.* Wister is also thought to have patterned his character, Trampus, after one of the valley's outlaws, Ed Harrington. Harrington admitted, and even bragged of, being a model for the novelist, but he insisted that it was the heroic character of the Virginian that he'd been a pattern for.

Harrington had come west from the Ozarks and was one of

the very early occupants of Jackson Hole, where he reportedly had a job, at times, feeding stock in the winter. He was also well known in Teton Basin, but primarily as a thief.

In 1887 Harrington, a man named Columbus Nickerson, and Jim Robinson stole a number of horses in the Teton Basin and hid them in nearby canyons. The owners, missing their stock, began a search that soon located the animals. This first search touched off a second one for the outlaws. Harrington got a warning that the officers were after him and skipped out, leaving his two partners in a remote cabin. A posse later surrounded the two rustlers in their cabin and called on them to surrender. Robinson ran out and was mortally wounded. Nickerson came out more peaceably and was arrested. Harrington had not run far enough, and was soon apprehended in Rexburg, Idaho.

While he and Nickerson were in jail awaiting trial, Mrs. Nickerson smuggled a revolver in to them. Harrington took the gun from her and turned it on the jailer, forcing him to open their cell. Before leaving the jail the pair released two murderers who had also been in custody. The rustlers then fled on horses the thoughtful Mrs. Nickerson had hidden nearby.

Harrington and Nickerson rode out along the south fork of the Snake River, but found it too high to ford. They stopped at a farm and foolishly bragged of their exploits to a farmer, who reported them as soon as the outlaws left. A posse quickly descended on the area and surrounded the rustlers in a marshy spot along the river bottom. The men resisted capture by hiding in the marsh all night. In the morning Harrington saw a deputy and took a shot at him. Harrington missed, but the deputy returned the fire, hitting the outlaw in the foot. It was all the inducement Harrington needed to surrender, and Nickerson quickly followed suit. The men were later tried and convicted. Harrington was given a long prison term, while Nickerson got off with a few months in jail.

Ben Driggs wrote that it was mainly through the efforts of Harrington's mother that her son was given a pardon four years later, but her efforts were wasted, because her son had not reformed. He continued his thievery, becoming known at this time as Ed Trafton. He also polished his growing skills as a dry-gulcher by harassing a sheep outfit and attempting, unsuccessfully, to dynamite a couple of sheepmen. Then, in an amusing turnabout and commentary on frontier life, Harrington was selected to be the first U.S. mail carrier in the Teton Basin. And while he apparently performed the job satisfactorily for the few months that he held it, he couldn't go straight.

He had a hideout cabin on the north end of Jackson Lake, and after committing one of his numerous robberies he used to walk all night to reach this cabin. Harrington, who looked somewhat like a plump Stan Laurel, had a surprisingly attractive wife and daughter. He left them on his Idaho place while he tramped the country picking up anything not nailed down.

In 1910 Harrington, who was much better known by this time as Ed Trafton, went to Denver to visit his aged mother. She had just received ten thousand dollars in insurance money following the death of her husband. When Ed arrived she had the cash in her house, and she asked her dutiful son to deposit it in the bank for her. But on the way to the bank Ed claimed he was robbed, for he and the widow's money never got there. Even Ed's mother disbelieved this yarn. She had him arrested, and he was eventually convicted and sent to the Colorado State Penitentiary.

When Harrington was released he returned to the Jackson Hole country. And in 1914 he brought off his most spectacular job. He waited on an isolated stretch of road in Yellowstone Park and one by one held up each coachload of tourists as it came by. Accounts differ as to how many coaches he eventually stopped. The Bonneys report fifteen, and Ben Driggs, nineteen. Because such holdups were not uncommon at the time, the particulars of Harrington's big day have become a bit confused. Some reports state that the unattractive little man offered to let some of the more comely female passengers keep their cash and jewelry in return for more intimate favors, but none succumbed to the inducements of the fifty-six-year-old bad man. Several, however, noticed instead the peculiar manner in which he held his rifle across his lap. When Harrington knelt down the old gunshot injury to his foot apparently caused him to balance his rifle peculiarly. This peculiarity helped to later identify him as the bandit.

Harrington got away that day with over a thousand dollars in loot. He made his way down into Jackson Hole, where he stole two horses. He then rode west across the Conant Trail. The Bonneys wrote that he tried to mislead his pursuers by going to the cabin of a man living on Conant Creek. Here he tried to ambush the settler in order to plant a fake confession and suicide note on the corpse. But, as happened so many times before, Harrington's scheme failed, and he was eventually arrested and tried. Found guilty, he was sent to the penitentiary at Leavenworth, Kansas.

Harrington served about four years there and was then released. He again came back to Jackson, where he bragged of his new plans for making films about his old exploits in the area. Later he went to California, where he tried to sell his story to the film studios. None was interested, and the aging outlaw eventually died there in 1924.

Harrington's dubious career helps to point out that the glorified, dusty street shootout was mostly myth. The killers of early-day Cheyenne favored the garrote to the six-gun—it was an affirmation of the belief in the ambush as a favorite way of eliminating enemies in the Old West. Burned Wagon Gulch just south of Jenny Lake is named for a furtive killing in which a wagon was burned in order to destroy evidence of the crime.

A few miles to the east, on Snake River, is the locally famous Dead Man's Bar. There in 1886, four Germans were attempting to placer mine for gold in the gravel deposits. According to the legend, one of the men, Tonnar, began suffering from delusions of persecution. To escape his fears Tonnar ruthlessly murdered all his partners with ax and rifle, then left their corpses partially hidden on the gravel bar. The remains were later found by an angler, who reported them to authorities. Due to the decomposition of the corpses the men who came out from Jackson decided to boil the victims' skulls clean in an old kettle so that they could be taken to Evanston as evidence. The kettle used for the grisly job is in the Jackson Hole Museum. But the results it produced were wasted, for Tonnar had left no witnesses to testify against him. He was released, and he quickly left the area.

Even today there is an undeniable ingredient of violence in Jackson Hole that still erupts from time to time. I have lived in Star Valley for over nine years and cannot remember a murder being committed here in all that time. But during the same period in Jackson Hole there have been at least five very unpleasant murders. Officers recently fought a gunbattle with suspects holed up in a Hoback River lodge that far surpassed the shootout two alleged horse thieves had with a posse at the Cunningham cabin in 1893.*

This latter event occurred at a small, low-ceilinged cabin in the northern end of Jackson Hole. The cabin has been restored as an historic site by the Park Service. Visit it and you can imagine the murderous emotions a man could develop if he were forced to spend a winter there. So, when the posse called the suspected rustlers out on that dim spring morning, they came shooting.

Recently it has been suggested that the posse acted hastily and may have killed innocent men. But Ben Driggs described the incident differently. He said that the story began when a few horses were stolen from the Poindexter and Orr ranch in Montana. Montana officials wrote to deputy Sam Swanner in Teton Basin about the theft, and he in turn checked with Johnny Carnes, who was in Teton Basin from his Jackson Hole homestead. Carnes said that two strangers were in the valley, but as the winter was breaking they would probably be moving soon.

* In the fall of 1972 the Teton County sheriff was shot and killed in a shootout not far from Moran Junction. Then his killer apparently committed suicide.

In response to information relayed by Swanner, a posse led by squaw man John Williams arrived from Montana. Williams recruited still more men as he moved from Teton Basin across the snowy pass into Jackson Hole. The men surrounded the little cabin early in the morning, and when George Spencer came out he was told to surrender. Instead Spencer drew a pistol and fired two shots before being blasted with a shotgun. Mike Burnett, the other suspect, came out of the cabin with a gun and was also shot down. The two men were hastily buried somewhere near the old cabin.

Also in the cabin that morning had been a youth named Hunter and a trapper and farmhand called "Swede" Jackson. This man came into Jackson Hole with William Arnn in 1885. He is the fourth Jackson to have been in the valley in early days, and the only one not confused with the valley's namesake, David E. Jackson.

Swede Jackson had been the only white man seen in the valley by the posse that came to Jackson Hole in 1885 looking for stolen steers. Swede was a peculiar man, often on the fringe of outlaw activities but never a proven participant. When he saw the posse coming in 1885 he hid under a haystack at John Holland's. Ever since it has been a valley joke, because Swede had unusually big feet and he neglected to pull them into the stack after himself. When the posse rode up one of the first things they saw was the haystack with a pair of big feet sticking out of it. In this case, as in the later one at the Cunningham cabin, Jackson did not appear to officers to have been guilty of anything, and he was released.

Nevertheless, when the posse dragged Swede Jackson out of his haystack they bounced him around a bit and threatened him with a real beating if he did not provide them with information. Such incidents of police high-handedness were common in early days. In those days law enforcement was a spotty business at best, and the men who worked at it were inclined to enforce it as they pleased.

Public sentiment tended to support such action, because when Spencer and Burnett were killed the whole region was an outlaw asylum. There was no Teton County as it exists today. The whole of western Wyoming, a strip over forty miles wide and more than two hundred twenty miles long, was part of Uinta County. The county seat at Evanston was at the far south end of the huge expanse. Travel was difficult, and Jackson Hole was about as accessible to the capitals of Idaho, Utah, and Montana as it was to its own embryonic state government in Cheyenne.

It was the remoteness of state government, and some appalling political machinations, that gave police power to the Wyoming Stock Growers' Association. For a time the association was more powerful than any single law-enforcement body in Wyoming excepting the army. In looking after its own interests the association's detectives overlooked other crimes, such as the stolen horses they found in Jackson Hole in 1885 and the widespread violation of the game laws they were supposed to help enforce.

Conditions like these led to a lot of do-it-yourself law enforcement on the frontier. One example is the case of Thomas Sewall, who was sent to the Wyoming penitentiary for killing a neighbor in South Park. It is also an example of a rare, man-to-man shootout. Sewall's ranch was eight miles south of Wilson. At the time of the killing he lived there with his pregnant wife and four small children. He and his neighbor, Paul Morse, who also called himself Charles P. January, had been on bad terms for some time. According to one account, Morse had taunted and abused Sewall until the latter had made it a habit to avoid his neighbor. This behavior convinced Morse that Sewall was afraid of him.

Relations between the pair stood this way in June of 1906, when Mrs. Sewall fell seriously ill. Her husband went out to catch a saddle horse in order to ride to Wilson for help. But, when he got to his pasture, Sewall found all his horses were missing. He followed their tracks and saw that they led to the Morse ranch. From there the horses appeared to have forded the flood-swollen Snake River. Sewall could also see that the river was too high for him to cross. This left him with no other choice but to go to Morse's house and ask about his horses. Morse came out and readily admitted driving off Sewall's horses.

Even the retiring Sewall couldn't take such abuse, and later testified that Morse "finally dared me to go and get my gun and fight it out and I accepted and went home and got my gun and came back and sat on the fence and waited for him to come out in sight and when he came we walked to within 150 yards of each other and exchanged five shots, my third shot got him."*

For other men the lonely valley of Jackson Hole became a self-chosen prison. Dick Turpin, the fiery, bushy-bearded pioneer for whom Turpin Meadows is named, is said to have come into the valley after murdering a man outside it. Uncle Jack Davis, who eked out a pitiful existence from a placer claim on Snake River, is also suspected to have hidden himself away for similar reasons.

About a year ago John Smith of the Moose Head Ranch took me to the top of a barren little knoll near Spread Creek. There some half-rotted timbers are lying in a crude rectangle to mark the supposed grave of an old settler. According to John, the settler had been murdered by two brothers over some long-forgotten bit of business. John didn't know exactly what the motive had been nor had he been told what the old settler's name had been. He knew the names of the killers, though—two hardcases who had never so much as been indicted for the alleged crime. It is normal for us to remember the criminal more vividly than we remember his victim (unless the victim is famous).

But to the people who were involved, the crimes and the criminals who committed them were hardly romantic. Though not widely known outside western Wyoming and eastern Idaho, the Whitney Brothers had deservedly bad reputations. It was said one of them could ride his horse at a good clip down the main street of a small town and hit every telegraph

---

* Sewall's statement is excerpted from a letter R. E. Miller wrote to the State Board of Pardons in which he requested a pardon for Sewall.

pole he passed with a slug from his revolver. One of my neighbors still vividly remembers the whipping he got when he forgot his parents' instructions and left the safety of his back-country cabin on a day when the Whitneys were supposed to be riding through.

It is better, I think, to remember the outlawry than to endure it. There are still places in the Jackson Hole country where homeowners never lock their doors at night and where a stranger will be admitted through those doors without first being examined through a peephole. Such trusting, honest homeowners are, by necessity, disappearing. And I miss them and their times far more than I ever missed any horse thieves.

The law-abiding descendents of some old-time outlaws are living in Jackson Hole today, but most of them prefer to forget their heritage. The bad old days are still recent enough to cause them undeserved pain. It might be more tactful to remember the men who cleaned out the outlaws: the sheriffs, soldiers, wardens, and, especially, the forest rangers.

9 / *Settling Pains*

Forests do not grow on glaciated plains, and for this
reason most of the floor of Jackson Hole is treeless. This area
of upland sage and grasses combines with riverine willows and
cottonwoods in an ecological transition zone. It was the place
the first settlers built their cabins, cut the native hay with
scythes, and began putting up the pole fences that have come
to be known as buck and rail fences.

What made this form of settlement possible was the next
ecological zone above the valley floor. It is the timbered mon-
tane zone that produces the abundant lodgepole pine, the
Douglas fir, and the aspen. It was this area, roughly between
seven and ten thousand feet in elevation, that also created the
need for forest rangers. In 1879 a tremendous forest fire burned
in Jackson Hole throughout the summer. The artist, Thomas
Moran, complained that he could not paint the Tetons because of the pall of smoke that constantly shrouded them. The
cause of this fire will never be known. It may have been set
by Indians, or the result of a lightning bolt. It was just one of
scores of other such fires that had raged in the mountain
West for years, many of which were the work of white men.
In the long run lots of these wild fires were not nearly so
disastrous to the land and wildlife as they seemed at the time.

But the governmental actions they triggered become more valuable every year.

First President Benjamin Harrison and then Theodore Roosevelt set aside increasing millions of acres of western forest lands to save them from a variety of disasters. But until a man was found to implement the new conservation practices, things went on about as they had before. The residents of Wyoming and other intermountain states often violently opposed the new forest regulations. And many of them came to hate Abram A. Anderson, who was known as the first colonel of rangers in the Yellowstone Forest Reserve. For it was the colorful Anderson who effectively enforced the new rules. Beginning in 1902 Anderson, as special forest superintendent, broke up his gigantic reserve into four much more manageable districts. These were the Shoshone, Wind River, Absaroka, and Teton divisions. Each one, in addition to making forest protection feasible later, provided the basis for the individual national forests that they were to become.

Anderson's rangers not only attempted to protect the timber and wildlife in their forests, but also took a firm hand in civil cases. Some of the early rangers in Jackson Hole were John Alsop, Rudolph Rosencrans, Ed Romey, and Charlie Deviney.

One wintry day about 1906, Alsop got word from Dubois, Wyoming, "that a man had hit a storekeeper in the head with a stove poker, robbed a safe and had stolen a horse and saddle." He was described as having a rifle in a scabbard, a six-shooter with a belt full of ammunition, and being headed for Jackson Hole.

Alsop continued, "Ed Romey was with me and we thought we were in a good place to catch him." Apparently the two men had waited for the outlaw somewhere in the Moran–Moran Junction area. But the outlaw didn't appear, so the two brushed out the existing tracks in the snowy road and returned to their cabin for lunch. When the rangers returned they found a set of fresh horse tracks in the snow. They set out for Charlie Allen's store south of Moran. Alsop wrote, "When we got to Charlie Allen's . . . he said 'John you are wanted on the phone.'

"Ben Sheffield, at the outlet of Jackson Lake, said over the phone, 'He is trying to cross the river now, has made two attempts but the river is so high he is afraid to tackle it.'

"By this time we were joined by two game wardens, a soldier, and Charlie Deviney, a new ranger who was helping me. We hurried to the spot but as we approached, the man took off through the swamp toward the park [Yellowstone].

"Charlie Deviney and the soldier reached the upper end just as the robber was coming out." By a ruse they got the drop on their suspect, who said to Alsop when he rode up, "So you're the big bull are you. What are you going to do to me now?"

Alsop explained, "We went back to Charlie Allen's, met the Sheriff's party from Dubois and turned the culprit over to them."

The soldier Alsop mentioned was from the Yellowstone Park detachment. Yellowstone Park had been established in 1872, and almost from its creation the park had been a haven for inept and corrupt administrators and concessionaires. The army was brought in to police the great park, and, as the army seems always wont to do, it wasn't averse to extending its authority and doing some policing in Jackson Hole, too.

The valley was beginning to be settled. In 1883 John Holland and John Carnes, who had a Shoshone wife, settled in Jackson Hole. As already mentioned, it was alleged that these men had supplied Teton Jackson and his horse thief associates with the necessities of life. Whether or not this is true, it is not necessarily a reflection on the two settlers. They may have had no choice in the matter. Carnes had migrated into Jackson Hole after an earlier attempt at settlement on the Green River near the present site of La Barge, Wyoming. According to a Forest Service record there were about one hundred head of cattle in Jackson Hole in 1883, and they were legally owned by John Holland.

The two men built their cabins on adjoining parcels of land north of the present site of Jackson. In the collection of W. C. Lawrence is an old snapshot of a cart with crude, solid wooden wheels that was built by these pioneer settlers. Such industry was necessary, since Jackson Hole was still accessible only by pack animals. The first farm machinery brought into the valley had to be completely disassembled, then packed in on horses or mules.

A year later, about 1885, Robert E. Miller homesteaded a short distance southwest of Carnes and Holland. Miller had already seen the valley in 1882, when he hunted and trapped there. He had come from Wisconsin, and was only nineteen in 1882. Vigorous, shrewd, and ambitious, Miller was to become one of the most influential men in Jackson Hole. In 1902 he was appointed supervisor of a division of the national forest.

To set the new supervisor straight (if he needed it), long-time Wyoming Congressman Frank W. Mondell wrote Miller, ". . . Personally, I have never believed that horses and cattle under the open range system would under ordinary circumstances be at all likely to overgraze a reserve. . . ."

Throughout his long congressional career Mondell was a champion of livestock interests. He was not a friend of either the Forest Service or the incipient conservation movement. Thus his friendly letter to Miller was a portent of things to come in Jackson Hole as they had already come to most of the rest of Wyoming.

The early forest ranger probably had no inkling of the machinations of the politicians. One of the requirements he had to fulfill before he got his job was to be able to pack a horse at, apparently, the Miller Ranch Barn. Then the prospective ranger would mount his saddle horse and lead the pack horse on a lope for a mile or so. If the pack did not come off he passed the exam. It was, and still is, a pretty good test for a packer.

Once he got the job, the ranger was expected to cover vast parts of his district every season. He did it mostly by horseback, and noted down the number of miles traveled each day. The ranger whose annual tally of miles fell short of his supervisor's expectations was likely to lose his job. When snow closed the trails, old-time rangers like Rudolph Rosencrans put on skis and traveled far into the wintry fastnesses of the mountains in search of poachers.

Rosencrans for many years was stationed at the Black Rock ranger cabin near the foot of Togwotee Pass. Here he helped pass the lonely winters by feeding and photographing big game. The ridge across from the station has been named Rosie's Ridge, and the old cabin Rosencrans used is now part of an interesting display beside the Teton National Forest Headquarters in Jackson.

The cabin has been tastefully restored, and on the day I visited it I noted, "There are displayed old Forest Service posters, charts, log books, scales [for timber estimates], maps together with packbags, saddlebags, compass, and dispatch case. The only incongruous thing was a small, short-wave radio identified as the backbone of Forest Service communications in the early 1900s. The set on display had operating instructions that noted *radar* and blasting procedures."

Rudolph Rosencrans lived a long, and at its end, not a particularly happy life. He was blind and alone for many of his last years, respected, even revered, by many in the community but not particularly close to anyone. While I was visiting W. C. Lawrence at his home on Jackson Lake, I was shown a number of scrapbooks. Turning the pages of one I came upon a large newspaper photo of young Rosencrans. He made a romantic figure astride a saddle horse, shirt sleeves rolled up over muscular forearms and a pipe between his teeth.

"There's Rosencrans!" I exclaimed happily.

Lawrence, with a twinkle in his eye, asked, "Did you know this?" He was pointing at a tiny news clipping fastened on the page containing the romantic picture. According to the undated clipping, Rudolph Rosencrans had been successfully prosecuted by William Simpson for the possession of fifty bull elk teeth. Rosencrans was found guilty and fined forty dollars plus court costs.

I could scarcely believe it. Rosencrans had become a sort of saint in Jackson Hole, and he turns out to have been a "tusker." Lawrence also said that Rosencrans, in his younger days, was quite a man with the ladies. To win their favor he poached marten and had the skins of the finest males made into chokers, which he gave to his favorites. Lawrence said he accused Rudolph of this fur poaching, but Rosencrans always denied it, claiming he bought the marten furs.

Poaching of furbearers like marten and beaver wasn't as vile a crime to most settlers as tusking. "Beavertooth" Neal was a beaver poacher of such guile and industry that he has since become a kind of folk hero. He used various devices to slip his illegal pelts by officers. One was to found the "Leader Fur Company" of Elk, Wyoming. Neal bought furs from outside Jackson Hole and then shipped them out again with his own, illegal pelts in the bundles.

He wasn't always successful. One winter day ranger John Alsop saw Neal with an illegal beaver. Alsop got a search warrant and served it early next morning. He found eleven beaver pelts in Mrs. Neal's trunk. Mrs. Neal's luggage had been a favorite hiding place for illegal fur.

Another illegal trapper wasn't nearly as slick as Neal, and apparently got caught a lot. The magistrate finally asked the fellow what he did all winter.

"I spend half my time in your jail and the other half walking back home," was the poacher's reply.

The tuskers were second-generation outlaws. The telephone, telegraph, and settlement had pretty well finished the Wild Bunch and the horse thieves, but killing elk for their tusks was an act that was not as sensitive to increasingly modern communications. The booty was also much easier to transport.

The Jackson Hole elk herd is a natural wonder and resource on a par with the majestic Teton Mountains. In the early days of settlement this herd contained at least thirty thousand animals. They spent their summers in the northern end of Jackson Hole, and particularly in the Yellowstone. As winter approached the animals began moving south. In an old account a hunter and a couple of state officials reported finding one herd in the Towgotee Pass region that contained about ten thousand elk.

Every elk has two canine teeth or tusks, one on each side and toward the front of its upper jaw. As a calf the elk has a temporary tusk, which is replaced by a permanent one during the animal's second summer. For a time the new permanent tusk is hollow, and considered worthless by most hunters. But as the animals grow older, the bulls develop especially handsome tusks.

A bull's tusks are shaped somewhat like a man's blunt fingertip. The tusk wears as the animal feeds, and in wearing it reveals an irregular bull's eye pattern on the end. With the passage of years the tusk takes on the color of old ivory, while the concentric circles darken to a contrasting brown and, rarely, black color. Many people regard these teeth as handsome trophies. And, unfortunately, this regard was highest among members of the B.P.O.E., the Elks Lodge. As a boy I can remember seeing many a rich-looking watch chain festooned with a gold- or silver-capped elk's tooth. At that time they were considered grand adornments, even though the Elks had already officially frowned upon their use by members.

In early-day Wyoming elk teeth were as valuable as gold. They were accepted as a medium of exchange in some areas, and storekeepers locked their elk tusks away in the same strongboxes that held their gold. In Jackson Hole it was a rare settler's range that did not have a tin cup of ancient coffee sitting at its back or in the warming oven. In the coffee were elk teeth being given some additional brown staining that the owner hoped would increase their value. Elk teeth were also carried in tobacco pokes to both stain and polish them.

Shortly after the turn of the century a good pair of bull's tusks were worth twenty to twenty-five dollars. Exceptional teeth brought three and four times as much. Even today a good set of bull teeth is worth twenty to fifty dollars. And since cow teeth never approached these values, the tuskers worked on the bulls.

Writing in the *Wyoming Tribune* many years ago, Stephen Leek said, "A settler in snowshoeing over an unfrequented part of the valley found eighteen bull elk killed for their teeth and saw in the snow the spot where the poacher had stood and shot them down. . . . In nearly all portions of the valley where the male elk range in winter and throughout all portions of the mountains in summer the carcasses are found. Unlike furbearing animals, the tusks are prime the year around, and can be sent in any numbers, by mail, to dealers under protection of the Post Office Department."

Leek continued, "One evening at dusk in early spring I was returning home from Jackson upon the public road when a shot was fired on the mountainside above. Looking up I saw outlined against the twilight sky an elk who staggered and then fell. A man walked up to it and it tried to rise and then lay still. The next day I climbed to the place and found the elk—with only its teeth taken."

There were very few officers in the area, and the tuskers could work with near impunity. Making their work even easier was the recurring tragedy of the starving elk in Jackson Hole. Civilization had choked off the animal's normal migration routes, and during severe winters they were trapped in Jackson Hole, where historically they had only remained in milder winters. Every spring the valley would be littered with hundreds, even thousands, of elk carcasses, each one containing a set of teeth.

Since the teeth were not contraband it was perfectly legal for citizens to go out in the spring and remove them from the elk carcasses. They could also possess elk teeth by lawfully killing the animals in season. This increased the difficulty of prosecuting the elk tuskers.

Today elk tusks are not so ruthlessly sought, but the bull elk still has a price on his head. The cape of any but a spike bull is worth twenty dollars, and the antlers, affixed to the skull, may bring sixty to one hundred dollars.

While most of the early settlers in Jackson Hole collected and sold elk teeth, they dealt primarily in teeth they had legally acquired. They were disgusted and infuriated by the professional tuskers who slaughtered the elk. Not only did the animals mean valuable food to the often struggling settlers, but the prime bulls the tuskers killed were just the ones free-spending dudes sought in the fall. And because many Jackson Holers guided hunters, tusking was not in their best economic interests.

Despite a few successful prosecutions the tusk hunters felt secure in Jackson Hole, where some residents actually feared them. One afternoon Ranger Charlie Lee was told by Pierce Cunningham, who ran a hotel in Jackson at the time, to avoid the hotel bar because Bill Binkley, Charley Purdy, and another tusker "are over there drunk and boasting they are going to hang a game warden's hide on the fence before night."

Lee decided to face the poachers. "He had his slicker buttoned up but pulled his arm out of his right sleeve and with his Luger pistol in his hand went in where the three of them were, two on the floor and one against the bar." Lee faced the trio but nothing happened. The three tuskers finally slunk out the bar's back door.

Slim Lawrence has pictures of many of the tuskers, and also of the tiny cabins where they used to hide out. Through the years he has found these cabins all over the northern end of Jackson Hole. They were invariably hidden in dense timber, away from streams and trails where they might be stumbled upon. One picture that caught my eye was of a smokehouse. Built deep in the timber, it was large enough to hold three or four elk. Lawrence said he doubted if the poachers fully smoked the elk, suggesting instead that they gave it a partial smoke to discourage flies and then packed it out to points of sale or transportation in Idaho. In the summer of 1971 I found a similar, though smaller, installation in the Gros Ventre. From its appearance it postdated the tusker period.

The tuskers are said to have also attempted to avoid detection by fastening elk hooves to the soles of their boots. In this way they hoped to fool officers into thinking elk had made the tracks. One story of tusking concerned a man who claimed to be able to drive elk into deep snow, where they became bogged down. The tusker then bulldogged the animals and pulled out their tusks without killing them. The truth of this story is reflected in the Wyoming Game and Fish Laws. A section states, in part, "Any person who . . . removes the head, hide, antlers, horns or tusks [from a game animal] . . . or mutilates any such game animal while alive by removing or detaching any tusk or tusks . . . shall be imprisoned . . . for not more than five years." Unfortunately, almost no one was ever punished to the full extent of this law.

According to an old Forest Service estimate the worst of the tusker gang killed about sixteen hundred elk. In light of subsequent figures, this estimate is probably minimal. Still, it was too many for the residents of Jackson Hole, who in exasperation finally met and formed a vigilance committee to chase the poachers out of the valley.

Some in the meeting wanted to summarily lynch the tuskers. But it was eventually decided to send the gang an ultimatum to get out of Jackson Hole within forty-eight hours, and a committee was chosen to deliver it. Receiving the ultimatum, the tuskers blustered but were gone within the specified time. According to a Forest Service record the tuskers took with them all the elk teeth they had collected, plus a wagon load of the best elk heads and a big moose head. Some of these heads were recovered by officers. When he learned of them, Theodore Roosevelt sent Theodore Palmer out to bring ten of the best ones east. These heads were supposed to have been mounted for the Smithsonian Institution.

As soon as the tuskers reached Idaho they boarded a train for California. William Binkley and Charles Purdy were arrested there and sent to Pocatello, Idaho, for trial. The pair pleaded guilty and were fined. One man paid his fine and the other elected to sit his out in jail. The men were also prosecuted for hunting in Yellowstone Park and drew convictions on that charge, too.

After he was driven out of Jackson Hole, Purdy put up in a cabin near Loon Lake, just west of the Teton Divide. Here he continued to hunt tusks until Prohibition arrived, which held out the more lucrative occupation of bootlegging to him. He took it, and thus helped end the worst days of tusk hunting.

While tusking was made financially attractive by the Elks Lodge, it was the Indians who founded the industry. According to an article in *Wyoming Wildlife,* the Indians regarded elk tusks as good medicine. The article adds that John James Audubon was given an antelope robe trimmed with fifty-six elk tusks, which he said was the equivalent in value of thirty horses. In the State Museum in Cheyenne I recently saw a dark-blue jersey dress, made by a Shoshone, the bodice of which is studded with elk teeth. A few of these teeth bear crude carvings. The article further stated that the Indians prized the tusks enough to make bone imitations of them when their supply of real ones ran low.

Of course, the Indians were not accused of killing elk for their teeth alone. They were often given passes to leave their Idaho and Wyoming reservations in order to hunt in Jackson Hole. The Indians understood that this was their right as granted by the treaty signed at Fort Bridger in 1868, which said that the Indians, Bannock and Shoshone, had the right to hunt on the unoccupied lands of the United States so long as there was game there to hunt and provided that peace be maintained between Indians and whites on the borders of the hunting districts.

Despite the treaty's provisions, the settlers resented the Indian hunting parties. As T. A. Larson says in his *History of Wyoming,* "Indians . . . had never been appreciated in Wyoming." Larson then quotes former Governor William Richards, who told the 1895 state legislature, "More large game is killed by Indians for the hide alone than is killed by our citizens for food."

With this sort of official sentiment abroad, the citizens of Jackson Hole were emboldened to enforce the laws as they chose and to try to stop the Indians from hunting in the valley. The Indians were unquestionably taking game at any season in defiance of state law. And this cut into the potential outfitting and guiding income of the settlers.

William Manning, late of Teton Basin, had been made the "Chief Justice in charge of Law Enforcement" in the valley. Manning was a tough old soldier and Indian fighter, but when he and a few others rode out on June 24, 1895, to stop some Indians from hunting, they found themselves outnumbered. They admonished the Indians to stop hunting, but the Indians paid no attention.

The settlers organized themselves, and, with Manning leading about twenty-five of them, they again went after the Indians. This time they found a camp of Bannock Indians in the Hoback Basin and proceeded to arrest them all. One posse member described the Indians as "sullen." Their attitude is not surprising, since there is considerable doubt that they had broken any law. Still, they allowed themselves to be herded over the mountains toward Jackson Hole. There are several versions of what happened next. Some say that posse members tricked the Indians into bolting so that they could shoot them down. Others say that the Indians did bolt, and this caused the shooting. But, whatever the cause, two Indians ended up shot. In one posse member's recollection a squaw on horseback was so frightened as her pony leaped ahead that she failed to notice her small child had been swept from his seat behind her. This baby was picked up and later sent west to Fort Hall with some of the Indians. The mother, however, went east, to the Wind River Reservation, and it was over a year before she and her child were reunited.

One of the Indians who was shot was killed outright, but the other, a boy, was only wounded. He had been shot through the arm and body and left where he fell. With nothing to eat but some dried meat, this youngster was days crawling to the ranch of a man whom he knew to be friendly. According to one account it was seventeen days before the boy received any medical attention.

The remaining Indians were taken into Jackson Hole, where they were found guilty of violating the game laws. Historian David Saylor says that most of the Indians' property was taken in lieu of the fine, which, as might be expected, the Indians could not pay.

The whole affair left a bad smell, and one report states

that "the Indian round up was a put up job to kill some Indians and thus stir up sufficient trouble to subsequently get United States troops into the region and alternately have the Indians shut out from Jackson's Hole." Both of the settlers' purported aims were realized, but in the interim a near panic swept the valley. Many Indians were still in the area, and the possibility of their revenging themselves on the handful of settlers seemed excellent. Crude forts were thrown up in the north end of the valley and in South Park. The people repaired to these, and in the meantime sent out a strident call for help. It was answered by a detachment of cavalry under General Coopenger, and also by a posse from Lander. Before the latter arrived false reports reached the nation's press that there had been a massacre in Jackson Hole and that everyone there had been killed. In fact, no one was killed but an old Indian.

The posse arrived after the cavalry, and in the words of William Simpson, who was a member, was composed mainly of men of good faith. But with these good men "there were a number of half-outlaws and tinhorn gamblers." These men robbed the John Holland ranch and also took everything owned by Jackson Holer William Arnn. Simpson and Arnn subsequently chased and caught up with these men as they were leaving the valley. They recovered the stolen goods and, to Simpson's surprise, an old pet horse he had previously turned loose on the Wind River. According to Simpson's account, it was only the coolness of Arnn, who drew his revolver and said, "The first son of a bitch that tries to pull his gun, I am going to kill," that prevented a gunfight. Simpson closed his account with the quotation at the beginning of this chapter.

The brouhaha over the Indians and the elk continued. Sheriff Ward of Uinta County arrested a Bannock for killing elk out of season. This Indian, Race Horse, lent his name to the ensuing court battles. He was exonerated by a United States circuit court in Cheyenne. But irate whites carried the case to the United States Supreme Court, where the lower court's ruling was reversed. The Supreme Court explained that the Treaty of 1868 had been repealed by the Act of Wyoming Statehood. This being the case, the Indians had lost their right to hunt on the big-game ranges of their ancestors. This case became a landmark in subsequent disputes over ownership and rights to wildlife.

The immediate result of the "Bannock trouble" spilled into Star Valley. One family believed the false reports of a massacre, and immediately threw their belongings into a wagon and hightailed it for Afton in the south end of the Valley. Near a tight defile called The Narrows, which almost pinches Star Valley in two, the family met a group of Indians. The Indians were just as frightened by the white wrath in Jackson Hole, and when the two parties met each was sure of the murder in the other's hearts. And both fled, terrified, in new directions.

Many of the troopers sent in to stop the nonexistent massacre of settlers were Negro. As soldiers will, some of these men dallied with certain of the Mormon girls in Star Valley. Such misalliances are particularly noxious to people of the Mormon religion, because the Negro's blackness is believed to be God's "mark of Cain." And, as less than equal spirits, Negroes are denied certain essential privileges of the Mormon faith. Thus it was for many years, until his death, that a Star Valley man, white-skinned though he was, was denied the Mormon "priesthood." Through an ancestor's indiscretion he became another sad casualty of the "Bannock trouble" in Jackson Hole.

After this trouble had been smoothed over, some of the Jackson Hole boys apparently decided to enlarge upon the actual events. When the great naturalist, Ernest Thompson Seton, came out in 1898 to stay for a while with Stephen Leek he got the "business." He was told that a band of Indians had been quietly surrounded somewhere along the Snake River early one morning. As soon as it became light enough to see, the surrounding whites riddled the camp with rifle fire, killing about "fifty" Indians. If this story is true, it is one of the best-kept secrets in Jackson Hole. What it seems to be, really, is a true story of dude-stuffing, which is an ancient and honorable Jackson Hole pastime.

A far more serious menace to the isolated valley than the Indians were sheep. They had been flooding into the West since the close of the Civil War. They were a curse to the cowmen, and a catastrophe to the range lands of Wyoming. Around the turn of the century the gnawing, nibbling flocks were increasing at the rate of hundreds of thousands per year. Some of the men who owned enormous flocks of sheep were politicians like Wyoming Governor B. B. Brooks and United States Senator Francis E. Warren. And as public servants they got away with all sorts of abuses of the public range. Vast sections of public land were illegally fenced, and, not satisfied, the politician-sheepmen also used devious if not dishonest methods to claim great chunks of public land for themselves.

Huge bands of sheep were herded across the western rangelands, spreading disease to the already dwindling wild game and trampling the forage into dust. For a long time little was done to stop these itinerant bands, which were simply thrown on the public domain and kept somewhere thereon all year long. John Alsop, the pioneer forest ranger, noted a trip south of Jackson Hole to Star Valley where he counted three hundred thousand sheep. The ranges could not begin to support such numbers, and naturally the sheepmen were constantly on the hunt for new territory.

In 1897 Jackson Hole cattlemen announced that sheep would not be permitted in the valley. Such ultimatums simply stung the pride of certain big sheepmen, and the rewards of sheep raising were great enough to sacrifice a few sheep and herders to probe the actual resolution of the cattlemen. In 1902 about thirty thousand sheep were pushed north, into the beautiful meadows of the Upper Green River. These flocks were attacked by a large number of men, and at least two thousand sheep were killed.

On the other side of Jackson Hole, in the Teton Basin, sheep herds were being turned onto the ranges formerly used by cattle and they, too, were raided. According to B. W. Driggs, a band of sheep was herded across the divide onto Mosquito Creek in Jackson Hole. Nean Christensen, the herder, was subsequently surprised in the early morning by three armed and masked men. They tied the frightened herder to a tree and then whipped him. Then other men began shooting the sheep; about three hundred were killed. Not satisfied, the attackers killed Christensen's horse and his dog, then burned his camp outfit. A year later Ed Trafton (Harrington) shot a sheep camp's team of horses and their saddle horse and then, as mentioned, attempted to blow up the sheepmen by planting blasting powder along the trail they used.

Early settler Lee Lucas said that on another occasion sheepmen drove a herd of four thousand sheep into Jackson Hole over a bridge they'd built especially for the purpose across the Snake River. Cattlemen destroyed the bridge and turned the sheep that had not crossed back into Idaho. According to Lucas, "The band that was already across the river was ordered to be taken out of the country by way of the Wind River region. This also was done and without any stop to rest and graze being allowed. They had to keep moving."

The dispute between Wyoming cattle and sheepmen was eventually settled. Many cattlemen had turned to the sheep business because of the much lower overhead involved, and because they had abused their ranges until only sheep could subsist there. But, while the means of the Jackson Hole cattlemen in keeping sheep out of the valley were questionable, I have no doubt that the results justified it. There are sheep today in Teton County, but virtually none in Jackson Hole. Half a dozen were kept in a tiny paddock on the outskirts of Jackson, but even these were eyed venomously by some old-timers who, by tradition anyway, will not permit a valley youngster to raise so much as an orphan lamb.

There are times, after I see politicians and unscrupulous businessmen conspire to successfully destroy some more of Wyoming's incomparable land or water, that I almost wish conservationists had the nerve of the old-time cattlemen.

I been lookin' at those mountains for thirty-five years and never made a dime outa' 'em yet.

JACKSON HOLE COWBOY

10 / Pioneers, a President, and Billy Owen

One of the privileges implicit in being an old-timer in any district is telling newcomers how tough things were before they came. A good deal of what a newcomer hears about the early hardships in Jackson Hole is true. There are elderly people in Jackson today who remember getting down on hands and knees as children and helping to cut wild hay with the only tools they had—butcher knives.

Settlers lived in tents while they farmed and built tiny cabins in a determined race with winter. And before they knew it the air that had been alive with mosquitoes was suddenly so full of snowflakes a man could wonder why he didn't suffocate. When the snow stopped falling and the sky cleared, the temperature plummeted. At forty-four below zero, the coldest I've experienced, everything stops. The dancing black and white magpies, one of the few dependable winter-resident birds, disappear. The horses stand next to anything they can find to stand beside, and they do not move. You might think them dead except for the little puffs of vapor seeping from their nostrils. Their backs are white with a heavy rime of frost, and the long, wispy hairs on their muzzles and eyes are coated white with ice. Thankfully there is no breeze, and the frozen silence engulfs you like an invisible cocoon. Such deep cold is so hard it has a metallic smell, and you must not exert yourself or your horses lest you freeze the linings of your lungs.

I think people stood those hardships in early days, not because they were necessarily better than we are today, but because they had to. A lot of them didn't know anything different, so they could not feel as sorry for themselves as some of us might today. And not all Jackson Hole's old-timers stood it. One fellow froze to death in an outhouse. Some went crazy and killed themselves or beat up their families. Others simply endured the winter until spring, then left and never came back. Jackson Hole still has a huge turnover in would-be residents; that first winter "inside" changes a lot of minds. The ones who stuck sometimes did so because they had nowhere else to go. Some old-timers really liked living in Jackson Hole, but others just lumped it.

The settlers who stayed and prospered were the most shrewdly practical ones. When they came into the valley they took up land where wild hay grew naturally and where it appeared that it could be made to grow even better by diverting water to it from adjacent streams. Not many of them gave a thought to building their homes so as to get the best view of the mountains. Look at some of the older homes left in the valley today and you will see that few of them were built with an eye toward the surrounding beauty. Not only do big windows let out heat, but they admit the looming landscape many come inside to escape for a while.

The less practical people, the ones who built sprawling, hard-to-heat homes on rocky hillsides and paid twenty-five thousand dollars for their mountain-view lots arrived later— after it was safe and possible to be impractical and appreciative.

All, that is, but one. John Sargent was among the first, if he was not the first, settlers in Jackson Hole. He is thought to have come into the valley with his friend, Robert R. Hamilton, about 1882. Sargent was a member of the respected Sargent family of Massachusetts, whose best known member was the portraitist John Singer Sargent. Hamilton also had a famous forebear, being descended from Alexander Hamilton, first

Secretary of the Treasury. Sargent was a remittance man, and quickly floundered when the money stopped coming from home.

But that sobering event did not happen until long after the men began building a remarkable building on the wild and lonely shores of Jackson Lake. It was a ten-room lodge, and the men called it Merymere after Sargent's eldest daughter. The lumber used to build it was obtained by laboriously whipsawing logs cut from the virgin timber. Slim Lawrence told me the frontier workmanship that went into the building was truly remarkable. In old pictures the lodge seems to me to be a little blocky looking, although it should be remembered that it was by far the grandest building in all of Jackson Hole when it was built and for some time thereafter. There is an unforgettable photograph of a woman standing just outside the lodge under a bower and backdropped by the wilderness lake and remote Tetons. She is playing a violin.

That tranquil scene was belied by the violence that sometimes flared at Merymere. First, Robert Hamilton disappeared and was finally found, drowned, in the Snake River below Signal Mountain. The mountain was named as a result of this incident, because of the signal fire that was to be built on its top when Hamilton was found.

Later two soldiers attached to the Yellowstone Park patrol stopped at the isolated lodge and found a badly hurt Mrs. Sargent. She was in agony, with two broken hips. Her husband, John, did not appear to be overly concerned about her, and he did not explain how such a violent injury had occurred. The unfortunate woman was taken into Jackson, where she died.

Subsequently, Sargent acquired another wife. Old photographs of her leave little doubt that she was wildly insane. Slim Lawrence said that the woman's well-off eastern family had bribed Sargent to marry her. Part of the sad agreement was that the laird of Jackson Lake take his new bride out to Jackson Hole, where she would never again embarrass her relatives. Once she became established at Merymere, the second Mrs. Sargent made herself a unique reputation. She found a large pine tree beside the Yellowstone–Jackson Hole Trail, the lower branches of which grew in such a way that it was easy to climb. Later these branches were sawn off to make a sort of natural ladder. On pleasant days Mrs. Sargent would remove every stitch of clothing and climb into the tree, where she sat for hours. For the lone saddle bum or packer riding the trail below the lady's perch, the sight of her there must have been at least memorable. The tree soon became, and is still called, The Naked Lady Tree.

Mrs. Sargent didn't limit her impulses to the tree, either. One early settler reported riding up to the Sargent place one day and finding Mrs. Sargent there and receiving matter-of-factly in the nude. This unfortunate woman was taken away before she could hurt herself or suffer the brutal fate of her predecessor. But Sargent stayed on, cut off from his family's purse and keeping his children in poverty and filth. To add to his now meager income he put up a store beside the trail, but sold little more than peanuts and candy. As might be expected, trade was slow and Sargent began conducting his business in absentia. Slim Lawrence found this sign in the tumbledown cabin that had been the store: *All under a dollar, leave it. All over a dollar, charge it.*

Rose Koops, Beaver Dick's daughter by his second wife, recently returned to Jackson for a visit. While there she remembered playing with Sargent's children when her family was camping in Jackson Hole many years ago. She mentioned that they had gotten candy at the "fort." Slim Lawrence was of the opinion that the fort Mrs. Koops remembered from so long ago was actually John Sargent's little store.

Sargent tried to run a hunting service at his lodge, but it apparently wasn't too successful. He had the first motorboat ever used on Jackson Lake, and ran it crazily over the waves with almost no knowledge of how to operate the gasoline engine. When people began moving into the area Sargent wrote the government complaining that they were killing elk illegally and were only squatting, not residing legally, on the land. In this case he seemed to be right, although little could be done about the poaching. Eventually Sargent sat down in front of the handsome fireplace in his romantic lodge and blew his brains out with a .45-90 rifle.

After Sargent's suicide Merymere fell into disuse, and was finally sold for a few hundred dollars for back taxes. On the death of one owner an eastern trust took over the management of the property, and one of its first acts was to have Merymere torn down and the whipsawed lumber burned. It was a stupid mistake. Since that time two more impressive log structures have been built on the property now known as the Berol or AMK Ranch. The newer of these homes I described in my notes: "On a rising bluff is the first log mansion I have ever seen. It is a long, one-story ranch-style house that I could only describe as RICH." This and one other property are the last private holdings on Jackson Lake. John Sargent's foresight exceeded his lifespan by no more than twenty years. The land on which he built Merymere is now worth a fortune.

Before World War II, land that the settlers considered far more valuable than the AMK's was selling for about seventy-five dollars an acre. That price reflected the income that could be made from it in the cattle business. Cattle ranching in Jackson Hole built slowly from the time the first herd of one hundred cattle was brought in by John Holland in the early 1880s; there were still only about one thousand cows in the valley by 1900. Jackson Hole is a tough place to raise cattle, for they must be fed hay five or six months out of the year. And these are the icy, vicious months when outdoor work is a numbing and exhausting effort. Even today the modern tractor is seldom a match for the powerful team of workhorses drawing a hay-laden sleigh, which starts more reliably on subzero mornings and handles better in the deep snow. Today's rancher does have the advantage of being able to truck his cattle out of the valley to market. The old-timers had to drive them out to rail-heads in Idaho or the Wind River country. They were epic and, with hindsight, romantic journeys, but they added to the overhead and helped to make cattle ranching less profitable in Jackson Hole than in other, more accessible places. After the boom prices of World War I the cattle market collapsed, and took a lot of Jackson Hole ranchers down with it. There was a certain recovery, but even today the number of ranches in Jackson Hole continues to slowly decline.

According to a pioneer's account compiled by Agnes Spring, there were only eighteen people in Jackson Hole five years after the first settlement. Of this group all but one, John Carnes's Indian wife, were men. In addition to some already named, the first settlers in Jackson Hole included Jack Shives and John Cherry, who founded the Hatchet Ranch near the entrance to Togwotee Pass. Emil Wolff—who, incidentally, had employed the violent German, Tonnar—had the Wolff Ranch. Dick Turpin, who as mentioned gave his name to Turpin Meadows on the Buffalo Fork River, later moved to a creek in the Gros Ventre. Pierce Cunningham ranched and later ran a hotel in Jackson. The Moultons, Cheneys, and Wilsons were three Mormon families who still have strong roots in the valley. In 1891 a diptheria epidemic took several lives, and Peter Hansen is still fondly remembered for the help he gave the stricken families. His son became governor of Wyoming and is now a United States senator. Charles "Pap" DeLoney started the first store in Jackson, and R. E. Miller followed with the first bank some years later. Stephen N. Leek founded a ranch just a short distance southwest of Jackson and also the famous Leek's Lodge on Jackson Lake.

Over the early years post offices were authorized at Elk, Wilson, South Park, Cheney, Zenith, Moran, Brooks (far up the Gros Ventre River), at Teton on the bench west of Moose, and at "Grovont." This spelling of "Gros Ventre" was the result of post office prejudice against places with foreign or double names. As time went on additional post offices were opened at Kelly, Slide, Hoback, Moose, and Jenny Lake in 1926. Today most of these have gone, and the buildings that housed them are gone, too.

Better remembered are the men who carried the mail over snowy and avalanche-prone Teton Pass. In one record from the archives at the Coe Library I find, "Brady Taylor, mail carrier from Victor, Idaho to Jackson, Wyoming drowned in Snake

River. Horse rolled over and over in the swift-running water. His body was found 4 days later lodged under the roots of a large cotton-wood tree." According to this same record, "George Kissinger, mail carrier from Jackson to Moran. Drowned in Grovont River. . . ." Other mail carriers were caught in avalanches on Teton Pass.

In the winter, covered horse-drawn sleds heated with small stoves were used by the mail carriers. In showing me a picture of one of these mail sleds, Slim Lawrence remarked that it had no windows, and thus rendered its driver blind to any avalanches that might roar down on him in Teton Pass. Before the covered sleds, men used to carry mail in and out of the winter-wrapped valley on snowshoes or skis. Some of the old skis are still on display in Jackson Hole. They were handmade and extremely long, perhaps eight or nine feet, and about the same style as the tusk hunters used.

Owen Wister had visited Jackson Hole several times in the 1880s, and naturally used the same means of transportation as the settlers. In 1971 I had the pleasure of meeting Owen Wister's son, Bill, while he was visiting in Jackson Hole. He recalled his first visit in about 1910, when the Wisters came in via Yellowstone Park riding saddle horses and carrying their gear in a wagon. On their next visit the family came by rail to Victor in the Teton Basin. Then they began an arduous wagon trip into Jackson Hole. At a place Wister called Canyon Creek there was a hotel of sorts, whose upper floor had been partitioned off into "rooms" by hanging cloths from wires or ropes. Such accommodations were also standard in Yellowstone Park.

About this time Owen Wister built a summer home, which still stands, a few miles south of present-day Moose. Here he spent some idyllic summers trout fishing and enjoying the valley. Bill Wister also told me how his father later toured in Europe with Ernest Hemingway and how they had read the galley proofs of *A Farewell To Arms* with a mixture of excitement and satisfaction. In the summer of 1928 Hemingway himself traveled through Jackson Hole.

"Duding" was one of the valley's first businesses. It began in

1888, when an Ed Hoffer brought the first dudes into Jackson Hole via Montana. And from then on the dudes kept coming in ever increasing numbers. One of the first and most august of this thundering herd was the President of the United States, Chester Allen Arthur. Arthur, who had assumed office after the assassination of President James Garfield, was a man whom Harry Truman later singled out as the only President to have maintained a professional prostitute in the White House.

Arthur's trip was a fantastic, private jollification conducted at public expense. Toward the end of his term, President Arthur gathered together a flock of political cronies, ranging from governors to senators and cabinet officers, and in the summer of 1883 the Arthurian party entrained for the West. Then, under the leadership of Gen. Phil Sheridan, this party began a pack trip at Fort Washakie that eventually terminated over three hundred miles away at the railhead on the northern boundary of Yellowstone Park. No civilian correspondents were permitted on the trip, and all the official accounts of the excursion's progress were prepared by Michael Sheridan, a military aide.

President Arthur was a Republican in a day when Republican administrations were perpetually rife with scandal. Before becoming James A. Garfield's Vice-President, Arthur had never held national political office. A successful lawyer, however, he was more of a behind-the-scenes manipulator than a simple party hack. His administration was noted mainly for reintroducing champagne and a certain elegance into the White House and for some civil service reform. While his jaunt through western Wyoming was primarily a fishing and hunting trip, Arthur is not remembered as either a sportsman or a conservationist President.

An early dispatch from the excursion's jump-off spot notes that Senator Vest, one of the party, had a parley with Chief Washakie and a large group of Arapaho and Shoshone Indians. At this meeting the senator tried to talk the Indians into taking their lands "severally" instead of holding tenure in common. This is an old ploy today. It is actually a divide-and-conquer plot to divest the Indians of their reservations by offering each tribe member land of his own instead of vesting title to the reservation land in the whole tribe. As soon as a tribe cracks and accepts land for each member, the way is open for all sorts of exploitation, none of it to the benefit of the Indians.

Fortunately for the Indians they turned down Senator Vest's scheme. They asked instead for permission to trade at the military store rather than at the Indian store, since buffalo hides brought ten dollars at the former place as opposed to seven dollars at their store.

The party left for the mountains at 7:00 A.M. on the morning of August 9, 1883. To maintain presidential communications a relay of cavalrymen was established along the route of travel so that messages could be sped in and out of the wilderness. Some records indicate that all supplies went by packhorse, but one stated that "go-carts" were also used to travel as far as practicable out of Fort Washakie.

This account—called *The Rajah, or the Great Presidential Sporting Excursion of 1883*—was a highly unauthorized one. It was further described as *A Burlesque . . . In Four Cantos*. It was written by "Unc Dunkam" with illustrations by "Dough-Raw."

The title page bears this rhyme:

Once reigned a great Rajah, in the Indian East
  He "fished" and he "hunted," he was fond of a "feast,"
A right frisky old Rajah, (as the Rajah books tell),
  And yet, all his people loved the Rajah, right well.

This verse is a portent for what is to come in the narrative poem.

According to the official dispatch the party made twenty-one miles its first day out. Correspondent Sheridan reported: "The President proves to be a good horseman, and came into camp like an old campaigner.

"Immediately after the arrival of the party at the camp, which is on a beautiful trout stream [the Upper Wind River] the President took his rod and soon killed the first trout . . . He enjoys camp life very much, and is up and out of his tent at 5 o'clock each morning, usually the first one and with flannel shirt and large hat enjoys it with the rest."

The unauthorized, poetic account of the trip includes the lines:

> *And thus that cavalcade mov'd on—*
> *As slowly sank the western sun—*
> *Along that mountain road;*
> *Three hundred "thoughtful mules," in line,*
> *All laden with the choicest wine . . .*

The author goes on to tell how a mule fell off the trail and "five hundred bottles broke!" No mule, then or now, could possibly carry so much wine, but there seems little doubt that a doubly staggering supply of spirits was packed into the wilds.

As the party neared Jackson Hole itself, via Sheridan Pass and the Gros Ventre River, Sheridan reported that, "Game abounds. . . ." Surgeon Forwood "returned to camp having shot an elk of great size and weight. The other hunters brought in two antelopes and a good supply of mountain grouse and wild ducks . . . but Gen. Sheridan has given preemptory orders that no more shall be killed than is absolutely necessary for the wants of the command."

From Camp Robert Lincoln on the divide between the Wind River and Jackson Hole, the President's party moved down to encamp near the present site of the Goosewing Ranger Station. Sheridan wrote, ". . . in the absence of fallen timber, rocky side hills and steep ascents and pitches, the ride would have seemed somewhat monotonous but for a single feature which actually glorified it. The party had climbed to the summit of a hill about five miles from Camp Arthur when there suddenly burst upon their view a scene grand and majestic. Below, covered with grass and flowers was a lovely valley many miles in extent, through which was breaking its way the river on whose banks the party had just encamped. Along the whole westerly edge of this valley with no intervening foothills to

obstruct the views, towered the magnificent Teton Mountains."

The author of *The Rajah* disparages Sheridan's description
of the Tetons by inferring that he took much of his material
from "old guide books." He goes on to tell how the President
and several of his companions all blazed away futilely at a
mountain sheep. But to the lowly soldiers, packers, and Indians
the excursion was hard work and no play.

> *By tugging, and pushing,*
> *And fasting,*
> *they made forty miles,*
> *In a day,*
> *But they* "blazed,"
> *With "U.S."* broken bottles,
> Every mile,
> *Of their* wilderness *way.*

The route taken by the Arthur party has ever since been
known unofficially as the Bottle Trail. Each camping spot was
given a name; Camp Arthur was on the lower Gros Ventre near
present Lower Slide Lake. Camp Teton was on the bench lands
near the present junction of the Jackson Hole highway with
the Kelly Road. This proved an unpleasant camp because of
the dust which blew into the presidential tents. At one
point the President, according to "Unc Dunkam," threw a
banquet at which the Indians entertained with war dances.
Perhaps due to too many trips to the "free tent," where liquor
was always available, one of the Indians:

> *Swung high in air*
> *His warclub, dire and dread,*
> *And would have* whack'd
> *Great Chester on the head!*

Whether or not the threat was real, it apparently seemed real,
and one of the party pulled a gun, thus establishing himself as
savior and protector of the President.

Following this episode the participants returned to the "free tent," which was described in a footnote as follows: "It was located in the center of the camp, and was *generously* supplied with all kinds of 'liquid refreshments,' except *'water,'* . . . These refreshments were to be had 'without money,' and simply for the asking, at any time of the day or night. Thus proving that Republics are sometimes *generous*, if not always *just*."

This tent, as might well be expected, became the object of much envy and admiration by the packers. Finally, late one night, they stormed the tent and set off a confused melee, which, according to the poem, resulted in the shooting death of some unfortunate mules who apparently were mistaken for marauding Indians.

The poem itself ends soon after this event with the following lines:

> *No more the* birchen *wigwam*
> *Is seen on Windy's side,*
> *No more is seen, the tent of skin,*
> *Where Venter's waters glide.*

> *For now, by stream and mountain,*
> *In defile and in pass,*
> *The red'men build their houses,*
> *Of* 'broken bottle' *glass!*

In reading the old poem today it seems to be a little too full of hurt and venom to be the successful satire it might have been. It leaves President Arthur before his excursion entered southern Yellowstone Park via the Snake and Lewis River route. Here, too, he fished, and Sheridan described the casting method of the President as contrasted with his crony competitor's: "The President throws his fly straight away from him, as a salmon fisherman naturally would, while Mr. Vest always throws his line to the right or left and sweeps the stream with the fly." Both men caught what today would be considered a shocking number of trout.

In a photograph taken on the journey the President appears as a somewhat red-eyed, fat man past his middle years. His pose is a bad attempt at the heroic. He had undertaken a strenuous trip, and while there was surely a lot of boozing en route it probably has been overemphasized. It just isn't possible to make such an arduous trip while constantly drunk or hung over.

The presidential excursion ended in Yellowstone, and the President, saying he had had all the fishing he wanted, entrained for the East on September 2, 1883. At the Republican Convention of 1884 he stood for renomination for the Presidency, but was defeated by James G. Blaine on the fourth ballot. Chester Allen Arthur died soon after leaving office.*

It is much too late to further criticize President Arthur for wasting public funds on his excursion. It probably cost the taxpayers more to have President Nixon in Jackson Hole for one day than it did to finance Arthur's whole trip. (Nixon's trip may also have triggered the Teton Dam project, a thirty-nine million dollar tragedy.)

The really sad thing about these junkets is that the politicians seem to get so little personal benefit and understanding from them. When President John Kennedy made his western trip in the fall of 1963 the Jackson Lake Lodge was reopened especially for his one-night visit there. At a press secretary's press conference it was announced that the President had looked out his window and seen a moose in the extensive willow bottoms that spread out below the lodge. One of the reporters, who are also fish in the desert on outdoor matters, asked what sort of moose it was. The press secretary, not knowing any more about moose than anyone else in the group, pondered for a moment and then decided that "it was a 'moosey' moose."

In the last dispatches from Arthur's trip it was mentioned that very soon the practicality of raising stock in Jackson Hole would be determined. The experiment began that very year, but it took the bust that followed World War I to prove that raising cattle in Jackson Hole was not profitable for all.

One promotional pamphlet written for the valley in earlier

---

* Recent research in President Arthur's papers suggests that he was an incurably sick man, and knew it, at the end of his term.

days stated that "dairying is destined to be the big industry of the Valley." This prophecy proved false. Hopes for development of the coal deposits found in the Gros Ventre were equally disappointing. And, while everyone knew there was gold in the valley and the surrounding mountains, no one has ever been able to find the "lode." There were many attempts to mine by washing gravel along the Snake River but none were rewarding enough to keep even one old prospector in the barest necessities.

After the turn of the century some residents of Jackson Hole realized that what they had in the area was recreation land. But, since they were not decided as to how it should be managed, youthful, ambitious Horace Albright was invited to Jackson Hole to discuss enlarging Yellowstone Park to include Jackson Hole. It had seemed a good idea, but the meeting ended in disaster and a beaten Albright slunk back to Yellowstone. Nevertheless, the seed of an idea had been planted.

At the same time it was becoming ever more obvious that something would have to be done for the elk. Settlement was rapidly closing the animals' historic, winter-migration routes onto the Green River and beyond. Thousands of them were dying of starvation in Jackson Hole every time the normally bitter winters became even more bitter. In the winter ranchers had to drive the hungry animals out of their barns, and others patrolled their haystacks all night trying to keep the elk from devouring them. Elk even made appearances at Jackson's old Crabtree Hotel, and four of them were regular visitors at the dam construction site on Jackson Lake. According to Elliot Paul they toured the mess hall seeking handouts, and the laborers named them Matthew, Mark, Luke, and John.

The dam on Jackson Lake was a symbol of one resource the valley did have to export—water. And America was entering the great age of the engineer, that miracle worker who could do no wrong and make no error. The ones who designed the first dam across the outlet of the lake should have served as a warning to all. It was a jerry-built affair of log cribs filled with rock. But for a time it held, and water needed for Idaho's ambitious Minidoka Project was backed up in the lake. Then, on July 4, 1910, this flimsy affair washed out. The glut of water caused damage throughout vulnerable areas in Jackson Hole, and the loss of the stored water threatened the livelihoods of Idaho farmers who depended on it.

In 1910–1911 Jackson Hole was still a remote wilderness, and, whether one approves of the final result or not, the rebuilding of the dam was a substantial miracle. Starting from scratch, an engineer or two with some willing clerks began recruiting men and material to rebuild the dam *that winter.* Just getting workmen was a problem in the still unpopulated West. Elliot Paul, who wrote a book, *Desperate Scenery,* about his part in the project, tells how every bindlestiff and bum riding the roads was recruited for the job. Tiny Idaho hamlets became supply centers, and storekeepers found their entire stocks bought out overnight.

Freight had never been easy to deliver into Jackson Hole, but now men were actually going to try to bring in huge boilers and great, iron headgates in horse-drawn wagons. The freighters used the slightly improved Grassy Lake Road, and they did their job. The boilers arrived and were used to heat the concrete and keep it from freezing while it set in the spillways. The huge gates were built in the East, with only a distant engineer's specifications to go by. Everyone wondered if the monsters would fit when they were at last hauled in and then wrestled into position. They did fit.

Ben Sheffield, who had been running a hunting lodge and store–post office at Moran wasn't especially happy to see the dam and its builders. Paul speculated that the newly opened road robbed Sheffield of what had been a private domain. The government had to get the land it needed for the project by condemning some of Sheffield's property. For Sheffield the old order was changing even before it had time to get old.

The dam raised the level of Jackson Lake several feet, and subsequent additions and alterations have further increased its storage capacity. Today, according to the Bonneys, the lake's high-water mark is thirty-nine feet above the old, natural one.

Raising the lake's level has also substantially changed its shore-line. Originally a little over eight miles long, Jackson Lake when it is full today is about sixteen miles long. In addition to holding water for Idaho irrigators the dam affords flood protection, especially to the area around Wilson.

Many of the old-timers considered surveying an even more important government function than reclamation, because until the area was surveyed it could not be filed on and claimed. One of those who surveyed land in Jackson Hole was young William O. Owen.

The second highest peak in the Teton Range has been named for Owen, who, by an act of the Wyoming legislature, is accorded the honor of having first climbed the Grand Teton. Owen was a prominent man in early Wyoming. In addition to his surveying, he was elected state auditor in 1892 and also served as examiner of surveys for the Interior Department. Owen was an ambitious, capable man—a good example of the politician–bureaucrat who used his skills to help open up the country.

But it is for his ascent of the Grand Teton that Owen is best remembered. On August 11, 1898, Owen, Frank Petersen, Jack Shive, and Franklin Spalding made a successful assault on the forbidding peak. Mementos, including photographs and metal banners, of that climb are on display in the Jenny Lake Museum.

At the time of the ascent, and for many years thereafter, the men credited with first climbing the Grand were Nathaniel Langford and James Stevenson. As mentioned earlier, they headed an expedition that Beaver Dick had guided to the center of the Teton group in 1872. Langford's published claims and descriptions of his climb up the mountain went undisputed until the Owen party reached the summit. They found no sign of previous climbers, and the characteristics of the mountaintop were not at all as Langford had described them.

And there began Owen's thirty-year struggle to be recognized as a member of the first team to have climbed the Grand Teton. He never claimed to have been, and was not, the first man in his party to reach the summit. The leader of the group was Frank Spalding, and his name was used first when the party's route up the peak was named. Spalding was a churchman, while Owen's other two companions were Jackson Hole ranchers. None of these companions ever worked for recognition as the first conquerors of the Grand as Owen worked. To establish such a claim meant convincing one of the leading mountaineering clubs of the claim's validity. And Owen had little luck with this until Fritiof Fryxell published an article supporting Owen's claim.

Until this article appeared Owen smoldered from what he considered the treachery of C. G. Coutant, the author of the first history of Wyoming. According to Owen's papers, Coutant had promised to credit Owen with the first ascent of the mountain. But when the book appeared Nathaniel Langford was given the honor. The photographer, William H. Jackson, let it be known that he supported Langford. This was important support, since Jackson had been with the 1872 party and was well respected. Nevertheless, Jackson's support of Langford's claims was not unequivocating. This and his own massive ambitions led Owen to pursue his claim until he was able to dredge out the charge that Langford had paid historian Coutant one hundred fifty dollars to list him as the first climber of the Grand Teton. Jackson apparently knew of this skulduggery, but remained quiet out of a sense of devotion to his old companions.

Over the years Owen continued to build up support for his claim until the Wyoming legislature officially recognized it in 1929. What spoils the virtue in Owen's reward is a letter in his papers dated April 3, 1899. It was sent to Owen from Fort Meade, South Dakota, by an army surgeon, Dr. Charles Kieffer. In his letter Dr. Kieffer described how he and two soldiers had interrupted a hunting trip to climb the Grand Teton about the tenth of September, 1893. This was almost five years before the Owen climb. In reading the original letter I was impressed by the doctor's obvious sincerity and the fact that he included on the letter a map of the route he and the soldiers had taken in climbing the peak. Since the doctor seemed entirely un-ambitious but simply interested in setting the record straight, I am inclined to believe that he actually was with the first party to climb the mountain. And since Owen kept this letter, but never publicly mentioned it, while trying to establish his own claim, there seems to have been some doubt in his mind, too.

The honor, dubious as it may seem today, never really did Billy Owen any lasting good. He lived into blind decrepitude, a terribly lonely old widower writing pathetic messages to Fryxell in script half an inch high.

It happened to more than one of the valley's first. Some moved away to California to get some warmth for their stiff old bodies. And one or two of those who could, or would, not leave sometimes sat by their wood stoves writing furiously—either the same sentence over and over or perhaps a denuncia-tion of the changes that had occurred in Jackson Hole since they came there as pioneers.

*There was no question that some-
thing had to be done. But making
Jackson's Hole into a National Park
was not what most of us wanted.*

EARLY SETTLER OF JACKSON HOLE

11 / Rockefeller's Range

Too many people have a habit in common with sub-
urban dogs. When they want to make a mess they go onto
someone else's place to do it. So it has been throughout the
West, and also in Jackson Hole. A case in point is the dam on
Jackson Lake. It has been a mixed blessing. Its waters have
produced a lot of Idaho spuds and surplus grains and kept a
lot of people on farms who might otherwise have ended up in
factories or city slums. The reservoir itself has proven to be a
fairly good fishery—though not nearly as good today as it once
was. Millions of dollars have been spent to develop and maintain the lake's recreational value. But I can remember the days
in late summer, or after mild winters dried the watershed pre-
maturely, when Jackson Lake was a flawed jewel set in a vast
mud flat. The mud flat was littered with black and ugly dead
trees, and this debris trimmed with the silted ejectamenta of
a decade of vacationers.

Over the years the woody debris has been cleaned from the
exposed shores of Jackson Lake. This has been a visual improvement, although the old trees did furnish valuable cover
to game fish. An agreement has also been reached with the
Bureau of Reclamation to keep the lake as full as possible
during the tourist season. Few people now see the lake in its

drained and ugliest state. And those few who advocate removing the dam are restrained by the knowledge that a reduced Jackson Lake would not recover its beauty for generations. These are only a couple of many factors that help determine whether or not the dam is the right thing for Jackson Hole.

When the dam was built, and for many years thereafter, there were no questions about its "goodness." After 1900 reclamation became a holy word throughout the West. Everyone automatically assumed that a government reclamation project meant more jobs and prosperity for another heretofore forgotten spot in the West. Western politicians have built whole careers on their ability to deliver dams to their constituents. Unfortunately for us all, there are a lot more politicians than there are suitable places for them to put dams. As a result, the Army Corps of Engineers and the Bureau of Reclamation have, in many minds, become the epitome of destruction, not construction.

But when the dam building urge was more universally popular, some feather merchants arrived in Jackson Hole and began laying plans to send even more water out of the valley and onto the farmlands of Idaho. There were also plans to drain Yellowstone Lake, but these didn't get as far as did the ones to tamper with the smaller lakes in Jackson Hole.

The basic damming procedure is as old as the settlement of the West. A dam is thrown across the outlet of a lake. At the same time the outlet channel is sharply deepened so that, while the capacity of the lake is increased, so is the capacity to drain it. A gate is placed in the dam, and when the farmers' water requirements increase the water master can meet them simply by opening the headgate. The people down in the valleys never see the desolation their projects have left in the mountains.

Hand in hand with the dams go the ditches, which are normally required to carry and distribute additional water. These ditches are sometimes superimposed on the old stream beds; often the latter are dredged and straightened to handle the flow more expeditiously. Not all canals are sterile pipelines, nor are all dammed lakes ugly. The fishing in some lakes can be improved by damming, although stream fishing is almost always ruined by channelization and diversion.

The average reclamation project seldom enhances the beauty of an area, and, when the one mentioned was nearly performed on the lakes of Jackson Hole, a few people protested. The promoters had lined up Jenny Lake and Leigh Lake, as well as Two-Ocean and Emma Matilda lakes, for drainage into Idaho. According to Saylor's *Jackson Hole, Wyoming,* dams were built on Two-Ocean and Emma Matilda lakes. Ditches were cut across the valley floor and the whole works seemed about to go down an ugly drain. Then the author–dude rancher Struthers Burt began to expose the scheme with the quiet but efficient help of Horace Albright, then superintendent of Yellowstone Park. Frank Emerson, later a Wyoming governor but at that time state engineer, was forced to recant on his plans to permit the drainage of Jenny and Leigh lakes.

Jackson Hole was saved from the devastation of reclamation, and at the same time the effort had put one more shot into the guns of the park people. A national park was the only way to save Jackson Hole from commercial exploitation. Almost from the time Horace Albright had seen and then become superintendent of Yellowstone, he had dreamed of extending his domain into Jackson Hole. Albright was a mixture of self-serving empire builder and superb public servant. Almost singlehandedly he pulled Yellowstone Park out of a slough of shabby commercialism and incompetent administration. At the same time he made it into the magical place that those of us over thirty-five remember it to be.

When Steven Mather and his bright young assistant Horace Albright took over the national parks prior to World War I, one of their first problems was to get people to use the parks. Albright did his job so well that his efforts have inadvertently placed some parks on the verge of destruction today. He is a man of great and contagious enthusiasms. An acquaintance ran into Albright last summer at Jackson Lake. He spent a few hours with Albright, who is now in his eighties, and came away with stars in his eyes. Evidently Albright is still the great mover and shaker that he was when he was fighting for the existence of the national park system.

It took a very long time and a tremendous amount of maneuvering by Albright and many others before the Park Service set up business in Jackson Hole. One of the landmarks in this long endeavor is at the Maude Noble cabin on the banks of the Snake River near Moose. As is well known, this is the place where, on July 26, 1923, Horace Albright met with Miss Noble, Struthers Burt, Horace Carncross, his dude-ranching partner, storekeeper Joe Jones, businessman Richard Winger, and Jack Enyon. They all knew that the handwriting was on the wall, and that if something was not done Jackson Hole was going to become a commercial sideshow.

For those who doubt this, in the Park Service library at Moose there is an old photo album prepared by Harold and Josephine Fabian. Its pictures show the cheap tourist cabins lining the road by Jenny Lake. There is a decrepit rodeo grounds at the base of the Cathedral Group of the Tetons. Broken-down squatters' shacks radiate the dead wrecks of automobiles, and garbage heaps grow beside dilapidated fences. Jackson Hole wasn't all this way, but too much of it was blistered with one-horse slums. The group gathered at Miss Noble's cabin had seen all this and more, and, while they only wanted to save the region as a recreation area, their original plans were swept up in the effort to create a new national park.

Today a bronze plaque identifies the importance of the Noble cabin. The door is unlocked, and when I walked through it a couple of years ago I was surprised to find that the cradle of Grand Teton Park verged on being a dump itself. There was some clever and interesting ax work on the logs that comprised the outer walls, but over the years shade-tree carpenters have remodeled—the place for a time was a restaurant, and they have added on as their desires and limited abilities dictated. The building is probably far down the list for restoration, and rightly so, but today it is a disappointment to all shrine fanciers.

As one long-time resident of Jackson Hole explained it to

me, there was no need for a park. He feels that the trashy camps and stores could have been closed or cleaned up. Recreational sites could have been developed for vacation homes, and all of this could have been done without seriously hampering the cattle business or the area's great big-game hunting. But everyone who lived in Jackson Hole had a different notion of how the area was to be saved or exploited. And there were hundreds of differing opinions, for Jackson Hole was speckled with the homesteads and ranches of rugged individualists. There are still over one hundred fifty privately held plots within Grand Teton Park. When the park idea was first being discussed there were even more, stretching from South Park all the way up the valley and almost to the boundary of Yellowstone Park. Not a few of these residents had taken up their land as sheer speculative property. And others, particularly some of the dude ranchers, had obtained their lands from the government in seeming violation of the spirit of the homesteading laws.

Even today these old laws, and especially the mining law of 1872, make it possible for public lands in Jackson Hole to be grabbed for speculative purposes. Now, as then, the federal government was not always able to assign its lands to the wisest uses. Often one bureau was at odds with another, and the effect of it all was to discourage hopes for a national park in Jackson Hole.

But although the first efforts inspired at Maude Noble's cabin were not especially successful, other conservation activities were having better luck. Stephen N. Leek came to Jackson Hole very early in its history. He established a ranch in the upper end of South Park, and later he built the lodge on the northern end of Jackson Lake that still bears his name. Leek was a pioneer photographer with still and, later, movie cameras. His favorite subjects were elk, which he fed in winter, and the Teton Mountains. Leek also had some skill as a writer, and he poured all these talents into a long uphill battle to save the elk of Jackson Hole.

Leek was instrumental in making the nation aware of the

plight of the elk. And he began to succeed, for in 1912 the National Elk Refuge was established. At that time it contained only 1,760 acres, but over the years it has been enlarged to enclose almost 24,000 acres of valley floor and foothill areas.

Even though the idea of saving Jackson Hole from commercial exploitation had no Stephen Leek to document it, Congress did decide to preserve its mountains and lakes. In 1929 the most spectacular portion of the Teton range, along with all the lakes at its base save Jackson Lake, were incorporated into Grand Teton National Park. The recent interest of John D. Rockefeller, Jr., in the area may have helped Congress reach its decision.

Rockefeller had first come to Jackson Hole in 1926. Guided by the astute and always park-serving Albright, Mr. and Mrs. Rockefeller had not only been shown the marvels of the region but also the effects of growing commercial blight. Rockefeller recognized the threat, and after his visit he began a very ambitious land acquisition program in Jackson Hole.

It was obvious at the start that, if the landowners knew who was behind the program, their asking prices would go straight up. To avoid this Rockefeller had the Snake River Land Company set up by one-time Republican National Committeeman, and lawyer, Harold Fabian. Early settler R. E. Miller, now president of the Jackson bank, was appointed to act as the firm's purchasing agent.

While the initial maneuvering was going on, Rockefeller remained anonymously in the background. But before his interest was made public, Rockefeller's influence was felt in Jackson Hole as it still is today, and many of the old-timers resent it. When a proposal was recently made to name the roadway between present Grand Teton and Yellowstone parks the John D. Rockefeller, Jr., Memorial Parkway, it was hotly condemned by an important citizen's organization. They said there were many people more deserving of the remembrance than was Mr. Rockefeller. (Despite the protest the road was officially given the Rockefeller name in 1972.)

This was probably true. John D. Rockefeller, Jr., grew up as the only son of one of the world's richest men. Even if he had wanted to, he could not have been like other boys. In reading his biography one gets the impression that the family was constantly on its guard lest young John forget the station to which he was born. For all his wealth I found no envy for Mr. Rockefeller. He grew up wearing a stiffly starched collar that became a part of his personality. His father had seized control of practically all the petroleum distribution systems in the United States. Many little gas-station operators who tried to compete with a Standard Oil station across the street knew what it meant to be ground into the muck like a medieval vassal. Mr. Rockefeller, Sr., might have been one of the country's richest men, but he was also way out in front as one of the most hated. This stingy-seeming doler-out of dimes was a living testimonial to socialism. By the time John, Jr., had finished college and was ready to go into his father's office, the Rockefeller fortune was under siege. They had to give it away or the government would take it away. Since Rockefeller and his advisers were sagacious in the handling of money, it was clear to them that giving away the money was the best course. There were all sorts of ways to put strings on their foundation dollars, and this fact has made the family at least as powerful now as it was in the old man's heyday.

The elder Rockefeller's fortune has been estimated at around a billion dollars. These were hard, uninflated dollars, and worth far more than the flaccid ones of today. And it was John, Jr.'s duty in life to give a lot of them away. He lived to be a very old man and his philanthropies were legion. What he spent buying land in Jackson Hole was a pittance compared with the sums he had invested in health, education, and the arts.

It is especially easy to hate a rich man who gives you things, one who practically forces gifts on a community, and John D. Rockefeller, Jr., was hated. In comparison H. L. Hunt and Howard Hughes are practically loved, primarily because they never did much for anyone but themselves. Rockefeller is still hated in Jackson Hole for this reason, and also because of the rugged western individualism that automatically tends to reject any meddling from "outside," especially if it comes from the East.

As an illustration, a wrangler I knew told about the pack trip taken by a very rich and famous easterner. The first night in camp the guide went down to the creek and lugged back a pail of water. The millionaire, seeing this, immediately seized upon it as his and washed his hands in it, fouling the whole bucket. The guide saw and resented this, and immediately told his dude that "by Gawd, you can dipper out what water you need like anyone else." The dude, of course, didn't feel that he was "anyone else" and made a bad trip of it.

Rockefeller lacked, or thought he lacked, the warmth to be at ease with westerners. As a result he tended to remain a gray eminence ever after it became known that he was backing the Snake River Land Company. He further complicated his problems in Jackson Hole by choosing "Old Twelve Percent" R. E. Miller as his buyer. Miller had grown wealthy on the frailties of other valley men. He held mortgages on many of the properties that Rockefeller wanted, and to acquire them he was not averse to exerting a little pressure. Not that Rockefeller can be accused of being a party to extorting the settlers' land; he was not. He paid a fair and sometimes premium price for everything he acquired. And eventually he replaced Miller with the more popular Dick Winger. Those, like the Hole's only female homesteader, Geraldine Lucas, who resisted his agents' blandishments to sell their land were not punished behind the scenes.

There was no need of that, for sooner or later, in one way or another, Rockefeller got nearly every place he wanted. Geraldine Lucas's land went to him after she died. Other lands were bought and then left in the previous owners' charge to operate as lessees holding long-term leases. The thing that John D. Rockefeller and his close associates knew and outsiders couldn't realize was that the family was a dynasty, and it would exist long after the Si Ferrins and Lucases were forgotten. Perhaps it would not be John D. Rockefeller, Jr., who got a man's land; it might not even be Laurance, his son. But the end result was inexorable. The Rockefeller empire was founded on an extraordinary money sense, and it could afford to work in geologic ages while the rest of us sweated out a 30-year mortgage.

John D. Rockefeller, Jr., spent about $1,400,000 to acquire 35,310 acres in Jackson Hole. Of this amount he eventually deeded 33,562 acres back to the United States for inclusion in Grand Teton National Park. This left a considerable amount of land still in Rockefeller hands, most of it comprising the JY Ranch between Moose and Teton Village. On today's market the lands the Rockefellers kept are worth infinitely more than John, Jr., originally paid for the whole block. A cynic might say that Rockefeller had multiplied the value of his land by buying up Jackson Hole and then giving part of it away as an alluring public park—one the public could see but not touch.

Perhaps the one thing that earned Mr. Rockefeller so much animosity in Jackson Hole was the easy arrogance of his power to do just as he pleased in the valley. While westerners are often provincial to the point of boorishness, they are very sensitive to any act they consider an attempt to manipulate them. And when the act is tainted with subterfuge, as they considered some of the Snake River Land Company's dealings to be, it only fanned the hatreds. As one lady put it, "It wasn't what he did so much as the way he did it."

And yet, if someone had not acted, there is every reason to believe that much of Jackson Hole would have been blighted by the kind of commercial crassness that has harmed the town of Jackson. Rockefeller was damned if he did and damned if he didn't. So he went ahead with his land purchases despite the mounting opposition that soon spread far beyond Jackson Hole. A second newspaper, *The Grand Teton,* was established to oppose park enlargement in competition with the *Jackson Hole Courier,* which was not averse to park expansion. The former paper used a good deal of syndicated news and was sometimes embarrassed to find items in its national news columns diametrically opposed to its antipark material written at home.

Wyoming politicians were almost solidly against park expansion. Very often they reflected the opinions of Wyoming livestock interests, who are historically reactionary. The politicians were also getting support from the outfitters and sportsmen of the state, who tended to oppose the park, too. After years of dissension Rockefeller finally gave then Secretary of the Interior Ickes an ultimatum. Either accept his land as the nucleus of an expanded national park or sit by and watch it be sold.

The government was forced to act, and by executive order the Grand Teton National Monument was set aside in 1943 by Franklin Roosevelt—an act that only made Jackson Holers more furious, for the government had done by fiat what it had not been able to do through legislation. Wyoming politicians immediately introduced bills to abolish the monument. They failed, and the new park, greatly enlarged by the inclusion of nearly two hundred thousand acres of federal land, remained. It took seven more years of compromising to make the area truly a national park, but this was finally accomplished in 1950 during the Truman administration.

One interesting part of the 1950 establishing act allowed the building of roads and hotels in the new park, something that had been prohibited in the older, smaller park established in 1929. The Rockefellers took almost immediate advantage of this provision and began building the Jackson Lake Lodge on a bluff not far from Moran. A friend recalled for me the displaced rancher who "would like to blow that son of a bitchin' hotel to hell."

But the public had a far different picture of the lodge. It was being built to accommodate the impending crush of tourism in the area. The new facility was to be a nonprofit endeavor, and I remember being told, "It's going to be a place where the man of average means can afford to stay with his family." This claim helped sell the lodge to the public. In a magazine article entitled "Teton Retreat," the kicker head read "Lodge a Nonprofit Project," and went on, "The new Jackson Lake Lodge is being constructed on ground within that park and is a non-profit development operated by the

Grand Teton Lodge and Transportation Company. Designed to absorb the rapid increase of tourists . . ."

The lodge is indeed a nonprofit operation. It is run by the Grand Teton Lodge Company, which is owned by the Jackson Hole Preserve, Inc. According to information in a letter written to me by Gene W. Setzer, the executive vice-president of Jackson Hole Preserve, Inc.: "Such funds as are received from Grand Teton Lodge Company are applied by Jackson Hole Preserve, Incorporated to the improvement of visitor facilities and to conservation purposes. . . . Because of the restricted season and high costs of operation, however, Grand Teton Lodge Company is very hard pressed to generate any income beyond that needed to maintain its physical plant."

Nonprofit is a word that has a lot in common with "reclamation." It often sounds better than it really is. For while the lodge may be nonprofit it is not inexpensive. In 1971 a double room in the lodge was listed at twenty-seven to thirty dollars per day. (Unofficial sources have reported far higher room quotations when they applied for reservations.) The lodge operates on the European plan, so meals, like activities, are extra. A moderately active guest should expect to spend almost as much on his activities and food as he does on his room. So, from my point of view, Jackson Lake Lodge does not live up to its original billing as a place for the family man of modest means. What is even greater proof of that is that this multi-million-dollar structure has only forty guest rooms, rooms that are listed for double occupancy only.

John D. Rockefeller, Jr., took a keen personal interest in the lodge's construction. He had chosen the site because of the magnificent view of Jackson Lake and the Tetons beyond it. When he visited the area he had often taken his lunch on a hill close by that has come to be a minor shrine known as Lunch Tree Hill. Rockefeller is said to have hoped to capture the view he enjoyed from his lunch spot in the great windows of the Lodge's lobby, or lounge, as the operators call it. If he did not, he came awfully close, for the view from the awesome windows is superb.

The lounge itself is a room of vast proportions. On the walls there are fine oil paintings of big game by Carl Ringius. The room's two great fireplaces are large enough to camp in. But I personally find the spaciousness a bit studied, too purposeful in its majesty and reminiscent of an old railway depot. It is not a particularly friendly room. But it is Xanadu compared with the functional lobby below it. This room has all the charm of a bus station rest room.

The rest of the public rooms are less memorable. When I visited at the lodge I thoroughly enjoyed the young, college-age kids who largely staff the place. They were bright, polite, and eager to please. I well remember the distress of a young waitress who found herself serving frozen rolls straight from the Lodge's subterranean food preparation rooms. I guess everybody there got those chilled rolls that night. The rest of the meal was only passable, and about half what a hungry man needed for survival.

I have since been told by former supervisory employees and seasonal park rangers that there has been labor trouble at the Lodge, mostly due to a dictatorial management. There had also been a problem with drug use among the staff serious enough to attract undercover narcotics officers.

One lady with many years of supervisory experience in good resort hotels said that the place was so hopelessly mismanaged that she had to quit in midseason. By another source I was told that lower-echelon Park Service employees were not welcome in the public rooms of the lodge. And it was said that, when a problem arose between the park and the lodge's top management, management bypassed the superintendent of the park and went directly to the Secretary of the Interior. Needless to say, this had a debilitating effect on relations between the lodge and park administrations. In 1971 a new manager was appointed at the lodge, and there seemed to be less criticism of the operation since he took over.

But the really tragic thing about the lodge is the building itself. It is by far the ugliest large building in western Wyoming, rising out of its ugly compound like a great steel and cement excrescence predetermined to be the ugliest of all it surveys. One day, while waiting for a Park Service hike to begin at the lodge, I made these notes: "This is surely one of the ugliest buildings in Wyoming. Shit brown in color and as slab-sided as Menor's outhouse, it looks like something the Nazis built to fortify their Siegfried Line.

"The long, covered entranceway has no majesty and is reminiscent of a freeway overpass. The 'native' stonework around the front doors looks like something the boss's wife had done one day when the crew was finishing early.

"The flattish roof is really a composite roof with layers shooting off at all angles. The sundeck [on the long portico] over the entrance is full of empty chairs of faded though vivid plastic[?] upholstery. These chairs are the most eye-catching feature of the lodge front.

"One loses faith in the democracy of the national parks when he visits the lodge area.

"The swimming pool, like the lodge, has no place here. But, (remarked an attendant), 'The water is 73 degrees this morning.' The house beside the swimming pool is a sort of Kaiser aluminum tipi with logs radiating around and down from its cone-shaped roof."

Seen from the hills to the east, Jackson Lake Lodge and its associated cabin complex and huge parking lot resemble nothing more than a heap of litter on the lake shore. The dark, squarish buildings are helter-skelter paper cartons and the cars in the parking lot could be the flashy sweep of beer cans and empty milk containers.

Virtually every commercial enterprise in Grand Teton National Park is connected with the Rockefellers. The only major exception is the lodge adjacent to the Signal Mountain campground. Every gas station in the park is affiliated with Standard Oil, and the gasoline prices in each are staggering. I have been buying gasoline near home, from the same Standard Oil refinery that furnishes the park stations, for up to seventeen cents less per gallon.

One of the other Rockefeller concerns is the picturesque

Jenny Lake Lodge, where a cabin for two runs fifty-eight dollars per day. The brochure for Jenny Lake Lodge reads, "This delightful Lodge has a special charm and is quite the most luxurious of all the facilities in the valley." A claim that is open to dispute.

Colter Bay Village has cabins that range from single-room jobs with semiprivate baths at ten dollars and fifty cents per day to two-room units costing as much as twenty-eight dollars a day. There is also a Tent Village, which features weird, hermaphroditic log and canvas shelters at a minimum of seven dollars per day. These shelters are the only ones in the Rockefeller domain where cooking a meal is allowed. And by my calculation they can only accommodate about three hundred people per night.

The family that either by desire or economic necessity wants to camp out in the national park uses government facilities. Because, from my point of view, camping out is an intrinsic part of any visit to a national park, I can't give the Rockefellers very high marks for successfully coping with the great influx of tourists to Jackson Hole—an influx that they were instrumental in creating.

I also happen to be one who thinks that a vast number of visitors to national parks would be just as happy and just as refreshed by a visit to one of the Disneylands. Instead, in places like Yellowstone and Colter Bay, we have tried to incorporate the best of Disneyland with the best of a park and the two just don't blend. But what many of us think does not carry nearly as much weight as what the Rockefellers think should constitute a national park.

There is no better example of this than at Colter Bay Village, where a fine, down-to-earth natural history museum was recently dismantled. I have been told on excellent authority that this act was the result of a deal made between George Hartzog, chief of the Park Service, and Laurance Rockefeller. It came about when the Rockefellers purchased a collection of Plains Indians' artifacts. The purchase was made with the admirable aim of placing the collection on public display. But to make way for it the natural history exhibit was ripped out of the Colter Bay Visitor Center. What was not realized by the Rockefellers was that their collection belongs in the Midwest, where the Plains Indians lived. It has no relevance to the Jackson Hole area, and should not be hauled out here. What makes the decision to do that seem even more willful and autocratic is that there has been a good collection of Shoshone Indian artifacts available for sale. And at last report this material, which very much belongs in Jackson Hole, was going to be sold out of state. The cost of setting up this Indian display has exceeded six hundred thousand dollars.

Then there was the matter of Menor's Ferry. Bill Menor established the ferry on the Snake River near Moose years ago at a place where he said the meandering, many-channeled Snake was "all together." The ferry is a pontoon affair that is fastened to a cable suspended across the river. When it was operated the river's current provided the power and the pontoons were manipulated to nose into the current in such a way that the ferry was forced back and forth across the river. It was a typical pioneer operation, and when winter closed it down a "brush" bridge was thrown across the open part of the river to allow passage.

The ferry was a landmark until a bridge replaced it in the late 1920s. After that the old ferry fell into disrepair, and it was not until several years later that the Rockefellers decided to restore it. The Park Service operates it now in the summer, but very often the operation is prevented either by dangerously high water in the river or a gravel bar that has formed along the ferry's course. As a restoration the ferry provides a link with the near past, but its present-day operation only titillates tourists. No cattle, wagons, horses, or even Model Ts are crossed on it. It has no useful function. But it is something that the Rockefellers have been interested in.

For several years the operation of the ferry has been just another one of the Park Service's free services. But in 1971 it became apparent that there wasn't enough money in the budget to operate the ferry *and* conduct all the nature hikes, too. From my point of view, and I think almost everyone else's who has one, the nature hike with a ranger is one of the finest of park activities. They are fun, informative, and the best way of all to see the park. Naturally, then, I was amazed when the staff at Grand Teton elected to *curtail* the nature walks in order to operate Menor's Ferry during the 1971 season. As bureaucrats whose prime interest is often self-preservation, they should have known that their nature hikes make as many or more friends for the Park Service than almost any other activity. But, like a lot of frantic lemmings, they bolted to fulfill the willful whims that money and power sometimes create.

Not all of the successful Rockefeller machinations can be attributed to bureaucratic spinelessness. Some of what has gone into Grand Teton Park is there because the Rockefellers stipulated that it be there at the time of the land transfer. The Jackson Hole Wildlife Park is one such feature. For some reason Laurance Rockefeller decided, with the New York Zoological Society, that a serious threat to the region's big game existed. So that it might be perpetuated and at the same time put on public display, the Wildlife Park was created near the Ox-bow Bend a mile or so downstream from Jackson Lake Dam. The area was fenced, and then buffalo and elk were put into the enclosure. At best the park was no more than a roadside zoo. It was over this Wildlife Park that the famed naturalist, Olaus Murie, is said to have broken with the Rockefeller organization in Jackson Hole. The Wildlife Park proved to be of no service to the animals. The buffalo have long ago walked through the fences and taken up new quarters in the Pot Hole area and in the Snake River bottoms, and in the winter the captive animals had to be artificially fed, and this was not always in their best interests.

Happily the Wildlife Park, or Range, has not been fully operational the last few years. It has long stood as a symbol of dilettantism that has no place in a national park. In a way, though, it also symbolizes the sometimes-curious foundation way of doing things. While one segment of the Rockefeller largesse has been devoted to planned parenthood and stopping the sad population spiral, another segment has devoted itself to substantially increasing the production of rice so that more people can be fed and enabled to propagate.

The Rockefellers today are not physically prominent in Jackson Hole. I'll bet Laurance Rockefeller, who has overseen most of the family's more recent activities in Jackson Hole, could walk through Jackson's square and never be recognized. When statements from the family are made they generally come through the manager of the Grand Teton Lodge Company or the Park Service.

The family has usually tried to get along in Jackson Hole. Unfortunately for both them and Jackson Hole it has not always known how. But the family has been held up to spates of public scorn and vituperation for some seventy-five years, and it has so far weathered every one. And even if one believes that what they have done in preserving Jackson Hole and enlarging the park was not done in the best way, about the only other way at the time led toward the chaos of billboard commercialism.

One of the major points of opposition to park enlargement had been the loss to Teton County of taxable land. To overcome this the government paid a subsidy in lieu of taxes to Teton County for twenty years beginning in 1950. In that time the tourist industry developed enormously and provided ample revenue. For a while, to improve local relations, all autos with Teton County plates were admitted free into Teton Park. There is still a great deal of livestock grazing in Teton National Park, and cowmen are permitted to trail their animals across park land to reach and then leave grazing areas in the Teton National Forest.

While it honors these commitments the Park Service makes no bones about its ultimate aim to return as much of Jackson Hole as possible to its original state. This includes everything from power-line removal to restrictions on horses in the high country. The general need for better planning in the national parks was wonderfully described in Edward Abbey's *Desert Solitaire*. Many of the finest parks were inexorably moving toward Coney Island status, but now, if the public can be made to understand the reasons for new operating procedures, it need not happen. Over three million people visit Grand Teton National Park every year. While a lot of us may think this is too many, the projections are for the tourist influx to be even worse, reaching five million by 1979.

Most of this will be the typical gawk, scratch, and drive-on tourism. It may be repulsive to purists, but it really isn't very harmful. What has been increasing in Teton Park are such things as mountain climbing. Hundreds now climb the Grand Teton each year. And the Park Service records show all registered climbs to have increased by forty percent in just three years! In 1970 there were 116,000 back-country hikers in the park. Boating on the lakes and Snake River has increased at an alarming rate. Winter activities are increasing, and the roaring snowmobile has already become a predatory slobmobile in too many areas. In summer, finding a campsite in Teton Park after lunch is akin to finding a four-pound gold nugget. But sad experience has already shown that developing more campsites is extremely detrimental to the park.

What John D. Rockefeller, Jr., gave to the American people as a gift is not without its headaches. Wouldn't it be ironic if the gasoline-powered motorcar, which made the Rockefellers their billions, were to be banned from some of the very lands that their money helped to buy?

*During the night I heard what I
thought were hoofbeats on the trail
between camp and the lake. I jumped
up and went outside the tent but, in
the bright moonlight, saw nothing.
Lady was still tied in her niche in the
trees.*

AUTHOR'S 1970 TETON NOTEBOOK

12 / The Teton Mountains

While many visitors to Jackson Hole are satisfied to sit
in a lodge or highway turnout and look at the distant Tetons,
an increasing number of others aren't so disposed. To my
knowledge all the significant peaks in the range were climbed
long ago. Books have been published describing the routes that
may be used to reach various summits. Some climbs have also
been rated as to difficulty so one may choose the route best
suited to his skill and spirit of adventure.

Mostly for novelty, and to get some publicity, a group now
attempts to climb the Grand Teton every New Year's Day. Because the peaks are traditionally storm-racked at this season,
the climbers are not always successful, but their publicity is.
The exciting if customary radio blackouts between the climbers' camp and park headquarters at Moose adds to the annual
suspense. Finally, though, the word gets through the snowy
clouds that the team is safe and packing out and the suspense
of a midwinter climb is over again until next year.

It is a stunt, although anyone who has seen the climbers'
corpses or even their photographs in the Teton County Sheriff's
Office learns never to take the mountain for granted. No one
has ever been hurt on the New Year's climb, but during the
otherwise delightful summer of 1971 bodies were caroming off
the Tetons like Ping-Pong balls.

The ones I saw pictures of had landed on their heads or had, at least, been struck very hard on top of the head during their fatal plunges. But the first thing you notice is the darkness of the skin. There is no deathly pallor—if you are killed in the mountains your face turns black. While the overall distortion of the head's shape is not great, there is still more than a subtle change. The features are puffy or pulpy, and the crown of the head has been pushed down to give the corpse a cretinous expression. They are hard pictures to look at. And, deriving as they do from the clean, exalting sport of mountain climbing, I find the incongruity between the two possible results of mountain climbing at once unsettling but also justified.

As a part of the research for this book I considered enrolling in one of the park-approved climbing schools. There, in a day or so, I would be taught enough about belaying and rappelling to go with a guide to the top of the Grand Teton. The whole experience can be had for about a hundred dollars. But once I actually went into the Tetons I became immediately aware that I was not and never would be a climber. In the Tetons words like "chasm" and "abyss" took on a new and much greater meaning for me. In trying to understand my anxiety, I finally decided that while falling was a very unpleasant prospect it was really the chilling unease I felt on the edge of a precipice that ended my mountain climbing before it ever began.

There are several places in the Tetons where a hiker may go, experience something of the climber's exhilaration, and still not suffer too badly from vertigo or acrophobia. The hike to Amphitheater Lake at the eastern base of the Grand Teton is a good example. I went with park naturalist Don Ester and a dozen other hikers. It is not a particularly long hike, but it is a steep one that takes time. We met in the Lupine Meadows before eight on a fine, cool morning in July. My notes for the climb began as follows: "The trail proved to be fairly steep, rising from about 6,750 to 9,700 in 4.8 miles . . . the whole group seemed to be reasonably experienced hikers."

This matter of experience becomes important on longer

hikes. In time a person develops a hiking pace that conserves his energy and wind while being the most comfortable for him. Getting stuck behind a slow hiker is almost as bad as getting ahead of one who is constantly treading on your heels.

Once, as we stopped for a breath on the end of one of the many switchbacks that constitute the trail, someone speculated on the haze that lay over Jackson Hole. Air pollution is supposed to be minimal in the valley, yet there are times when the air seems to be a bit thick. Our ranger-naturalist commented that an automobile engine used about a ton of air in burning a gallon of gas. My notes continue:

"About halfway up we began to see Jackson Hole stretching out below us. At the end of one switchback we stopped and could see Jenny, Jackson, and then Two-Ocean lakes below us to the north. East we saw Bradley and then Taggart lakes and, of course, most of Jackson Hole.

"Flowers along the way were red monkey flower, split-leaf painted cup (a close relative of paintbrush), coral root orchid, and bog orchid. Higher up we saw moss campion.

"Surprise Lake is just a short distance above the last switchback. We had to wade across some rotten snow en route. It is a very small lake—maybe an acre and a half. It was still 90 percent ice covered. Crossing more snow—the trail was largely obliterated by it—we came to the cirque at the base of Disappointment Peak. In it lies Amphitheater Lake. It is about 3½ acres and it, too, was mostly ice covered. (We had met an eager youth, rod in hand, on the way up and I imagine he was quite disappointed.)

"The water coming from Amphitheater Lake is clear and marvelously cold. I bellied down and drank some at the outlet and thought it delightful. Some of the best I ever drank, yet there is a certain danger that this and all the Teton waters are polluted and signs are posted at trail heads to this effect.

"As they travel along the people become more and more friendly. It is an interesting metamorphosis.

"The pink algae that grows on the snow [giving the drifts a distinct blush] is supposed to taste like strawberries . . .

others said it tasted like watermelons. My vote would be with the watermelon group. While we are waggishly admonished to avoid yellow snow, pink snow is a survival food, though it more often serves as a refreshing bit of chilled salad.

"After lunch we climbed the Surprise Lake Pinnacle, which rises above Surprise Lake. It was a very easy climb, and when I reached the top I got a surprise—even though I'd been warned. Below the Pinnacle there was nothing but hundreds of feet of space—Garnet Canyon. When the magnitude of the spaces below me at last registered I felt a trifle shaky and sat down, but not until I moved off the edge of that abyss did I feel completely comfortable.

"While the Grand Teton from a distance looks solid, up close it appears cracked and broken; from grayish-blue at a distance it turns a buff color. This is one of the best places a hiker can choose to get a climber's notion of the Tetons. I decided I had no desire to climb any of the peaks. It made me nervous just to see members of the group standing on the brink of the chasm, let alone watch the youngsters happily scrambling around on it.

"But if I took my eyes off the deadly drop into Garnet Canyon I could see all of Jackson Hole and a grand array of the Tetons' most impressive peaks. We could also see the Teton Glacier and much of the moraine that it has formed.

"On the rock cliffs above Amphitheater Lake are big, dark but shiny stains. A biologist in the group said this was a blue-green algae, a form that reproduces asexually, by spores. This stain is what I heretofore may have mistaken for seeps on the rock faces."

On our way down we met "some other hikers, four of whom were bound to climb the north face of Grand Teton . . . despite their beards, long hair, head bands, and beads I had to give them grudging admiration, for it is not something I would do—no, sir! The Grand's north face looks straight up!"

This encounter with "hippies" was one of several I was to have in the Tetons. Only these mountain-variety kids with their repetitive "mans" and "beautifuls" are not the freaked-out, "bird"-flipping garbage of the city streets. In time a lot of them will revert to the middle class that made them, while others may be broken by the same society. The rest, and there are never enough, will try and perhaps succeed in making all our lives a little more meaningful.

After agreeing to write this book, but before actually beginning it, I wrote my editor, Angus Cameron. I told him that I hoped the book would say something to the many young people who flock to Jackson Hole and the Tetons every year. It was my opinion that many of them regarded the mountains as a kind of Alpine Lourdes, but that the majority of seekers there didn't seem to know what it was they were hoping to find.

Angus liked my allusion to an Alpine shrine, but did not comment on my implied aspirations to omniscience. He probably knew what I learned in writing the book, which was that I would not find any great, revealing truths to pass on to young people. I sat every night for a month in a mountain tent and tried to convince a young fellow that the formula by which I'd grown up would keep him from going back to jail and also out of the clutches of organized religion. The boy must have had other options, but from what he told me of his life I didn't think so.

What I forgot during our sessions was that, while this boy was wellborn, he had fewer choices of what to do with his life than I'd had at his age. He was not as free as I had been. At the time neither of us realized that, in the mountains, making such choices was unnecessary. Perhaps that was the formula I should have expounded, but it seemed too simple.

Actually, it is the kids who have said something to me. Theirs is a great, welling feeling drawn equally from youthful wisdom and their equally youthful ignorance. They are being cheated. A college professor who spends his summers as a naturalist said, "It isn't the rioting and the violence that surprises me—on the whole, I'm far more surprised by the restraint the kids have shown." I am, too.

There have been any number of grand pronouncements about preserving this animal or that vista, "for future generations." It has mostly been a sorry lie. A young person has no chance today of seeing the Yellowstone and Jackson Hole that Lieutenant Doane saw less than one hundred years ago. He can see only a fraction of some of it. In one way or another, most of this wilderness has been impaired or completely destroyed.

In the Tetons, some of what once was still is. The most spectacular part of the range has been incorporated into Grand Teton National Park. Within this incorporation are three specific zones. The southern part of the range, from the park's south boundary to Indian Paintbrush Canyon has been completely developed, with good trails, footbridges, and designated campsites. From Paintbrush Canyon to Webb Canyon several miles north there are no developed trails. This is a pristine wilderness, seldom visited and then only by experienced backpackers. While I was camped in Moose Basin I met a young fisheries biologist, who had backpacked from Jenny Lake to the western side of the range, from where he worked his way north to the high basin where we met. In all the time I spent in the Tetons this pleasant young man was the only one I met who was thoroughly traversing them.

At Moose Basin he was in the third zone: the Park Service describes it as having "primitive trails." This means that trail maintenance isn't very regular; nearly all streams, bogs, and gulleys are bridgeless; and, within reason, you may camp where you please. The scenery isn't awesome. Unless you leave the trails, a practice the Park Service restricts to groups who have climbing permits, there is only one spectacular viewing point.

Where the trail crosses Moose Basin Divide you can look out over much of the area to the east and southeast of Jackson Hole. Looking down toward Moose Basin itself the old lava flow that encrusts the backbone of the northern Tetons glitters in the sunlight. Farther south the tops of Mount Moran and the Grand Teton loom on the rugged skyline. The divide is just above timberline, and a few clumps of scraggly, stunted pine rise up to contest that fact. Flower line is a bit higher.

During August the big yellow sunflowers are beginning to droop sadly and to shed their golden inflorescence. But in the basin itself the bluebells are thriving. At their best, they grow to my waist, and I felt a guilty pang or two when I had to force my way through them to reach the swift creek.

A strange thing about this vast, down-tilting basin is that a horse will eat very little of its abundant vegetation. Being there recalled another time when I was walking with a horse wrangler through thigh-deep wild flowers that he referred to as "these damn weeds." What grass there is often occurs as little blue-green spears, each individual several feet from the next. At the small boggy seeps along the hillsides there are dark, lush sedges, which I fed my horse. These are not plentiful enough to feed even a few horses. And before long their shod hooves would cut the soft, moist ground into mush. Such conditions make this marginal horse country—especially if you go there with a nervous, homesick mare like Lady.

Of course, a backpacker has no such equine worries. He can go as far as his little packets of edible powders and woody chips of dry food permit him to. A packhorse, despite the extra work and care it requires, carries everything, even its own food. There is room in the panniers for the big heavy cans of peaches that taste so good after a hot, tiring hike. And it is really astounding how far, and over what kind of terrain, you can pack a fresh, raw egg. You can take canned ham and slabs of bacon and even pancake flour and biscuit mix. It is always wise to have a jar or two of something that seems exotic—say, potted cheese, fancy pickled peppers, or raspberry jam. These usually prosaic items become tempting delicacies in the mountains. The thought of them helps you to push on during the day, knowing that you can unpack and enjoy them in the early evening.

One of the best, most self-indulgent times I ever had for myself was on lower Berry Creek. It was on the last leg of a walking-pack trip into the northern Tetons. I had come down Webb Canyon from Moose Basin. In my notebook I wrote, "Got up before 6 A.M. It did rain lightly in the night, and a few drops fell while I was getting dressed, so I cooked breakfast in the tent.

"By the time I got packed up the sky was mostly clear.

"The trail down Webb Canyon was OK, much better than Owl Creek, but it was rocky and the maintenance hit and miss. A third of the way down there is a fine waterfall on the N. Canyon wall. . . .

"Lots of huge spruce. The stream assumes torrential aspects in certain places. I had to wade it twice—knee deep and then some. Feet got soaking wet (boots, too), twice Lady stepped on my heels and for a while I really hobbled.

"Got wet again crossing Berry C., near the R.S. Went over to dry out socks, but no ranger.

"The trail to the lower Berry Ck. meadows is fine and I have encamped on a wooded knoll near the stream."

While making these notes I was lying on some canvas with my head and shoulders propped against my rolled sleeping bag. At my right hand was a tin of pilot bread, which I was eating after liberally spreading it with a tasty, soft cheese. I had taken my damp boots off and hung my wet socks on the limbs of an adjacent pine. No Garden of Delights could have been any more delightful to me at that moment. The really happy thing about such moments is that the older you get the more you enjoy them.

If you think about it, there are two special kinds of satisfaction to be had from camping in a mountain wilderness. The first comes from just overcoming the doubts as to your ability to do it at all. This is a city-bred insecurity that can be cured a thousand ways: building a campfire with only one match and no paper tinder, cooking on a one-burner gas stove and being able to serve each dish hot and unburned. You can also enjoy this satisfaction by remembering that, despite any number of perplexing mishaps, you completed the trip and got home safely.

The other sort of satisfaction never comes to me on a two- or three-day trip. Because in that time I'm still experimenting and worrying and wondering. But by the fourth day I've come to terms with the things that bothered me earlier. I can begin doing everything I've done all along, but can now enjoy doing it as quickly and neatly as possible. The stove is familiar now, so not only is my cooking good but I can pride myself on having done something clever with leftovers. I have at least momentarily convinced the obstreperous Lady that not only can I pack her by myself but that I can do it despite her objections. When I throw my diamond hitch it is a full, fifty-eight facet beauty—a thing of perpetuity and symmetry that will ride beautifully all the way to the next camp.

The central part of the Teton Range is not suited to horses and is almost exclusively the backpacker's domain. A Sierra Club trip into that trailless area is advertised as difficult and not for beginners, yet it is sold out months ahead of time. I have only been around the edges of this silent world. I've had peeps and long-range views that are the looks of dreams and magic mirrors.

This is especially so if you boat slowly along the west shore of Jackson Lake. Steering south from the little lakeside camp at Berry Creek to the Warm Springs camp I eased my skiff through the wooden debris and beached it on a tiny strand. "The shore is lined with old logs and stumps but should provide a nice beach when the lake recedes . . . the meadows are lush with many kinds of plants—a few in blossom. It is also alive with humming, singing insects. I walked up and down the shore perhaps 500 yards looking for the Warm Springs. I didn't find them, although I did hear the rush of a stream farther back in the timber. It is certainly the edge of an untracked wilderness here, and I would not have been surprised to have come on a bear—even a grizzly." I saw none that day I made those notes. The meadows were filled with robins.

At length I reembarked and continued south along the lake's western shore. "Above me were timbered, wild-looking mountain slopes with here and there a big rocky ledge or outcropping. Beyond jutted the infinitely more rugged outline of the Teton group. Early in the morning, with the rising sun on them, the Tetons' features become very clear, and even at long distances you can see much detail.

"I stayed out about 250 yards from shore and I began to see

open, green swards on the timbered slopes. I hoped to see game, but I saw nothing. In this stretch the mountain range could almost be called rolling; then, in a very abrupt change it becomes the familiar, rugged Teton peaks.

"Coming on the first glaciated canyon—Colter, I think—I found it so huge that I seemed to be in a motionless boat, for the great canyon went by me almost imperceptibly. On the north side [of the canyon] is a stupendous rock wall rising up hundreds of feet above the talus slopes. Below them are narrow, twisting lines of timber. These lead down into a green draw that has a half stream–half waterfall threading down it in three places. The falls are so high up on the mountainside that I wondered how barren-looking rock could produce so much water."

As I putted along below the great range, I noted, "The scene has become so magnificent that it would be easy to get a crick in your neck from constantly looking up.

"Well south of me I noticed a fast boat cutting capers across the water and leaving a semi-rooster tail in its wake. On a fine morning under these towering peaks such frenzied activity seems juvenile.

"Next is Waterfalls Canyon, and the south wall is even higher than the one I had just been awed by. Mt. Moran looms ahead now. I cleared some shoreline and could see it in all its bulk. It is a white-spotted colossus. It seemed that in going down the range here the 'show' got better and better as each new 'act' rose up to overshadow the previous one.

"The colors of the peaks close up are in grays that grade to bluish gray and almost black from a greater distance. Deep down in the formations there are streaks of buff, almost a rusty color. The waterfall called 'Wilderness' is high up in the canyon and has the shape of a billowing horse's tail. It is narrow at the top and then flares out to many times its width as it disappears behind a trace of timber."

Going on, I wrote, "A deep snowdrift lies like thick icing on the ridge above this canyon. It surrounds and emphasizes a smallish rock spire near the ridge's summit. It looks like an Arabian minaret incongruously enveloped by snow.

"The falls, which had disappeared behind a tree line, re-appear and are wider still. These falls can be seen from across the lake, but they are better seen here, and still they are a long way off.

"As always, every few feet you move along this range the visual angles change and give the canyons and peaks a very different appearance." Mount Moran is a sharp-seeming spire from some northern aspects and not at all like the stolid, flat-topped peak we're used to seeing from the valley. That bright morning the few clouds were "little cotton puffs, shining on the horizon. I noticed one had gone aground on Mount Moran.

"Moran Canyon is vast. And the upthrusting mountains here appeared to have been formed of quick-setting plastic. How else could rock be set in such curves and rounded angles?"

In Paintbrush Canyon there is a block of stone that lies at an unbelievably precipitous angle near the sharp edge of a very high ridge. It looks like a mammoth steamer trunk that has been perfectly balanced on the cornice of a skyscraper. Sitting on a convenient rock beside the trail it gave me the feeling that if I waited long enough that great block would eventually teeter and then come crashing in a great display of gravity and billowing dust. But it did not move. I drew a picture of it in my notebook. It cannot last the night, and yet I know it will probably last much longer than all my nights.

The Park Service, fully realizing that the Tetons are the chief and most arresting feature in Jackson Hole, has made special efforts to preserve the range's foreground. It is a sad thing to drive up through the beautiful South Park area, see the Grand Teton exquisitely framed in the angle of Leek's Draw, and roll on into the sadness of a propane farm and a roaring gravel yard. The scene is similar at Jenny and String lakes, where many of the trails into the south and most spectacular part of the Tetons begin. Coming back is much worse than going up, for in going up you have begun in a crush of recreating Americans. The kids, suckled on TV westerns, leap out to pat the packhorse; they never realize that the packhorse, like most horses, has absolutely no desire to be patted. But mostly it is the crowd and its aloofness that grate on me: the frozen-faced women spooning out picnic fare from brightly colored tin cans, the rattling sacks of potato chips and Fritos, the pop cans, and the foolish, impractical clothes that nearly all park visitors now wear.

As you walk, you get farther and farther from this roadside hubbub. The people on the trail become fewer, the saggy-breasted women with sculptured hairdos fall behind, and step by step it gets better. But coming back is the reverse of this. Your welcome home from the wilderness is the babble rising out of the garbage, the leaky faucet, the dirty privy, the auto with its hood up, the fat man in his undershirt.

The campground milieu can be avoided by coming back before 9:00 A.M. The crowd hasn't yet formed, since it is a relaxing, vacationing body that flourishes best in the heat of the day.

Another way to avoid it is to begin your hike at one of the jump-off spots farther south. The White Grass Ranger Station is such a one, and the Phelps Lake trail head just off the Moose–Wilson Road is another, although this latter beginning point isn't too good a choice for the short-term hiker anxious to see the most of the mountains in the least amount of time.

For him there is little choice but to begin at the String Lake or Jenny Lake trail heads and march up Cascade Canyon. This marvelous, glaciated canyon lies immediately west of Jenny Lake. It is one of the hanging canyons mentioned earlier. The approach to it is steep, but once you are in the canyon itself the trail hardly rises for several miles. Near its head the going is steeper and eventually the trail forks. The south-tending way leads to an open forest of large and rather unusual white-bark pines, while the other fork passes Lake Solitude en route to the often snow-closed Paintbrush Divide.

The day I chose to hike to Solitude began with the cool pink and blues that often denote the passing of a summer rain-storm. I was camped on the edge of the Gros Ventre and noted, "Driving down off the bench I thought the misty clouds lying in the Snake River bottoms resembled a giant lake of pinkish blue.

"The weather looked favorable, but I did carry a raincoat, and lunch of two sandwiches and four Space Food sticks in my knapsack.

"Cascade Canyon was awesomely beautiful, and I was again struck by the violent power of the avalanches that have swept down from those towering walls. In one area there was a cemetery of golden stakes; they actually were the snapped-off trunks of myriad conifer saplings. In another place the snow from an avalanche still remains drifted across the trail.

"There were some 'fuzzy-wuzzies' in the camp along Cascade Creek, but they either didn't hear, see, or just chose to ignore my 'Hi!' and wave.

"From the rocks beside the trail a pika emerged and gave me an opportunity to study him at close range. He was much like a gray-brown guinea pig with larger ears and somewhat smaller overall size.

"As I went up the canyon the clouds began gathering and lowering over the canyon ramparts. The sunlight filtering down was diffused and almost dreamily soft. En route I overtook and passed a cheery, raincoated party of elderly people; two of the ladies had accents and bright Swiss[?] faces. These people all looked to be in their 60s and one especially alive lady in the group was probably nearer 70. This group moved slowly, but steadily, and *they got there*." At this point in my journal keeping I recall being prejudiced against the car-bound tourist. It was only occurring to me that everyone simply cannot visit the Teton Range. Rugged as they are, the mountains cannot long retain their pristine state under the pounding of growing thousands of Vibram soles.

"I reached the lake [Solitude] at 11:30 A.M. It had begun to rain when I was about a mile from the lake, and it continued intermittently all the time I was there. This did not enhance the lake's appearance and a further detraction, for me, was that the lake was still about 65 percent ice covered. The ice was rotten and half submerged. I estimated the lake to be about 3 acres in size. . . . It lies in the bottom of a three-sided basin or cirque. The surrounding cliff tops were all shrouded in leaden clouds. The wind was blowing, and I soon was wearing my raincoat over a down vest while I walked around the lake shore.

"The basin is still mostly snow covered. The second thing, after the horses' hitching rail, I saw at the lake was a big snow bank and a blue-clad fellow bounding over it, ice ax in hand. The meadows around the lake were still muggy wet, and water was running or standing in numerous places.

"As the clouds lifted a bit I walked out on some large rocks that jut out into the lake. I could see down into the lake here and found the water clear and deep. I counted four small streams waterfalling down the cliffs and emptying into the lake.

"It is apparent that horses' hooves have chewed up the soft vegetation surrounding the lake. It will take years for this briefly summered area to recover." This is the reason for the hitching rail. The Park Service requires that horses be kept away from the lake. Needless to say, the area around the hitching rail was pretty well used up itself.

"There are mere wisps of timber threading in narrow stands up the basin's north side," my notes went on. "These are mostly white-bark pine with a good mix of alpine fir." Since my days of college botany, alpine fir has become "subalpine fir" because it also grows at lower elevations. Some loggers call it "ranger fir" because the Forest Service has recently encouraged its greater use. If you cut into one with an ax the odor released will explain why alpine fir is also called "piss fir."

"Farther up the sharp ridge separating this canyon and basin from Paintbrush Canyon there is a solid row of weather-frazzled, white-bark pines. Below them, the slope is gentler and quite green. Cutting in a sharp diagonal across this slope is the trail to the Paintbrush Divide."

There were three or four small, blue alpine tents, the type popular with most backpackers, pitched at sites around the lake. The campers I met were all very chipper despite the rainy weather. "While I sat on a flat rock I had overturned to get a dry seat two boys, 19 or 20, with lank, wet hair came pegging in, looking tired, more tired than I felt. One of the boys brushed the long hair out of his eyes with his fingertips in much the way a girl would, throwing his head back at the same time.

"The clouds began to part a bit, and as they raced across the sky strips of sunlight beamed down to light the snow-fields in fast-moving sweeps. I was reminded of the effect of the big multimirrored balls that used to sparkle and dazzle as they turned above old ballroom floors.

"Looking away from the lake, down canyon, I could see a great peak; it was probably Teewinot. Above me on the south wall were two, much smaller, peaks with flat tops. The snow lies here, old and gray and many feet deep. Eternal snow.

"On the soft lake margins a small white flower was bloom-ing—it *may* have been 'sandwort.' On the way up I passed large plots of bright yellow lilies. While this is certainly an alpine setting, the rough cliffs above the lake look more like the 'real alpine' country—Spain, Whymper, Hemingway—all that.

"While I was making notes the two long-haired boys cast about and eventually pitched their orange tent in the area I would guess is most exposed to weather. The boys will surely know if it is cold tonight.

"Looped in the cliffs above the lake are what look like three hanging canyons. I saw a hiker coming down the switch-backs below Paintbrush Divide. From where I stood he ap-peared to be about one inch high—tiny and only visible when he passed by a backdrop of snow."

While I was hiking back down the trail, "the sun came out and showed me the slopes covered with low huckleberry in a brilliant green that was vibrant—almost beyond belief."

Not surprisingly, I do much better going down a mountain trail than I do going up one. As I swung along, "I began to meet the multitude. I passed one group after another. I re-member two girls laboring up under huge packs. One was a bright-faced kid, maybe Irish, and I could tell she was a nice girl. Her companion was Chinese and she, too, was nice. Shy nice. Then a fuzzy-haired, bearded Negro and a nice-looking white girl—with a look of old money and old family about her.

"There were hippie types, and even one lad who came along lugging a cased guitar. There were men in shorts and straw hats. Way down the canyon near the west boat dock on Jenny Lake one woman stood blocking the trail and haranguing her companions so loudly that I could hear her far down the trail. She was way past the no-bra age, for her nipples and navel were in a direct horizontal line. Most hikers are nice, a cut above the average tourist, but when there are so many they spoil it simply by the sheer weight of their number."

I arrived back at my camp in the early evening. While I wrote up my day's notes I paused and looked out toward the Tetons. "The sky tonight is a miracle, golden-layered clouds, thick like a quilt with just a few small puffs of gray in the foreground. The golden quilt has a straight bottom edge that is just far enough above the Teton's rugged horizon to expose the bright band of blue that is backgrounding the mountains. As I write, the quilt is turning to a deep, soft orange. This is the loveliest sunset I have ever seen in the Tetons. Now the gray clouds look like puffs of paint spilled on a pane of glass. And already this fantastically beautiful sunset is fading. The orange-gold quilt is turning to waste gray; the orange color is quickly running off its lower edge.

"Now it is gone and unless you were here you would not believe it had ever existed." The tourists were largely forgotten and I concluded the day's notes: "There is the memory of the storm cloud's rear guard boiling and pouring over peaks that gleamed wetly from the shower just passed. The mountains *all* are beautiful—there are very few beautiful people— maybe for today just the old Swiss lady who was genuine from the smile on down."

Cascade Canyon is as beautiful going up as it is coming down. The stream, Cascade Creek, has many placid pools in the level stretches of the gorge, and it is common to see moose browsing beside them. Unlike Cascade, some of the other canyon and alpine trails are more scenic and easier to traverse going in one direction than the other. The booklet *Teton*

Trails shows all the trails in the park, and makes some recommendations for hiking trips. My copy is strangely bent and badly worn from the many miles it has traveled in my hip pocket.

One of the most memorable of its suggested trips begins at the White Grass Ranger Station. Close by the famous old White Grass Dude Ranch, the ranger station is hidden deep in the timber at the end of a rough, single track road. During the summer of 1970 the seasonal ranger there was frequently visited by a black bear who came up on the cabin porch looking for handouts.

The trail system permits considerable variations, but the one I chose is a great loop to Marion Lake near the southeast park boundary, then north to Sunset Lake and Hurricane Pass before turning west again over the Static Peak trail. The latter trail joins the Death Canyon trail, which in turn leads back to the White Grass station.

By mid-August most of the snow had gone off the high passes and the first crop of hay in the valleys had been cut and stacked. This allowed my friend and neighbor, Darrel Jenkins, a few days away from his dairy farm to make the trip with me.

Darrel brought a bale of his very finest hay for Lady, the black mare who would be packing our outfit. Forage is short in the Tetons, and Lady is not a particularly good forager anyway, so we were almost compelled to pack the hay. A bale was more than Lady would need or could carry, so we took some hay out of the bale and then re-tied it in two bundles before packing it in a burlap sack. When we put it on top of Lady's already big load and then covered it with a canvas pack cover, our mare resembled a tiny elephant with a huge howdah on her back.

Since the only real test of a pack is to travel with it, we started out. In my notes I wrote, "We started and also started our troubles with the pack. First the two parcels of hay slipped and fell down over the mare's nose. From then on it was slipping pack and repack—often from the bare horse out—all day long."

The Open Canyon Trail, which we took after leaving the

White Grass station and hiking up to the west end of Phelps Lake, "is uphill all the way to the Mt. Hunt Divide—which is signed at 9,700! It was a tough day. Much of the trail passes through timber and the far wall of the canyon is obscured much of the time. The scenery—even over Mt. Hunt—is pleasant but hardly spectacular."

As we toiled along we drank from the tiny rivulets running out of the old snowdrifts. I looked in vain for the mountain sheep, which are said to be sometimes seen around the divide. This section of trail, not one of the most popular, had not been maintained in about three years. I wrote "There were trees across the trail and just below the Mt. Hunt divide about 20 feet of the trail had slid off the mountainside and into the abyss. I led Lady across this with my heart in my mouth and never looked down or back. One of us sent a huge boulder careening down into the canyon below." We had hoped to reach Marion Lake before dark, but the slowness of the trail plus our constantly slipping pack precluded that. We camped instead in the canyon that splits lower down to become Open and Granite canyons. I had time to note:

"There are still lots of wild flowers although the main show is about over. Monk's hood, split-leaf daisy, helianthus, lupine, paintbrush, gentian, groundsel, and still some scarlet gilia high up." That night we ate hamburgers and fried potatoes and fell into bed.

I got more rest than sleep and got up fairly early to find "a fine crisp morning. I let Lady loose on hobbles, but all she did was run for the horse camp below. I finally tied her up and built a fire."

After breakfast we packed and found that "it was a steep climb to Marion Lake. On seeing the lake we regretted we had not made it there the day before. It is a cirque lake and lovely green in color, surrounded on three sides by lush green slopes and backgrounded by a tall, rocky cliff.

"Beyond the lake the trail climbed again, and we had to stop frequently to catch our breath. Eventually we topped out into a high, wide alpine meadow. The Grand Teton loomed ahead and was a magnificent sight all along the way." This section of the trail is called the Skyline Shelf. Walking along it toward the distant Grand Teton is like walking along a plain toward a fabled, towered city that gleams in the distance— only no such city exists outside the illustrations in a book of fairy tales. For me those few moments spent hiking toward the Grand Teton group were among the most memorable in a lifetime.

"We reached the head of Death Canyon about noon and camped in a copse of alpine fir above Pass Lake—a pond really less than an acre in size. Just a few steps from camp is the deep cirque where Death Canyon begins. It is a beautifully green, glaciated canyon curving eastward toward Jackson Hole. On one side is the Death Canyon Shelf and on the other some green, gently sloping highlands, under long, square-topped mountains of sedimentary rock.

"Our camp was lazy until I looked up to see Lady far out on the bench to the east. Somehow she'd got untied and had hied herself off. I ran for a pan of oats, but by the time I got out where the mare was Darrel had caught her." The previous day had so done us in that we were happy to camp here after only about a five-mile morning hike. I made notes and puttered while Darrel read a paperback novel, carefully tearing out each page as he finished it and placing the sheet in our little campfire.

"From Pass Lake you get one of the few views of a sunset on the Tetons." In Jackson Hole the Tetons are between you and the setting sun, and really spectacular, colorful sunsets are rare. I noted, "It was a pleasant camp."

The next morning "we were packed and on the trail toward Alaska Basin about 10:20. Most of the trail is level or nearly so, and we made good time." Darrel took some photographs and we traded off leading the mare. It is peculiar how sore and tired an arm can become from simply holding it slightly back toward the horse for hours at a time. "There were deer tracks in the trail—one a tiny fawn's.

"At the head of the Shelf we came down a series of steep

switchbacks, called on the map Sheep Steps. Part of the trail here had given way and there was a detour." The trail in this section actually passes out of Teton Park and into the Targhee National Forest. "It was a narrow trail over loose rock. Lady insists on walking on the edge of these trails, and coming down the steps I felt myself leaning in toward the mountain in a hopeful effort to move her over onto a safer track.

"On the Shelf we saw some curious boulders that were almost spiky, like the mace of a medieval chain and mace." These large stones probably were algal heads that have developed from vegetation that grew in a shallow sea eons ago. "Also on the Shelf are several small creeks that flow into gaping holes in the ledge and disappear. One sinks into a muddy pool the way water swirls down a bathtub drain. It is a little eerie.

"Off the steps we came into Alaska Basin. It is a west-sloping basin, layered with rock outcroppings and interspersed skeins of conifers. It isn't really what I would call a basin, and Darrel said he was disappointed in it." The name I think is drawn from the bitter weather that often exists on this windward side of the range.

"We passed the Basin Lakes area, where there is a fine campsite, and climbed on up the steep ridge and then down again to Sunset Lake. It lies under a brownish-gray wall rising as much as 1,000 feet above it. Around the lake, except for a rocky edge on the east side, is a green, rock-studded meadow. There are a few chucks [marmots] here, and someone has apparently killed a black one and left it on a rock top. There are some pebbles around it and yellow flowers wilting on the carcass.

"It seems to me that the horses brought in here are allowed to roam too much." A horse will generally eat more than he needs, and it is unfair to other travelers to use up all the grass.

"After lunch Darrel proposed going up to Hurricane Pass; I would have skipped it." I had already been there, but my reluctance was mostly sloth, and it would have been very unfair to Darrel not to have gone. "We went up the switchbacks and across the open, rolling, gravelly slopes to the pass. I was glad I went, for the Tetons, Grand, Middle, and South, are as ever magnificent. Above the pass we met some pleasant hikers who recommended that we go out on the slope along the top to the wall. It was a climb of half a mile and the view from there was superb. . . . I could see a small lake below the Teton group and to the west a bit of Jackson Hole and the Wind River Mountains. But being out there on that precipice also gave me the willies, and I didn't venture near the edge as Darrel did. It was very hazy [smoky?] off to the west in Idaho but still the vastness is almost incomprehensible. There are peaks and buttes in almost every direction.

"The weather has been bell-clear and wonderful—even hot —all during the trip. I have seen many wild flowers, including some new ones I can't identify. All the old, familiar ones are here, too, even though many are past their prime.

"There are also ravens, coyotes, I heard one howl early this morning, and chucks. Plus a few golden-mantled ground squirrels and small, drab birds I can't identify. This has probably been the most scenic day of our trip. Tomorrow it is a long haul home. I bathed my feet, and it felt wonderful, then put on clean socks in anticipation."

It was here that I heard the sounds described at the beginning of the chapter. I got up the next morning and looked in the trail dust for tracks, but found none but deer prints. Then I saw what I had heard in the night. Small rocks far up on the cliffside rising above the lake would become dislodged and come bounding down. Their echoing sound was a little like hoofbeats. Horses' hoofbeats. The deer pass by, but they do not leave a sound.

*When the elk are fat and sleek they
belong to the government of the
United States. When they are starving
they belong to the people of Wyoming.*

ATTRIBUTED TO WYOMING GOVERNOR
J. M. CAREY

13 / The Wildlife

The little mule deer buck that cautiously investigated
our camp near Sunset Lake was the antithesis of the old guber-
natorial claim. His delicate, two-point antlers were still in
the velvet, and the buck himself was painfully thin. His
wasted coloring made him appear even frailer than he really
was. This deer, like many of the deer in summer, had faint,
bluish-purple shadows on his cheeks and under his eyes. I
suppose this dark coloration is attributable both to the animals'
light summer coats and to the innumerable insect stings and
bites they receive.

There are many kinds of wildlife in the higher parts of the
Teton Range, but none is especially abundant. On rare occa-
sions you may sight a bachelor band of tremendous buck deer,
but far more often the animals are solitary or in groups of two
and three. Forage at the mountaintops is not abundant, as
the little buck's condition suggested.

Darrel Jenkins and I did not see a lot of wildlife on our
trip. We had especially hoped to see bighorns near the Mount
Hunt Divide but missed them. The wonderful scenery partially made up for that lack, and by the morning of the fourth
day we were both ready to go home.

The trail out to Jackson Hole rises gradually as it crosses a rocky ridge below Buck Mountain. And, as it rises, it offers a fine view of Alaska Basin and the Death Canyon Shelf. We could not see the great Teton group from this trail, however, and that made our hike up to Hurricane Pass the day before an even brighter memory. Much as I can enjoy the national pastime of criticizing our governmental bureaucracy, I must also mention the creativity that has been shown in siting the trails in the area. Whoever was responsible is every bit as fine an artist as the ones who have been painting these mountains on canvas.

I made these notes on the last day of our trip along these routes. "There were many small but firm snowdrifts across the trail. We had no trouble crossing any of them. The trail rises steadily to Buck Mt. Divide where signs are posted to mark the Teton Park–Targhee Forest boundary.

"The sedimentary rock we had seen farther south has long been replaced by granitic rock. There is no timber. As I stood on the pass I could see the Static Peak trail crossing the half-basin below Buck Mountain and then rising and rising to the craggy, forbidding top edge of Static Peak. It is a long, jagged-topped mountain whose serrated spine reminded me of some ancient reptile's back. As the trail bore ever up on this mountain, I wondered if there was an alternate route. The way we were going seemed to be leading us out on a fly-walk above Death Canyon's dark abyss.

"But there was no easy alternative and so up we went, me leading the docile but fast-stepping Lady. As we climbed it was reassuring to see the width of the trail, about four feet, and to think about the many hikers who must have success-fully preceded us. When the last slope gave way to a trail blasted out of the sheer moutainside my reassurance began to fail. There was nothing below but a chasm so deep and sheer that I could not see its bottom. I walked carefully and slowly —so slowly that the mare put her forefoot across my heel and ankle and nearly tripped me. It wasn't a place where I wanted to stumble even slightly or be given an impatient shove in the back by the mare. I had to keep my gaze down on the trail immediately ahead; it was the sort of place I'd have preferred to crawl over. Darrel and I exchanged scarcely a word as we wound up and up to what at last was the trail's apex on Static Peak. It was a breathtaking view, but I didn't tarry there. We started down almost immediately and soon passed a sign that announced the elevation at over 10,700 feet."

This segment of the trail was an unbelievably long series of switchbacks. Part way down we met some backpackers coming up, and their high packs frightened the mare. Fortunately, she's the sort who calms as quickly as she blows up, so we had no trouble. Darrel helped some of the girl hikers to scramble around us in the worst places while I held the mare. Throughout most of our Static Peak journey I had held Lady's lead rope very lightly between thumb and forefinger. If she decided to pitch over the brink I wasn't going to try to hold her back. This fear had some foundation, because as we walked along the load on Lady's back occasionally banged hard against the mountainside, causing her to momentarily bounce and sway. The canvas pack cover was severely abraded in several places where the jutting rocks had cut into it. In a few of the tightest places I even feared the manila lash rope might be cut, dumping our duffle into infinity and precipitating an equine panic. She would not have been the first animal to have plunged over that sobering brink.

None of my fears materialized, however, and we eventually reached the canyon bottom. We stopped there for a quick lunch beside the stream. It would have been more pleasant but for the flies that arrived and tormented us all. The longer we sat there the worse the flies became, until we had to leave to get away from them.

In Wyoming's mountains there are times when it seems that you can encounter every sort of biting insect known to entomological science. Big, green-eyed horseflies hover along the forest trails like menacing helicopter gunships. Being rather sluggish chewers, they don't usually get all the way into a man before he realizes he's being attacked. But, when I have been bitten by one of these flies, the result has been a large, itching sore the size of a half-dollar. There is also a much smaller fly, called *Symphoromyia hirta*, that not only pesters the elk but whose bite can win the undivided attention of any man. These charcoal-colored little monsters bite and leave a sore welt that often festers during several days of alternate itching and aching.

One sunny afternoon hordes of these vicious flies rose out of the lush Gros Ventre vegetation to virtually ruin a lavish picnic my wife had prepared. What made it worse was that the picnic had been prepared for an officer, and his wife, of our publisher's firm. Fortunately, they were good sports, and together we raced through the food, trying to eat it before the flies ate us.

At such times I've heard leathery westerners wonder out loud: "The good Lord made us all and I 'spose he had a purpose—but why did he ever make these goddamn flies?" I've wondered that myself, and also why we need the vast clouds of mosquitoes that are sometimes big enough, a wrangler said, "to breed a tom turkey."

There does seem to be a reason. Watch a bunch of horses, shiny in the summer sunshine. They're never still—they flip their tails, cow-kick their stomachs, and shake their manes. The insects keep them moving. It is the same with game. By tormenting the animals the insects drive them from one range to another, thus helping to preserve the forage. Insects help to drive deer, elk, bighorns, and even antelope from depleted winter ranges to lushly vegetated higher country where the lambs, calves, and fawns are born. They encourage the animals to scatter over the summer range, and in dispersing make it more difficult for predators to find them.

Mosquitoes are probably more abundant now in some parts of Jackson Hole than they ever were in the early days due to the irrigating that goes on all summer. But they have always been bad, and Beaver Dick Leigh's diary contains many references to mosquitoes and how their numbers sometimes forced him to move his camps. The Indians were also affected by the mosquitoes, and they moved around the country to escape them. Today some tourists and summer residents plan their time in Jackson Hole with an eye toward avoiding the mosquitoes. I've been told that one wealthy man who owns an opulent summer home in Jackson Hole refuses to use it except in August.

One hitch in such vacation strategies is that wildlife is far more visible in Jackson Hole earlier in the summer. By August the heavy traffic has helped the insects to push the game away from the roaded areas. Then, about the only place a tourist can see an elk from the main highway is the Exhibition Pasture just north of Jackson. The antelope that have been appearing on the sage-clad Antelope Flat area move back toward the untraveled foothills or go across the Snake River into the Pot Hole area.

Most of the antelope in Jackson Hole do not stay there year round. They winter in the plains areas south and east of Jackson Hole and then cross over the Gros Ventre into the valley in the spring. At one time this migration was a tremendous thing. Historian Ben Driggs visited the valley many years ago and reported that it teemed with antelope. Nowadays relatively few antelope migrate in, and some stop short of Jackson Hole in the high, open swales along the Gros Ventre. Some of the does bear their fawns along the way.

One day in early June I was crossing Antelope Flat and stopped to watch the curious activities of a doe antelope. Later I wrote in my notes, "She had one fawn with her. She got up and lay down again two or three times while I was getting to a spot where I could watch without disturbing her. I thought she might be having her second fawn."

If she was, the fawn I could see was oblivious of the fact, for he frisked around demonstrating the innocent delight that apparently bursts within these small creatures. Later I saw a doe antelope with a pair of fawns in that same area, but there is no assurance that it was the doe I'd been watching.

Doe antelope are very careful to leave their newborn fawns well covered, and the fawns themselves are instinctively great hiders. You can drive for hundreds of miles across Wyoming during the antelope fawning season and see literally thousands of antelope, scarcely any of which will be fawns. This secretiveness makes it all the more worthwhile to stop and watch when you finally do see a fawn or a pair of them with their mother. They add wonderful new meaning to the words "frisking" and "joy." Watching them always delights me.

The sad note about the antelope who migrate into Jackson Hole is that some of them never leave. They stay in the valley too long and then are trapped there by the winter's deep snows. A few will survive on the sparse forage they find on the windswept buttes, but the rest perish. Unfortunately for Wyoming's antelope, the typically vicious Jackson Hole winter was played all over the state in 1971–1972. Some antelope populations disappeared in the blizzards, and their loss may affect the numbers migrating into Jackson Hole in the future.

This ebb and flow of game is natural. But the game's environment is not so natural any more. What with vast strip mines gutting more and more Wyoming ranges, and atomic explosions, in search of natural gas, threatening to poison forage surrounding the lands, the wildlife populations may not be able to recover from less violent "natural" calamities. By the sheer weight of his numbers man is eliminating the chance of other species to survive. William Faulkner wrote that it was not fission that would be our undoing but a vulgar verb that also began with the letter *f*.

Time and again wild populations have demonstrated to us the possibility of our own tragic fate if we would only see it. Overpopulation means inevitable catastrophe. But, because man is a dominant animal, a great many lesser forms of life will go down before we do. It is a chain reaction that, past a certain but imperfectly known point, will rush on to its merciless conclusion no matter what we do to stop it.

A similar phenomenon happens to Jackson Hole moose. These big animals with the seriocomic countenances were virtually absent in early-day Jackson Hole. This may have been due to the animals' inability to withstand unlimited Indian hunting along with a climatic, vegetational, or some other factor, such as disease, that helped limit the moose population. When the white population ended free Indian hunting and almost simultaneously gave moose legal protection, the animals began to increase. In the 1920s the numbers were sufficient to allow hunters to shoot a few bulls. They kept increasing until today about four hundred moose of either sex are shot by hunters every fall in Jackson Hole.

Most of these animals die outside Grand Teton National Park where they are not protected. Inside the park moose have been so well protected that biologists recently conceded that the park's moose habitat is full. There literally was no place to put another moose. The decimating effect this large and hungry herd has on its winter browse supplies results in a periodic die-off during more severe winters. These die-offs by starvation typically take far more moose than succeeding conditions might require. But a big die-off assures that the willows on which the moose heavily depend will get sufficient respite to revive and replenish themselves. Lately, some park biologists have come to regard this periodic starvation of moose as a normal form of herd regulation. Their point is well taken, but I have seen the wraithlike moose calves struggling in the winter snows and can't help thinking that a bullet would be a more humane solution to their overpopulation problem.

Even if this "natural" solution works with moose there is no assurance that it will work with other game. This is because, while the willows that are so important to moose will come back, other species of plants on which other kinds of game depend often disappear under heavy foraging. There is good evidence that there was more grass in Jackson Hole in early days than there is now. Overgrazing encouraged shrubby plants, and these, in turn, encouraged deer, which originally hadn't been too numerous in the area.

I have wondered if the increase in moose has been helped, too, by overgrazing, which tends to encourage the coarser kinds of plants on which moose thrive. The virtual elimination from the area of such predators as wolves and grizzly bears also aided the moose buildup.

Most descriptions of the Wyoming or Shiras moose are quick to note that this animal is the smallest member of the moose family. Size, however, is a relative thing. I remember one early morning on the upper Yellowstone when I was wrangling horses. I found the shadowy band in the meadow and started them toward camp. It was just light enough to see that I had two herd-quitters in the bunch. Try as I would, this pair could not be made to stay with the other horses. When they trotted into a clump of willows I dashed after them, and only then did I get near enough to see that I'd been trying to herd a cow moose and her calf into camp. Considering that they were wild animals, I had had more success than one might expect.

Often the big animals are not particularly afraid of humans, and many an old-timer in Jackson Hole can tell how a moose tried sleeping on his porch one winter. When outhouses were common, people en route to them sometimes found moose blocking the way. These moose have chased innumerable fishermen up into trees, and one especially cantankerous bull is supposed to have charged, head on, into a Yellowstone tourist bus.

On the whole, however, I think the belligerence of the moose has been exaggerated. It is always dangerous to interfere with a cow and her calf, and the bulls are particularly sullen during the rut in October, but usually they will either just stand and watch you or go prancing off. Unless they are hurt or aroused, moose are quite easy to kill. Most of those I have seen shot accepted their fate with a pathetic, dumb curiosity.

Like most other hunters, however, I had to experience this for myself. I applied every year for one of the limited moose-hunting licenses and finally succeeded in drawing one. Since it might be my only chance to hunt moose, I decided to try for a bull that was large enough to be a decent trophy and small enough to furnish some good meat. Eventually I found three bulls all lined up and standing for my inspection and selection. I shot what I thought was the best one, and my neighbor,

Delos Sanderson, helped me to dress and quarter the carcass. No more care is ever lavished upon a prize-winning Kansas City beef.

With the meat laid carefully on elevated poles to cool we began removing the antlers. I used an ordinary carpenter's crosscut saw to cut the antlers out of the skull. When we lifted out the antlers the moose's brain was exposed. Never a pleasant sight, this bull's brain made me ashamed. The intelligence center of this great animal was scarcely larger than an ordinary deer's brain. No wonder they are such phlegmatic, deliberate-seeming creatures. What often appears to be boldness on the moose's part is more likely stupidity. Now that I have killed my one moose I can readily understand why another man might wish to shoot his first one. But the person who wants to shoot a second moose is beyond understanding.

The venison isn't that good, either. In fact, the meat that Delos and I handled so carefully was the worst game meat I have ever brought home. It had a queer, marshy-metallic flavor that grew progressively less palatable. The moose meat my wife and I put down in brine and "corned" was delicious, however. And I finally found, after trying all sorts of wine and spice flavorings, that soaking the moose steaks in milk rendered them edible, even good.

The elk, on the other hand, is the real star of Jackson Hole's big game, and their flesh is ordinarily excellent. They were a staple item of food for the early settlers as well as the Indians. When a limit was finally put on, it restricted the hunter to two elk a season. The old-timers then customarily shot a cow for its meat and a large bull that provided both meat and salable tusks and antlers.

Even to this day the Jackson Hole elk can be as controversial as they are precious in the valley. In 1925 Frank Lovejoy wrote a letter that helped to explain the root of some of these elk tribulations. Published in a Wyoming paper, the letter stated, in part, "In the early days when there was no hay available . . . I have walked for a mile on dead elk lying from one to four deep. . . . They would be very poor and would . . . roll to the foot of the hill and never get up. I know a rancher who, one spring, pulled 450 dead elk off his hay meadow.

"One rancher put lighted lanterns around his haystacks thinking it would keep the elk away. A big bull carried one of the lanterns on his horn the rest of the winter. One hard winter . . . a bull hooked the telephone line, pulled it off the poles for more than a quarter of a mile and carried it out across the big swamp above Jackson. . . . I have seen at night upwards of 500 elk in the streets of Jackson."

Farther on in his letter Lovejoy wrote, "The elk have not drifted down this year as they usually do on account of the big landslide we had last June up on the Gros Ventre River, which cut off their trail coming to the winter range around Jackson. . . . The elk used to cross here onto Sheep Mountain, then over to Flat Creek to the government elk refuge. . . . Last evening over 3,000 head came out of the hills at Antelope Point about 10 miles north of Kelly."

In very severe winters the elk historically moved completely out of Jackson Hole to the sage plains south and west. Once settlement and shooting blocked off the traditional migration routes to the sage plains, the elk were confined to Jackson Hole. Lovejoy wrote, " . . . Every seven or eight years we have a winter that will cut them back. If we get a snowfall of 18 or 20 inches the latter part of November or December, followed by a warm rain for three or four days, then a drop of 30 to 40 below zero, the elk range will freeze up so the elk can get no feed."

The weather conditions Lovejoy described seem to be occurring more often in recent years. In both the winters of 1970–1971 and 1971–1972 almost the exact conditions he mentions occurred. But this time the elk were on winter-feeding lots throughout the area, and most of them survived. Elk increasingly winter on these lots, and the Wyoming Game and Fish Commission has reported some difficulty in buying enough good-quality hay to feed them all.

On the National Elk Refuge, which has the greatest concentrations of elk but only about a third of all the animals in the area, more than forty tons of hay are fed every day of the winter. While emergency feeding is only begun after the elk can no longer forage naturally on the refuge, it is not a perfect solution to the elk's problems.

Many years ago the annual loss of elk on the feed grounds amounted to as much as ten percent of the herd. This and other elk problems were what brought Olaus Murie and his wife, Mardy, to Jackson Hole in the late 1920s. Murie was a government biologist, and his studies of the elk were to help make him world famous. The young biologist began his work by taking his devoted wife and their small children with him into the wilderness while he studied the elk. More work was done on the refuge, and Murie eventually was able to make contributions of knowledge that led to better management of the elk herd. Don Redfearn, presently the elk refuge superintendent, told me that winter losses are now around one percent.

In 1951 Olaus Murie published his book, *The Elk of North America*. A prize-winning volume, it continues to be the standard work on elk. Later Olaus Murie left government service to become president of the Wilderness Society. It was a job that he could do and still live in the picturesque log home he and Mardy shared near Moose. When Murie died in 1963 Mardy continued to make their home a haven for conservationists. She is presently a consultant to the Wilderness Society. Her book, *Two in the Far North* and another she wrote with Olaus called *Wapiti Wilderness*, have become perennial favorites.

One of the things that has brought the Muries public acclaim is their warmth. Murie was not an unfeeling biologist, and he wrote in *The Elk of North America*, ". . . sport shooting . . . that kind of hunting, by many considered the highest type is pursued today. The trophy hunter is generally one who organizes a packtrain, with guide and helpers. . . . Generally a comparatively long period is spent in the mountains, and the sportsman is not in a hurry. He is in search of the finest head . . . and the killing done for this reason is a negligible factor . . . in elk conservation."

Many hunters, particularly the nonresidents, who are legally restricted to shooting bulls, profess to be trophy hunters. But very few of them will pass up a yearling spike if it is the only alternative to going home without shooting something. In a few areas heavy hunting pressure has reduced bull elk and resulted in a ban on spike shooting. The recent and overall policy, however, has been to allow more killing of elk, and the harvest in Jackson Hole has been rising. In both 1970 and 1971 more than six thousand elk were taken in the seventeen hunting areas that make up the Jackson Hole unit. These are record kill figures, and constitute a third and more of the annual elk kill in Wyoming.

Some people think too many elk are being killed, while others would increase the kill even more. Certain officials have proposed that about one thousand additional nonresident hunters be allowed to shoot cow elk. Throughout the nation, and even in Jackson Hole, there are a growing and vocal number of people who would prefer to do away with hunting. I think this latter group is too often ruled by emotion. But they do have a point, and the very best reasons for banning hunting are hunters themselves. Too many of them, resident and nonresident alike, are boorish, ignorant slobs.

In West Germany, where there is amazingly good hunting, a person must have one hundred hours of hunting-related classroom training before he may even sit for his hunting license examination. This examination is difficult, and many applicants fail it in spite of their hours of study. A prospective hunter must also win the approval of the local equivalent of a game manager before he may hunt in the latter's district. There are no such requirements in Wyoming, where, as in most states, anything warm and with a few dollars in its hand can buy a license to kill. Right now the writers of articles justifying hunting in sporting magazines are being terribly self-righteous vis-à-vis the attacks being made upon hunting. They would be far wiser to recognize that a problem does exist among their constituents and start agitating to eliminate it.

Many tourists passing through Jackson exclaim over the distinctive archways at the corners of the town square. They are made of elk antlers, and some people believe that the animals were killed to provide material for these structures. Of course they were not. Bull elk shed their antlers in late winter or early spring, and the arches as well as dozens of other Jackson Hole items are made from them. I think most of this stuff, including the arches are Wyoming *kitsch*, but no animal was sacrificed to provide the raw material for it.

The annual pickup of shed elk antlers grew out of a problem on the refuge. The bulls' antlers often fell off in the hay fields, where mowing crews inadvertently ran into them the following summer. Since, by current law, the elk belong to the people of Wyoming, the state game and fish people were asked to remove the antlers. As soon as they began, the collected antlers became prize trophies as well as the basis for handicrafts. Eventually the rights to collect the antlers were given to local Boy Scouts.

Every spring the boys are taken out to the refuge, where they scour the wintering areas for shed antlers. To spur the searchers on antlers are picked up beforehand, marked, and then re-hidden. Boys finding these antlers redeem them for prizes. Later the collected antlers are auctioned off to the benefit of the scouting program. The bidding is usually spirited and also usually dominated by Asians, since in the Orient it is believed that the powder obtained by grinding the antlers is an aphrodisiac. Many of the westerners who scoff at this belief are the same ones who think that a few mountain oysters bolster their manhood.

Another sort of misapprehension exists among some summer visitors. These people are disappointed to find that the vast elk refuge is virtually empty of elk when they drive out hoping to see some. For this reason a few representative elk are kept in the fenced pastures beside the highway just north of Jackson. Refuge personnel are very aware of the menagerie aspect of this display. The superintendent told me that he simply hasn't funds to spend on aesthetically improving this display —although even if he had the money I doubt that much could be done to improve the looks of the roadside pastures. Shade-giving structures have been provided in the exhibition pasture, but it still pains me to see these animals confined to a treeless pen during the hottest summer months. It would be to the benefit of everyone, including the elk, to do away with this display, whose only apparent purpose it to mollify the questioning taxpayer. Besides, elk can nearly always be seen, at daylight and again at dusk, from the roads between Signal Mountain and Moose.

So great is the attraction of Jackson Hole's elk that the area's other wildlife is sometimes overlooked. Actually Jackson Hole is one of the very few places in North America where bighorn sheep may be seen from certain highways and back roads. These highly prized animals were once abundant. Then overgrazing, livestock-borne diseases, and overshooting decimated them. They have not responded to modern management techniques, and their populations have either remained static or been in a slight decline.

In Slim Lawrence's collection there is a photo of Cissy Patterson in western togs. In the picture the flamboyant young woman is romantically framed under her big sombrero and with a dead bighorn ram on either side. She is supposed to have bagged the pair. Years ago the erratic heiress owned a retreat far up Flat Creek in the Gros Ventre Range. When her life became too hectic Miss Patterson, who had married a count, used to come out and hole up for a while at her place in the mountains. The property is still called the Countess's Place and the surrounding area is still pretty good for sheep.

Some of the problems of the bighorn may be due to the mule deer, which have increased in Jackson Hole and usurped some of the sheep's winter range. In the winter and early spring scores if not hundreds of deer can be seen on the hillsides around Jackson Hole. Just south of Jackson a new highway cut has apparently exposed a mineral the deer enjoy, for I have frequently seen them standing there both at night and in broad daylight a few feet off the busy highway. And while I was encamped at various places throughout Jackson Hole, researching this book, I often awoke in the early morning or looked out at dusk to see deer outside my door.

In my notes I once wrote, "A doe, yearling I think, came

just before 8 P.M. She came from the direction of the road, and while coming hesitantly, with flicking ears and switches of her tail, she progressed rapidly to within 20 feet. She raised her head and then quickly lowered it, all the while with her thin, graceful neck extended to the fullest. She did not like my camp."

Finally, after some deliberation, she decided to pass by the camp, and then "she paused and gave the side of her muzzle a long but careful scratch with the toe of her right hind foot.

"She has a slight split in the top of her right ear, perhaps I will see her again." [I did.] "She is wearing her brown coat but her big ears, grayish brown at a distance have a distinct purplish cast close up."

Hiking earlier the same day I "saw a golden-crowned kinglet on the edge of Emma Matilda Lake." The forests of Jackson Hole are not ordinarily full of large numbers of many species of birds. But during the annual migrations you sometimes can see many birds. As I noted, "A few days ago in the places where I was traveling I saw all kinds of western tanagers; nowadays, I see none." On another day I was hiking with a park naturalist who happened to mention that blue grouse were becoming rare in the park and might even be absent. In no time we came around a bend in the trail and found a blue grouse pacing importantly through the trailside vegetation.

June, while it has a deservedly bad reputation for bringing chilly rains, is a good month to see a wide sampling of the area's wildlife. Trumpeter swans sail majestically on several of the valley's ponds, where they often nest. The rare birds are also seen on Flat Creek just outside the Jackson City limits. In the forests little, pink-sided juncos flit along the trails establishing their reputations as the most numerous of the smaller birds. In the meadows goldfinches flit brightly through stands of willows sometimes to the croaking of sandhill cranes. In wooded areas chickadees hang upside down from conifer branches and look for food. Around wooded springs, especially where aspen trees grow, there is a good chance of seeing ruffed grouse. At certain times the females will sing a little, clucking warning song to their young that is captivating. Earlier, of course, the males can be heard drumming in the forests.

One June day in the Mount Leidy highlands my wife and I came upon a lonely pond that had three pairs of scaup swimming on its surface. For us, at least, it was a surprise to see ducks that aren't particularly common in the area sailing around on an even less common pond at eight thousand feet elevation.

Mallards are probably the most common ducks in the region. They can be seen at the lowest elevations in the valley as well as thousands of feet up in the surrounding mountains. Goldeneyes are another common species, though they aren't as widespread as the mallards. The peculiar whistling sound of the goldeneyes in flight makes them easy to identify.

Mergansers are common on the Snake River. They are fish eaters, and seldom hunted, but they still buzz speedily away from intruders, often maintaining neat ranks without ever taking flight. Canada geese are among spring's first migrants, and are common along Snake River.

Until very recently it was also possible to see numbers of bald eagles along the Snake. A few nested there while others came and went, playing their roles as scavengers on the deer that winter along the river. The recent campaign allegedly sponsored by a few greedy sheepmen against all eagles has apparently helped DDT eliminate many of these birds. As if to explain the attitude of many stockmen toward predators, I heard one say, "I don't think eagles really do that much damage—but if they *was* doin' the man damage, why then he had to git rid of 'em."

The Cowboy State often reflects a cowboy point of view. One winter a couple of young men took advantage of a rise in the price of coyote pelts and had some "fun" running the animals down on their snowmobiles. According to witnesses they harried the fleeing coyotes to the point of collapse and then killed them by running the snowmobiles back and forth over their bodies. Some of this was done in Grand Teton National Park, and reports at the time said such incidents had been fairly common.

Despite all sorts of warnings and appeals, the growing army of snowmobilers persists in harassing big game. One stunt of the hot-rodding snowmobile driver is to chase a deer through deep snow until it collapses and bogs down. The snow slob then leaps from his machine onto the deer and bulldogs it. Such senseless abuse often results in deep shock that can kill a wild animal. And while it is illegal, snowmobiles are frequently used by unscrupulous hunters to corner game so the animals may be shot.

Snowmobilers occasionally join touring clubs whose bylaws and pronouncements about not molesting game are widely published. What few of the members seem to realize is that their howling, motorized safaris into the back country cause as much stress and discomfort to game as the intentional kind. Much of western Wyoming is perfect snowmobiling country, and people come here from all over to go touring. Guided tours based at motels and lodges cover hundreds of miles of back country. And in late winter, when this sort of touring is best, the game animals are at their physical worst. The pregnant females cannot stand any unnecessary pushing around. Some officials of conservation agencies say the snowmobiler's chivying of elk is so bad in certain places that the animals have been driven completely off their traditional wintering areas.

Residents of remote areas in Jackson Hole really need their snow machines. I don't begrudge them these. But the rest of these machines and the engine-revving louts who run them should be barred from all public lands—at least until thorough studies of the effects of their machines have been made.

This disregard for wildlife's welfare is nothing new. Shabby zoos, roadway menageries, and similar sleazy displays of animals have become a kind of seasonal custom around Jackson. In earlier times a few private citizens of the valley even kept elk. In a recent newspaper story about cutter racing there is an old photograph of a frightened-looking little spike wearing a harness and hooked to a racing cutter. Two horsemen flank him, each with a rope around the elk's neck. Attempts to race an elk failed, but did succeed in bringing the animal's plight to the attention of authorities.

Most residents of Jackson Hole recognize the great value of the area's elk. "Their" elk may not be appreciated so much for an aesthetic resource as a money-making one, but the possessive interest is there, nevertheless. Each nonresident hunter for an outfitted elk hunt can't do it for less than a thousand dollars.

It is interesting to visit the commercial airport north of Jackson and see the hunters arriving in the fall. The outfitters and guides who come down to meet the sports are typical masters of rustic suavity. The dudes eat it up. Some of them try to out-"manly" their manly outfitters. They do it either by making a pompous show of their affluence or by condescending to their hosts while explaining, as if to a child, some piece of their equipment or facet of their trip west. The guide, who is likely computing to himself the possibility and size of his guest's tip, smiles and bobs his head in feigned admiration. The whole ritual of airport manliness is an amusing exposition of the Hemingwagian theories on cojones. It is ridiculous, but I guess necessary to a host of budding Francis Macombers.

Hunting also provided a great deal of the basis for disagreement over enlarging Grand Teton Park. Many of the elk killed at that time were shot in areas that would be taken in by the proposed park. The National Park Service is historically opposed to hunting within its domain, and brochures handed out at Grand Teton state, "Hunting within the Park is not permitted." This is only a matter of semantics, for every year about twenty-five hundred hunters are deputized as temporary park rangers and each is assigned the task of removing one excess elk from the herd as it moves into and through the park. The deputy successful in killing an elk is permitted to keep it, thus completing the shabby fiction by which he hunted in the park.

The area of hunting is restricted, and because the elk being sought are mostly migrants coming down to winter range, finding them in these areas isn't always possible. Sometimes, though, the hunting is too easy, and the elk are slaughtered. This can happen anywhere, but is often worst in some of the open meadows immediately adjacent to the elk refuge. The animals will occasionally try to walk through a hail of bullets to reach the sanctuary. Overall, however, public hunting in Teton Park is a better way to reduce excess elk than by the ranger reduction program that caused such a furor in Yellowstone Park.

When former Secretary of the Interior Walter J. Hickel visited Grand Teton Park during the summer of 1970, he was asked about allowing hunting in Yellowstone. He had once declared himself open to at least considering such an idea—but in Jackson Hole he quickly rejected it. It has become a political maxim not to allow hunting in national parks. Nevertheless, the ban on hunting is a very *unnatural* thing. I do not see any basic difference in killing a beautiful trout and killing a mammal inside a park. But, considering the generally shabby state of American hunting ethics, the ban is justified—although it is hardly fair to the elk who spends his summer learning to let camera-bearing tourists come ever closer to get his picture, and who then unwarily steps across a park boundary line and is blasted.

While the management of Wyoming's game is a state responsibility, it is often shared with federal agencies. Right now state authorities are scared silly that Congress will make into law the recommendations made by the odious Public Land Law Review Commission. Most conservationists have condemned this commission's report for what it is—a bald attempt by private interests to grab publicly owned land and resources. One of the report's lesser but nevertheless dangerous proposals is to do away with various state controls over nonresident hunting. While democratic in tone, such a proposal, if adopted, would doom Wyoming wildlife in a year or two. Neighboring states are even now taking steps to repair the damage done to their wildlife by selling too much of it to all red-hatted comers.

Wyoming, while guilty of coveting the nonresident's license

dollar, has not been as guilty as many others. The state has a better game and fish setup than a perusal of its woefully deficient and antiquated game code indicates. Considering the obsequious deference with which the game commission treats the livestock industry, its employees do a good job of maintaining the state's wildlife. The department is well financed, mainly by the sale of nonresident hunting and fishing licenses. Its monthly magazine, *Wyoming Wildlife,* is among the country's best conservation journals. Unfortunately only about ten thousand copies go to residents, while thirty-nine thousand are mailed out of state. This magazine promotes recreational money-spending visits to Wyoming, but it also carries a sound conservation message in a customarily beautiful package.

One of the real weaknesses of the politically appointed Wyoming Game and Fish Commission is that it is overwhelmingly composed of ranchers. Some of these commissioners are competent, but others are not; rather, they are on the commission to represent interests often inimical to wildlife. Apparently the commission employees are able to lead their policy-making commission along paths of righteousness. Nevertheless, the scandalous slaughter of eagles in Wyoming seemed to completely have escaped the commission's notice.

The growing demands on the western environment are much too dangerous to permit inept, selfish men to determine the fate of wildlife. The problems today make the old ones with tuskers and beaver poachers seem like kid stuff.

Take, for example, the dam on the Teton River. The Teton is a lovely, medium-sized stream that heads into the western Wyoming portion of the Teton range. Running west through a canyon in Idaho's Teton Basin, the stream is somewhat inaccessible but very good fishing for the increasingly rare cutthroat trout. In winter the canyon is a haven for deer. Over a thousand of them wintered there during the terrible storms of 1971–1972. When a dam was proposed on the river, it was condemned by conservationists and tax watchers alike as a boondoggle, economically and ecologically unsound.

Rogers Morton, Secretary of the Interior, said the dam would not be built. Then President Nixon made a flying, one-day trip to the area and somewhere got together with old party wheelhorse and ex-sheepman, Idaho Senator Len Jordan. Jordan had a favor coming from Nixon, and he got it in the form of the Teton Dam.

Not long ago I saw a TV newscast about the work that was beginning on the dam site. The newsman asked the construction company spokesman what environmental safeguards they were observing. So help me, the hardhat said he was making his crews throw their lunch wrappers in garbage cans and refusing equipment maintenance men the right to spill the drain oil on the ground. Deer and trout don't stand a chance in the face of such callous stupidity.

I admit to a chronic optimism when it comes to the preservation and restoration of Wyoming's wildlife. But, more and more, I'm forced to admit by the facts that my feelings of optimism are mostly derived from man's instinctive belief that "Tomorrow will be better." Tomorrow has not been better for most Americans, and it certainly has not been better for wildlife. Virtually no one, probably not even repellent Congressman Wayne Aspinall, who manipulated the Public Land Law Review Commission, consciously wishes to destroy our wildlife. But the great majority of us consciously and sincerely want to be rich. Our materialistic preoccupation with resource exploitation, combined with the gutlessness of most politicians on most environmental issues, bodes no good for other species. One day, an old-time game warden, long retired, stumped into the barber shop where I sat waiting. He was old and mostly forgotten, and understandably sour about it. "You know," he said to the group, "our wildlife hasn't got one good friend any more." Maybe the old man exaggerated, and maybe he was just another barbershop biologist, but I think he was at least partly right. Like it or not, we have a habit of remembering the truth when we hear it.

*. . . you will never find another place
that will compare to Wyoming's Snake
River Country.*

WYOMING FISHERIES BIOLOGIST,
quoted in *Wyoming Wildlife*

14 / *Whose Bounteous Waters*

Late in the summer of 1971 my neighbor, Mike Hanson,
and I drove to the end of the Pacific Creek road on the south
boundary of the Teton Wilderness. There we packed a camp
outfit on Lady, the mare, and started up the trail. By the time
we reached the big, mile-long flat that parallels the creek, the
pack had turned a little and it was time for lunch. We tied
Lady to a tree and removed her burden down to and including
the packsaddle. It was one of those late summer days when it is
hot when the sun is out but almost chilly the minute the sun
slips behind a cloud.

Several miles up the valley a big, gray cloud of smoke was
billowing up hundreds of feet into the sky. As we ate we
watched the smoke; planes droned in from beyond the distant
ridges and flew bravely into the pall. Since Mike is a forest
ranger he was able to give a blow-by-blow account of the fight
we were watching. Because the blaze was in a wilderness area it
had to be fought without tanker trucks and bulldozers. Planes
could be used to bomb the fire with retardants, and the sweat-
ing crew on the ground could use power saws to make their
firebreaks, but mostly it was shovels, Pulaskis, and pack strings
that fought the fire.

My wife had made big, meaty sandwiches for us, and to wash

them down we periodically scrambled over the creek's steep bank to fill a cup with water. "You better take it easy on the water," Mike said. "If any of those fire retardant chemicals have gotten into the water they could give you the trots." The water in the back country of Jackson Hole is so uniformly and delightfully pure that I had not given a thought to its safety.

Until recently some of the boatmen who operate float trips on the Snake River impressed their guests with the stream's purity by drinking directly from it. Maybe it is not such a good idea today, but it is still safe to drink from the Snake's headwaters. It is little wonder that such good water is the basis for what has been one of the finest trout fisheries in North America.

Mike and I finished our day by setting up camp at Gravel Lake, a good-sized lake almost completely surrounded by thick timber. By judicious tightrope walking on a semisubmerged log, and even more care with his backcasts, Mike managed to catch two cutthroat trout practically at our doorstep. Despite my protestations about not caring much for trout, Mike insisted that I share his catch at breakfast. The largest fish was no more than thirteen inches long. But, like the other, it was firm and full-bodied, with red-orange flesh. Perhaps it was the seasoning of hunger, but the trout I ate was delicately delicious. I had forgotten a trout could be so good, and I attributed a lot of its flavor to the limpid lake water.

Mike and I were several more days in the wilderness. On our second day we were beset by a heavy rain that lasted all day. It was a day I spent in the tent desultorily reading the *Journals of André Gide* while delving periodically into a sack of miniature chocolate bars that Mike had bought in Jackson. While I was thus engaged Mike put on his long slicker and hiked around the lake, fly fishing. But the storm had queered the fishing and he caught no more trout. If he had, perhaps the one I'd already eaten would not have been half so well remembered and appreciated.

It used to be that my youthful memories of the outdoors were based largely on how much game I had killed or on the number and size of trout caught. This isn't to say that I now regret the countless hours I have spent pumping a fly rod; actually, that time has been priceless. But now there are other times in my memory when I have enjoyed and been alternately thrilled and charmed by the waters of Jackson Hole without ever having fished them.

The Snake is too big and unrelenting, even in its slow meanders, to be called charming, although there are many charming spots beside it. For a good part of the spring and summer the river is under very apparent manipulation by the U.S. Bureau of Reclamation engineers at Jackson Lake Dam. The current is fine for irrigating in Idaho, but much too fast for fishing in Wyoming. It is even too swift for casual wading, and more than one unwary person has had his feet, or even his horse, swept from under him by the powerful currents. Fishing in the Snake is really only practical early in the spring and again in the early fall after the Idaho crops have received their last watering and the dam engineers reduce the flow from Jackson Lake.

Until recently the condition of the Snake in summer caused almost everyone to leave it alone. Other than a few anglers sitting in folding chairs below the Jackson Lake Dam spillway, the river was almost empty. Then someone got the idea of floating dudes down the river in big war-surplus life rafts. The first of the big rafts were used by the Grand Teton Lodge Company. Putting in below the Jackson Lake Dam, the rafts, with twenty or so passengers aboard, cruised the meandering byways of the Snake River above Moose.

Every season these float trips became more popular. New trip operators proliferated, and some even set up ticket booths on the streets of Jackson. Today you can arrange for any sort of trip from a three-dollar cattle boat voyage lasting an hour or so to an all-day outing with an ecologist who feeds you fine cheese and choice wine for lunch. In just the last half of the 1960s traffic on the Jackson Hole segment of the river zoomed from fourteen thousand to over fifty thousand people, with the end of the increase not in sight. The Jackson Lake–Moose segment, along with stretches in lower South Park and the upper portion of the Grand Canyon of the Snake, are most popular. But it is generally possible to find a float trip going down any part of the Snake, from the dam to Alpine at the mouth of the canyon.

The traffic has become a bit too heavy on the more popular sections of stream, forcing the Park Service to restrict landings and take whatever other measures it could to protect the river and its shoreline wildlife.

Outside the park, and inside it to a lesser extent, the customer is pretty much at the mercy of his float trip outfitter. The Snake is legally a navigable river, and what a man decides to use floating down it is pretty much up to him. There are a few mighty old-looking rafts still in use on the river, and, while there have been remarkably few accidents, the last bad one involved an old surplus raft. The better operators have their inflatable boats made to order, and they are a far cry from the war surplus stuff. Custom-made rafts of eight- to twelve-passenger capacity cost about twenty-five hundred dollars, exclusive of fittings and accouterments.

The accouterments in a Barker-Ewing raft, for instance, include a spotless, pale-green nylon carpet in the bottom of each boat. Dick Barker and Frank Ewing are two remarkable young men who operate one of the oldest and most successful of the Snake River float trips. Their boats are nineteen feet long by eight wide, and each one has ten separate air chambers. The boatsmen stand in the center of the boat and handle the oars while their passengers, up to twelve, sit in the ends of the boat.

Barker and Ewing float the ten miles of river between Dead Man's Bar and Moose. The trip lasts about three hours, and I think it is a bargain.

This trip begins at Moose and, as I noted, "They arrived, four Land Rovers all pulling big, olive-green flat-bed trailers loaded with canvas-covered rafts. The drivers wheeled into the parking area like charioteers and drew their Land Rovers up in a neat formation abreast. It was a smart arrival.

"Mr. Ewing, whom we recognized from his photo in the company's brochure, met us and began checking names, shaking hands, and assigning us seats in the Land Rover."

Ewing is a bronzed, lithe young man in his thirties with sun
streaks in his blond hair. Raised in Kentucky and educated at
Yale, he speaks beautifully, with a distinctive accent. Since he
makes the same trip several times a day, all summer long, I
wondered how he could maintain his jolly graciousness. But
Frank Ewing seems to do it.

We took our seats in the Land Rover with Ewing's other
passengers and were soon on our way. My notes continue: "The
Land Rover is not a quiet machine, and I noted that ours had
47,000 miles on its odometer. Still, the vehicle was very clean
and in good repair. Turning off the highway just north of
the Snake River Overlook, we drove down a steep dirt road to
the river's edge. With much dispatch and precision the boats
were uncovered and given a few pumps of air with a giant hand
pump. Then the trailers were backed down to the river's edge
and the boats quickly unloaded.

"All the equipment was good stuff in good condition. Our
boat was carpeted with a pale-green material that was spotless.
Ewing, estimating our weights, assigned us all places in the
boat. There were 12 passengers; 2 families with 2 kids each
and 2 mid-teenagers plus my wife and me. When everyone was
comfortably seated around the big air chamber that was the
boat's gunwale, Ewing stepped into his rowing cockpit in the
craft's center. There are inflated, tubular transverse sections
that form the cockpit and provide the foundation for the
wooden rowing frame that is fitted into the boat. Into this
frame, at the center of the boat are fitted the oarlocks in which
the twelve-foot oars are placed.

"Ewing is well spoken, very courteous, and almost painfully
solicitous of our comfort. He was wearing a blue shirt with a
small, brownish-red figure, worn-looking corduroy jeans, and
sneakers. He looks a little like John Updike, the novelist.

"He handled the big raft with deceptive ease. We float side-
ways and the boatman stands, or kneels, facing downstream. He
holds his oars up and at right angles to the raft when he is not
rowing. Rowing is done mostly to guide the boat. The current
is swift and the boat moves rapidly on it."

We had chosen one of the early evening trips in hopes of

seeing as much wildlife as possible. "Ewing noted that the swallows darting above us were of the bank and rough-winged varieties. Then he pointed out some alpine fir and Douglas fir on the steep eastern bank and told how the lingering snow, moisture, and cold supported these trees in this unusual, for them, location.

"Mostly the ride was smooth, we bounced lightly over a few riffles, and some of the passengers were excited by them.

"There was a swarthy minister, his nice wife and two daughters in our end of the raft. The preacher had a fancy camera with telephoto lens, and from this and their nice clothing, plus the details we heard of their vacation, I had to conclude that preaching is a pretty good racket nowadays.

"We didn't see much wildlife until we reached the bald eagles' nest. The area around it is well signed by the Park Service to keep people away. There are 3 young birds in this nest, which Ewing says are 14 weeks old. (This was on July 27.) They have been flying for 3 weeks. He also said that the nesting pair has been returning for many years, usually producing 2 young. These birds have a territory that extends 12 to 15 miles along the river.

"Ewing said that DDT was damaging osprey and that they had declined here in the past 12 years with only one pair in 5 or 6 now nesting successfully.

"Ewing also said that a white-tail deer had wintered on Miller's Butte last winter. As we floated down I found Ewing a biological nonpareil. The information flowed easily from him—biology, geology, ecology, some history, and it seemed just about anything else you might want to know.

"Someone pointed out a spruce leaning out over the river, and Ewing explained how geotropism caused many of these trees to grow up straight again. And indeed we saw several whose tops were now growing straight while their lower trunks still leaned out over the river.

"We saw a beaver, moose, and elk. We also had a glimpse of an otter along the river bank. The otter had warned us of his presence with a series of loud chirps.

"At one point we smelled a new, unusual odor that had a slight heaviness about it. Ewing said it came from a moose, and, sure enough, we soon saw a bull moose on the bank. I did not think the odor unpleasant."

The evening grew a bit chilly, and part way through our float "we stopped and Ewing passed out cups of hot cider and homemade muffins. The cider, slightly spiced, was especially good. I was constantly struck by the man's efficiency, the preparations made in the raft, blankets, ponchos, bug dope, and binoculars stowed in two big Coleman coolers. Lord knows what else he might have furnished had anyone but asked.

"At several points the river runs in a number of channels, and Ewing steered us through these with a minimum of pulls on his long oars. About three hauls were all he needed to set us around a new bend. Sometimes he braced his feet against one of the transverse sections and really leaned into a stroke, but all the while he was talking and laughing and making the whole thing look easy. Once he very easily guided the raft between two dangerous-looking snags when it appeared to me that he hardly had room to pass. We ground slightly on one bar, but never touched the river bank.

"It wasn't a physically thrilling ride, and much of the time I was more interested in what Ewing was saying than in the willows, cottonwoods, and spruces gliding by. It was almost dark when we reached our landing just above the Moose Bridge. This, too, had been effortless, and, after securing the boat, Ewing walked us up the hill a way and was almost diffident about collecting his fee. He refused to be tipped. The minister, whether by design or carelessness, tried to short Ewing five dollars when he settled up. It was a trifle embarrassing."

My wife and members of her family have since floated the Snake with Dick Barker, and they all found their "trip" highly enjoyable. For those who want a longer trip and wilder water, Denny Becker and a partner have been operating float trips in the Grand Canyon of the Snake.

Frank Ewing is one of two or three outdoorsmen I have met

in the course of writing this book about Jackson Hole who have thoroughly impressed me. I don't consider myself easily impressed.

Crowded as the river has become, it is a generally observed regulation that no boat push off until the one ahead is around the first bend. This practice enhances the wilderness character of the trip and most passengers truly think they are all alone on the river. But one day in the late summer, when I walked to a secluded spot and then climbed down to fish from the river's western bank, I found how crowded the stream really is. No sooner would I get a cast worked out and my fly working when a rubber boat or kayak or even an inner tube would come bobbing along. "How's fishing?" or, more commonly, "Did another boat go by here?" was the persistent question. "Yes," I could have answered, "any number of boats have gone by and fishing is lousy."

Some of the old-time fishing guides on the Snake River blame the decline of the once-fabled cutthroat trout fishing on the float trippers. I suppose the boats have some temporary effect on a trout's inclination to rise and strike, but there is more to it than that. The fishing in Snake River isn't very good any more because the trout are fewer. Some of the blame lies with the dam on Jackson Lake. Not only does it form an insoluble block to trout migrating upstream to spawn, but it has been used at times to cut off too much of the stream's natural flow. Biologists say that flood-control diking in the Wilson area has destroyed spawning areas and also that other spawning tributaries have been blocked off by irrigators. The sport catch may have been too heavy; certainly, it is much higher overall than it was in the delightful days when Owen Wister spent his vacations fishing the Snake.

Because the river is the home of the Snake River cutthroat trout, a unique subspecies, the Wyoming Game and Fish Commission has sought to maintain this fish throughout the area. It has been only partially successful. The cutthroat trout is still the principal trout in the Snake River, but brown and rainbow and even lake trout are also caught in the Snake and its tributaries. The Salt River, which flows near my home and enters the Snake today at Palisades Reservoir at the mouth of the Grand Canyon, was a cutthroat stream. There are still cutthroat in the Salt, but there are probably as many brown trout. Which isn't to say that there are lots of either, any more. Wyoming has never enacted a stream protection law, and landowners may, and do, rip and gouge the streams of this state into barren, silted sluiceways.

Studies throughout the western Wyoming–eastern Idaho watershed show that many of the principal trout streams have become silted. A certain amount of silt washing down a trout stream in the spring is normal in the West. "High and roily" is a description I can remember since stream conditions first began to be carried in newspapers. But the two go together. The high water of spring tends to keep the silt load moving so that it can neither fill in trout habitat nor settle on delicate trout eggs buried in stream gravel. But overgrazing, excessive clear-cutting of timber lands, road building, and destruction of stream bank vegetation have all contributed to too much silt in our creeks and rivers. There are places in Salt River where the silt is deposited four and five feet deep.

A few years ago my wife and I were invited by a district Forest Ranger to examine a road-building project in the Lower Hoback Canyon. It has been a perpetual tragedy and mistake to parallel the West's most beautiful streams with highways. But the ranger wished to show us how many careful steps were being taken to protect trout habitat during the course of this project, and indeed the planning was commendable. But being a cynic, especially when it comes to politicians and contractors, I said, "These plans look fine, but it only takes one jerk on a D-8 cat to spoil them all."

The ranger sincerely tried to persuade me to be a little less cynical, though he must have found it difficult, for a huge gout of silt was even then flowing where the Hoback River used to be. And sure enough, when we got to the construction site there sat a jerk on a D-8 cat in the middle of the stream, happily backing to and fro across what remained of the stream channel.

The Hoback has never been an exceptional fishing stream. It has a fairly steep gradient and not many pools where trout can feed and hide. What's more, portions of the stream freeze solid in the winter, reducing the trout's already limited habitat. Still, the gush of silt could only be damaging to the existing habitat and to trout-producing areas of the Snake River.

Fishing float trips to most of the larger streams in the area can be arranged. Depending upon the distance from Jackson Hole, the daily fees run fifty to seventy dollars per day for two anglers. A good fishing guide earns this and more, but a non-fishing float trip can last as long and be considerably less expensive.

For the person who just wants to fish, the shore of Jackson Lake is as good a bet as any. Sometimes the trout bite and sometimes they do not. The angler who aspires to derrick in one of the lake's thirty-pound mackinaw trout will have as good or better chance of success fishing through the ice in winter. Many residents of the area enjoy winter ice fishing as much as they do boat or bank fishing in summer, and a few ice-fish exclusively.

The best of the ice fishing often occurs late in the winter, and a few anglers will take great risks on the rotten ice to catch a fish. One fellow told me about snowplaning on the lake when there was almost as much melt water on top of the ice as there was lake water under it. It was late in the afternoon when he decided to stop fishing and hurry off the ice before it melted even more. He started for shore, and immediately the water was flying in a great spray from his machine as it roared across the ice. Visibility was poor. Suddenly the fellow heard a great *whump* and the snowplane sagged in its flight. He had struck a patch of open water. Only the machine's momentum took them on across. Another fellow landed a ski-plane on the lake, and after a few hours fishing found the surface too slushy for a takeoff. He taxied the plane across the mushy ice while his passenger had to literally wade in off the lake. The Park Service now prohibits airplane landings on the lake.

Many residents of Jackson Hole habitually carry fishing

rods in their cars and trucks. Whenever their available time
and a likely spot coincide they'll stop and walk down to the
water's edge to make a few casts. If the fish bite the anglers
will continue fishing until they stop biting. If, as happens more
often, the fish do not bite, the angler will quit after a few casts,
wind in his line, and go on about his business. I've never been
able to quit so easily. I believe that the next cast, a subtle variation of all those that have gone out before, is the one that will
catch the big one.

There was one moment at Jenny Lake when I did have just
a few minutes to fish. It was early in the spring, and the ice had
only recently gone off the lake. Old, crystallized snow was still
lying in deep drifts in the shaded timber. I flung out a spoon
and began reeling it in. The water is quite shallow on the
eastern shore of Jenny Lake, and you must retrieve a spoon a
bit too fast or have it lodge forever among the rocks under the
surface. Suddenly there was a heavy pull on my line, followed
by the surging run of a heavy fish. I knew I had hooked a big
mackinaw trout. Then, just as quickly as it had come, the fish
was gone. The hook had pulled free. As I was reeling in, a
middle-aged couple hurried down to where I was standing and
began fishing. I hooked my spoon in a rod guide, clambered
back up to my car, and drove away.

Jenny Lake, ringed with dark and quiet stands of timber
and shining brightly under the ruggedest Teton peaks, is one
of the most beautiful lakes in the world. Its waters are clear
and generally placid. At its northern end there is a lovely sort
of grotto, where the waters from String and Leigh lakes come
flashing in. On its western shore, just a few steps from the
lake, Hidden Falls plunges down in a haze of spray and a gush
of white tumbling water. In June, when the melting snows
are contributing their utmost, the two hundred fifty-foot waterfall is most beautiful.

It may be my imagination, but I have felt that the hordes of
early summer mosquitoes are not as thick around Jenny Lake
as they are in other places.

Years ago there was a Jenny Lake dance hall, store, and post office. Canvas-roofed camper cabins stood in regimented order along the road. There was also a rodeo grounds and grandstand, and at the wild Saturday night dances men were known to shoot off their pistols. The Rockefellers saw some of this when Horace Albright guided them through the area in 1926, saw it and primly disapproved. Rustic revelry wasn't the Rockefeller style.

It is all gone now, the camper cabins, everything—as forgotten and vacant as long-ago pistol shots. Folks had some good times there, and the times seem even better now because those who remember them are getting old. And being young in Jackson Hole has always been a little bit better than it is in other places.

Today there is a small museum with an interesting collection of rocks of the area together with memorabilia from early-day climbing parties. There is also a gift studio and a small ranger station, behind which is a "tents only" campground. A short walk from these log buildings is a small boat dock with a wooden walkway extending across the lake's outlet. Boats may be rented here, and it is also the place where the large inboard cruisers dock to pick up and unload passengers from the Hidden Falls landing across the lake. Except for these party boats only small, open boats with low-powered outboard motors are permitted on Jenny Lake.

A short distance from the boat dock, down the stream, is the Jenny Lake horse corral and the Exum Climbing School. Glen Exum and his climbing instructors have long enjoyed a good reputation both in teaching people to climb and in leading climbs up various Teton peaks. Just beyond the northern end of Jenny Lake, in a peaceful enclave all its own, is Jenny Lake Lodge and its guest cabins. There is also a stable, and I have often met their wrangler leading equestrian parties along the local trails.

Linking all this together is a narrow paved road that loops off the old highway east of Jenny Lake. The loop road passes the climbing school, then turns directly into the large, and usually crowded, parking area around the museum and ranger station. From there the road parallels the eastern shore of

Jenny Lake until it enters the timber a bit south of Jenny Lake
Lodge. Beyond the lodge the road forks, one fork going down
to String Lake and the other leading back out onto the highway
to Signal Mountain and the Jackson Lake Dam. In the summer
of 1971 there was road construction in this area, and my description may have been somewhat altered by the contractors.

It doesn't really matter. In my opinion it is not the road
conditions that are ruining Jenny Lake, it is the roads themselves. All day long, all summer long, the traffic growls and
howls past Jenny Lake. If you walk along the eastern section of
the trail that circles Jenny Lake you will do so in a haze of
smelly auto exhaust. Maintaining this road is like having a
drive-in at the Louvre. The tourists could putt-putt by the
Winged Victory, the Mona Lisa, and Venus de Milo and never
miss a munch on their potato chips.

The Park Service has attempted to maintain a self-guiding
nature trail along Jenny Lake's east shore. A number of the
more interesting and prominent plants of the area are dis-
creetly identified, and without the cars it could be a fine experience for people who aren't familiar with trails and native
plants. The thought of taking a walk on a self-guiding nature
trail was a lot more embarrassing to a natural-born westerner
like me than was the actual walk. I not only enjoyed it but
learned something.

It was not at all like the experience motor travelers have
at the park-provided scenic turnouts overlooking Jenny Lake.
One day I noted:

"A Texas car drew up.

"Texan: 'Boy! Now they's *fish* out there!'

"Pennsylvanian: 'How do you fish for trout?'

"Texan: 'How would I know? You can tell from our plates
we ain't from around here.'

"Second Texan: 'Well, let's roll—I ain't had nothin' to eat
since seven this mornin'.' "

The water-taxi service on Jenny Lake is even less admirable
than the hungry Texan. The big boats drone back and forth
across the gentle little lake all day long. It is no great boat ride,
and most of those who take it would be better off hiking

around the short trail to Hidden Falls. They can hire better boat rides on Jackson Lake.

The Park Service staff numbers some critics of its own, as revealed in the service's recent Grand Teton Master Plan. Not only is the wisdom of commercial boating on Jenny Lake questioned, but the horse corral business seems about to be properly transferred to a less congested site in the eastern part of the park. The old dictum that "parks are for people" has been amended to say that "parks are for people up to the point that people become too numerous and begin destroying the parks."

A segment of the park-using population will nod approvingly at such statements. And they will be furious if the Park Service later waffles on its stated aims. But what the cult of conservationist–ecologists often fails to take into account is the great bulk of park users. If visits to Grand Teton were limited to dues-paying members of the half-dozen leading conservation organizations, there would be no crush. More people, three million, visit Grand Teton each year than belong to the nation's six leading conservation groups combined.

Listen to the questions this public asks at the Park's Visitor Centers. You will hear the rangers answer mundane stuff about fishing or shops. Not many of our citizens are given to thoughtful ecological queries. Horace Albright deserves much of the credit, or blame, for the average American's love of his national parks. Albright encouraged them to hop into their flivvers and "See America First." In Yellowstone he put on wild animal shows and personally conducted impromptu park tours to win over the unimaginative public. The vast park system we have today is proof of how successful the promotional efforts of Albright and his successors have been.

The strange thing about national parks and natural wonders is how the former seems to magnify the latter, and the synergistic result is an influx of people. As an example of the storied "forces of nature," Lower Slide Lake is hard to beat. But it is across the valley, off the general tourist beat, and comparatively ignored.

Unless you have seen the catastrophic results of the landslide near Hope, British Columbia, the slide that occurred on the end of Sheep Mountain in 1925 is vastly impressive. The slide poured down and choked off the Gros Ventre River and created a lake almost five miles long. Old-timers maintain that the slide was precipitated by a series of minor earthquakes. It seems plausible that these temblors helped to send the wet and greasy-slick shales typical of the area plunging down the mountain. On top of them was fifty million cubic yards of overlying sandstone and other debris.

Two years later this dam was breached by the rising water and the top sixty feet of it was carried away. The little town of Kelly was all but washed out, along with six of its inhabitants. Now a self-guiding trail has been built on top of the remaining portion of the dam. Not only are indigenous plants identified but other unobtrusive signs point out results of the forty-seven year old landslide. Other features of the area are a rest room that verges on the luxurious and, when funds permit, a summer naturalist to answer visitors' questions.

The lake itself has never been one of my favorites. For most of the summer it is off color, as a result of the upstream runoff. Blackened old snags lurch up out of the water as tangible ghosts of the trees that once grew beside the river. Very often the rises of numerous fish dimple the lake, but these are more likely made by introduced Utah chubs than by game fish.

The Forest Service has built a small but attractive campground beside the lake, and it is full most of the summer.

The paving ends very near the entrance to this campsite. From there on the road is narrow, rough, and greasy slick when it is wet. When it is dry it is very dusty. If you follow it about eleven miles you will reach Upper Slide Lake, which formed as the result of a number of minor landslides. Like its larger counterpart downstream it is turbid throughout much of the summer. Though smaller than the other lake, I would rate it as being considerably uglier.

The streams of Jackson Hole have attracted prospectors for

over one hundred years. Now, however, the prospectors along the streams are not looking so much for gold as they are for ways to grab the land. This grabbing and use of public land is allowed under the antiquated mining laws of the United States.

These laws recently allowed an Idaho corporation to file on so-called "corridor" lands lying adjacent to the Snake River between Grand Teton and Yellowstone National parks. The key to establishing a claim is to be able to prove that the mineral in the land claimed is of such value that a prudent man would mine it. It doesn't take much imagination to see how many interpretations of this regulation there can be.

Even though I have it on the best authority that the Idaho corporation never had any intention of seriously mining their claims, they announced that work would proceed. In one of the most unctious and fatuous statements imaginable, a corporate officer said, "Fortunately the owners and management of the company are natives to the intermountain area and love and respect the environmental aesthetic values abounding here as much as the next person or group."

Since there is no known method of mining the firm's claims other than with a dredge, the statement, under happier circumstances, would have been hilarious. Fortunately, the project was halted at least temporarily by a Forest Service order banning all heavy earth-moving equipment from the area.

At stake in these nebulous claims is not gold but land that is becoming increasingly valuable. And, while the ploy to grab prospective recreational land in the corridor seems to have failed, others have not.

In 1967 the Bureau of Land Management announced that the old survey of land along the Snake River was in error. According to published reports, the Bureau was going to claim title to these riparian lands. Naturally, residents of the area who had always thought they owned land beside the Snake were in an uproar. This uproar became a holocaust when it was revealed that ex-Wyoming Congressman Teno Roncalio, with several associates, had filed mining claims all along the contested twenty-mile stretch of river. Roncalio was accused of having inside information about the bureau's intention to reclaim the land.

Roncalio's attorney later denied this charge, saying that his client had obtained the information properly from an obscure but available publication of legal opinions.

Despite charge and countercharge, the mining claims were on record, though not yet patented. Involved residents refused to allow government surveyors on their land—not for spite so much as to force a court test of their claim to the land. In the meantime Roncalio was, after a two-year hiatus, re-elected to Congress. As a United States congressman he was in the position of being accused of using his office to help protect his claims. He did defend some of his claims against a state attempt to discredit them.

Later, when Roncalio visited Jackson he was quoted in the *Jackson Hole Guide:* "I don't know what I'm going to do with them [the claims] but I assure you that there will be no mining on them *while I own them.*" (Italics are mine.) In answer to repeated questioning, Roncalio referred vaguely to a "state park" or that making the area into a wild river was "something I might do."

Congressman Roncalio during his first term had one of the worst voting attendance records in the House. Lately he has worked for the Washakie Wilderness and become something of a doyen of conservation. He strikes me, however, as a man made in the same mold as a number of his Wyoming predecessors in Congress. He was nonplussed recently when he found that about as many Jackson Hole voters did not want a larger airport to accommodate jet planes as did want it.

I think it was Cicero who said, "Politicians are not born, they are excreted."

*Ours is a small and select guest ranch.
We cater to not more than 40 guests
who stay in 16 modern western log
cabins. We are all on a "first name"
basis, and we try to make your stay
here one you will never forget.*

JACKSON HOLE DUDE RANCH BROCHURE

15 / *The Dude Wranglers*

Many years ago I was involved with several other young fellows in a penny-ante poker game. We were all terribly amateurish players. And as such we were all trying to act as though we could play as shrewdly as the cowboys in the movies. At one point in the game a technical question arose. None of us knew the answer, but as our bewilderment began growing into an argument our host's parents came home. They had been out to dinner and a show with their houseguest, a lady who ran a dude ranch in Jackson Hole.

We put our problem to the lady from Jackson Hole, and she quickly and correctly answered it while being helped off with her stylish coat. It wasn't that the lady was a poker buff so much as it was that her background of dude ranching had prepared her to solve practically any question or problem that might arise.

While dude ranchers are essentially innkeepers, they have established a tradition of entertaining and even pampering their guests that goes far beyond simple innkeeping. They also perfect the delicate ability of extracting large sums of money from their guests and make them like paying it enough to return for another visit. While the average dude spends about a week at a dude ranch, there are a few well-heeled fans of such places whose bills run into the thousands of dollars.

The dude business is said to have begun in 1888 when Edward Hoffer brought some travelers down from Yellowstone Park. Actually, nonresident sport hunters had been guided into the area before that time. But hunters don't quite come under the category of dudes—not dude ranch dudes, anyway. A man named Louis Joy started the valley's first guest ranch in 1908. According to Struthers Burt's delightful *Diary of a Dude Wrangler,* Joy liked to begin a season with an eastern partner. The easterner would be manuevered into paying most of the bills, in addition to getting his eastern friends out to stay at the ranch. Once Joy was assured of a bankroll for the season he declared a psychological war on the unwary partner that usually succeeded in driving the fellow off without a fair share of either the business or the profits.

The JY Ranch on Phelps Lake was started by Joy and eventually became the property of the Rockefellers after they had been luncheon guests there in 1926. Struthers Burt, a Pennsylvania dude himself, soon abandoned his partnership with Joy and formed another, this time with Dr. Horace Carncross, another easterner. They homesteaded land on the Snake River not far from present-day Moose and eventually became famous as operators of their Bar BC Ranch.

Dude ranches were quickly and sometimes wildly successful. Years ago people came out from the East to spend their summers on one. They fished, went on trail rides with colorful wranglers, ate Dutch-oven dinners by campfires, and square-danced in the ranches' main lodges. Not a few of the dudes stayed on and bought dude ranches of their own. Many were successful because they had learned the ropes from rough-edged westerners without forgetting their eastern manners. Of course, some dudes preferred salty old hosts who swore at the community dining table and ordered their guests around as though they were bunkhouse cowboys.

Most ranches had a few head of cattle, and the dudes would be employed to move the "herd" from one pasture to another. A few days later they would all troop out and put the cattle back where they'd been in the first place. Some guests treated their rancher hosts as father and mother figures and followed their advice on the most fundamental, even childish matters.

Years ago Marion Budge wrote briefly about the area's guest ranches: "They are simply country homes, kept up for occupancy during the summer months, by eastern people.

"The dudes and dudines, as they are known, contribute much to life in Jackson Hole. They are always out in full force at the Rodeo (usually called 'Frontiers' in early-day Jackson) and keep some very good racing animals. The running horse from the JY ranch, rode by a dudine, won the first money last year, while the second money was won by a horse from an honest to goodness ranch and ridden by its owner, a Jackson girl, Parthena Hansen."

The noun "dude" includes both genders today, although I have heard a woman referred to as, "that dude lady." To most westerners it is a word that carries, at best, a hint of derision. To others it is the vilest thing they can politely call another human being in mixed company. For this reason most dude ranches prefer to be known as "guest ranches."

Like many westerners I seldom thought about dude ranches, but if I did it was with the notion that they were on the sissy side. They were refuges for the rich, and they glorified phony pretensions by calling themselves "ranches."

Then, in the summer of 1971, I got a chance to see for myself when I booked in for a week at the Moose Head Ranch. Like the White-Grass, the Four Lazy L, and the Triangle X, the ranch I chose has been established for many years. Fred Topping homesteaded it nearly fifty years ago, and while he operated it it was as well known for outfitting hunters as for duding. When Floridians John and Eleanor Mettler bought the ranch from Topping's widow they dropped the hunting camp.

The first thing I had to do, or thought I had to do, was what countless dudes have done before me. I stopped at a couple of shops in Jackson and bought a pair of boots and some chichi-colored Levis. I tried to buy a new belt at Scott's Saddlery, but the only plain one they had was about eight years too small. All the rest of their saddle-leather belts had been embossed with the ghastly, pouting, wilting designs almost universally demanded on a western belt. So I made do with my old, plain one.

Levis are a phenomenon that did not become universal until about the time of the Second World War. They used to come with a leather tab sewn to the waistband that identified them both as to size and maker, Levi-Strauss. On one hip pocket was stapled a big oilcloth certificate that was a promise to replace the garment if it ripped. The leather waistband tab is now plastic and the oilcloth warranty has become paper, but they are still Levis—the most popular pants in the West.

If reasonably clean, they are suitable dress for almost any occasion in Jackson Hole. The clerks in Jackson stores that sell Levis (a few others stock different brands) will tell you that nothing really fits like Levis.

Blue jeans that wear as well as any are still available from, surprisingly, a major mail-order house. The ones of theirs I've had will outwear other makes by at least two to one and they don't shrink. Before writing this I got up and examined the pair I have on—they are three or four years old—they may not fit me as well as some others, their blue color might be a little off the shade we remember, and these pants never fade to the pale blue of oft-laundered Levis. But they really do wear and they cost about a dollar less than some other kinds.

As an item of equestrian apparel, Levis and their imitators have one cardinal virtue. Their high, tight cut acts as an athletic supporter and keeps the saddle from getting in a lick below the belt.

Pants are so universal in Jackson Hole that the sort of uni-sexuality wearing them creates is taken for granted. In the winter some women who'd rather be warm than stylish wear jeans under their house dresses.

The dude's uniform often includes a wide-brimmed hat and a pair of boots. Some of the girls at the dude ranch sub-stituted their high-fashion boots for cowboy boots and no one seemed to mind. When I went riding I wore my tough, lug-soled hiking boots, but when relaxing and socializing in the lodge I wore my new, semi-high-heeled cowboy boots. That way I was comfortable in both situations. Most cowboy boots are made for wider feet than mine and I wrote in my notes, after finally finding a pair that fit, "Only ducks wear 'cowboy' boots; 'B' or 'C' width is almost impossible to find."

Dollar for dollar you don't get as much value in a cowboy boot as you do in a good hiking boot. One night I sat listening to a couple of wranglers discuss their boots—they wore expensive Tony Lamas. Mostly the men described how they ripped their boots to shreds in a matter of months. But they would not wear anything less. The person who is going to make occasional forays to dude ranches is just as well off with a pair of lower-priced Acme boots. Cowboy boots do give your foot some support in the stirrup, as will any boot with a steel shank in the sole. They are streamlined and thus a little less likely to hang you up in a stirrup, but this feature has been vastly overrated.

Like most western wear, the cowboy hat is nearly as susceptible to style changes as high-fashion clothing. When Jackson Hole ranchers were protesting the enlargement of Teton Park, many of them wore what amounted to a snap-brim felt with a slight glandular condition. The style was called a San Fran, Jr., and they are no longer sold. The nearest thing to it is the "LBJ," with a lower crown. Now a trend is back to the big sombreros popular with dude ranchers and sheepmen forty years ago. But the main demand is for a rakish job called a "Pecos" with its Rodeo Cowboys' Association crease. This number is, approximately, a cross between a ten-gallon sombrero and a schoolboy's paper airplane.

A good cowboy hat of "beaver" quality, but rabbit felt costs at least twenty dollars. They wear almost forever. Since most dudes don't want a cowboy hat for eternal use they either get wool felts or straw hats. The latter is probably the wisest choice. You can get a very good straw hat for the price of a mediocre wool felt one. Straws are generally appropriate for summer season wear, and, if you lose or give it away at the end of your vacation, you're not out much.

Nothing is surer to reveal a dude to a resident than a wool felt cowboy hat. No westerner above the age of eight will buy or wear one. Some pretty rugged outdoorsmen, however, buy baseball or golfing caps for summer and fall wear. They don't look like cowboys, but in several respects their caps are as good or better than the traditional Stetson.

At the Moose Head Ranch I learned that one of the few house rules required riders to wear hat ties. I had not seen one of these corded chin straps since I saw my last Buster Crabbe western. But they do keep hats from falling off where they may roll under the horse and cause him to buck.

The rest of the dude ranch routine is flexible. Meal hours are announced by the ringing of an old-fashioned bell. At some dude ranches the meals are served family style. But in the Moose Head's dining room the tables are separated and the guests usually eat with members of their own group.

When I was there the guests who were riding sauntered down to the immaculate corral around nine for their morning ride. The horses would all be standing saddled and ready. Near the door of the tack room stood a step-stool affair for riders who couldn't quite get their feet up in the stirrups.

There were fifty-two horses on the ranch. They were "dude" horses—which can mean phlegmatic plugs or good, gentle animals with large "idiot" factors. The Moose Head horses were all fat with the big "hay bellies" soft horses develop. But the thing that surprised me about all the mounts I had was that they were good horses. To be sure, they needed riding, but they were better animals than most dudes could appreciate.

The same was true of the tack. Each saddle had its own neatly made rack in the tack room, and each was also clean and in good repair. A lot of dude outfits will buy any second-hand saddle they can find so long as the price is low enough. Their saddle pads and blankets are often in matted tatters. But none of this was true at the Moose Head, and none of their horses had the big sores I've seen on many "for hire" horses. The latter attribute was due as much to lack of use as to abuse. But I did notice that whenever a guest's horse showed the least sign of developing a tender back he was immediately replaced with another horse.

Sometimes the rides would be arranged so that at noon a pickup truck from the ranch met us at some prearranged spot on a back road. The truck bed was filled with all sorts of picnic fare and the young wranglers would cook hamburgers and wieners for the dudes over a wood fire. For the youngsters in the group there was always a bag of toasting marshmallows. On another day-long ride to a spot where we couldn't rendezvous we carried bread and a variety of very good cold meats in saddlebags. We drank water from a *bota* and fashioned our own sandwiches. On still other days the rides were shorter and the guests could be back for lunch in the dining room. In the afternoon they might ride again, or be driven into Jackson for sightseeing and shopping. Or they could just sit and take it easy.

Cabins at many of the Jackson Hole dude ranches are not fancy. They are often small and not particularly well-furnished or lighted. There is basic plumbing and a little air-tight wood stove for heat. At the Moose Head Ranch the cabins were much nicer. I had Cabin B and after moving into it I noted that "it proved to be most attractive, with a marvelous view of the mountains."

My cabin had electric heat, which I used in preference to messing with the little wood-burning stove. Closet space and other storage was ample. Towels were changed daily, and the bed was made up and the room quickly and unobtrusively tidied every morning. In the afternoon the ice bucket was filled, and my supply of instant coffee replenished.

Most of the big staff at the Moose Head were college students. They were bright, willing kids and fun to be around. Like other summer help they were not paid high wages. This is partly because summer help is plentiful, but also because many of the youngsters have no experience in cleaning, waiting tables, or helping in the kitchen. Ranch operators usually add a bonus to the wages of kids who stay and work throughout the summer. Tipping also adds to their earnings. It is often paid them in the form of a ten to fifteen percent surcharge added to the bill. At the end of the season the pooled tips are divided equitably among the staff. Having been on both sides of the tipping question, I think this method is the best and fairest of all.

The Moose Head is about the last of the privately owned guest ranches in Grand Teton National Park. There are several other establishments operating in the park, but most have been sold to the Park Service under a life-tenure agreement. Under this method the owner of a property is permitted to live on it and operate his business until he dies or retires. Then the property may be occupied by members of the owner's immediate family until they die. Only then does the land revert to the Park Service. It is one of the few ways I know in which a person has his cake and eats it, too. The only "bad" effect of the acquisition program is to increase the value of the remaining privately held lands in Jackson Hole. The Moose Head is an extremely valuable property today.

Which is not to say that a dude ranch owner can expect to recover his investment quickly, if ever. There is always plenty of overhead in running such a business. These costs went on in 1971 when a recession was felt at the dude ranches perhaps more than in most other Jackson Hole businesses. I visited one fine old ranch during my stay at the Moose Head that didn't have a single customer. The Mettlers' business was only a little better.

In addition to the customary maintenance, the Mettlers had bought a property that they felt needed considerable renovation. The old lodge, which had also housed the post office called Elk, lacked space and light. Its dining area was also dark and small, and the kitchen facilities were inadequate. So the Mettlers built a new lodge. It is a huge building, although its size is not so apparent from the outside. In addition to a modern institutional kitchen and staff dining room there is a big guests dining room that could easily accommodate sixty people.

The whole west wall of this room consists of huge plate

glass windows that rise to the high ceiling. These are interspersed with supporting log pilasters. Outside the windows the cottonwoods of the Snake River bottoms frame the Tetons, which rise in the near distance. In addition to the fine view, guests at breakfast are treated to the sight of forty or so horses being trotted in from the green meadows for the morning ride.

Off the dining room are two lounges—the smaller with a bar and small library plus a great table that was layered with what seemed to be most of the periodicals printed in English. Adjacent to this room is a smaller one where kids (staff or guests) can play Ping-Pong. This lounge also contains a great stone fireplace whose size is best comprehended by comparing it with the huge bull elk's head mounted above it. Besides the books and magazines there are a writing table and a couple of card tables.

Down a short flight of stairs from this lounge is another, even larger room. It, too, has an enormous fireplace. One of the staff lights a fire in it on chilly mornings and the ensuing warmth soon fills the room and then spreads even beyond. This room features a bull moose head mounted over its fireplace. It is furnished with comfortable, solid wood and leather furniture. Between the large windows making up one wall are soft-colored Hardy prints of trout and trout flies.

The older guest cabins are used by the staff. A number of the almost opulent new ones are of duplex construction, about fifty feet long by twenty feet wide, and they cost in excess of twenty thousand dollars each. Between the lodge and the cabin where I stayed are a series of trout ponds. The water had been stocked with large fish. But although the ponds were open to fly fishing, and the fish could be seen rising every evening, I preferred to sit in the camp chair on my cabin's porch. From there I could alternately watch the swallows sweeping the skies for insects and contemplate the Tetons.

Being one who enjoys the outdoors I found life on a dude ranch a pleasant blend of elegant exertion and languid luxury. As in most cases in the Jackson Hole area where recreational vacations are on a person-to-person basis, I found the service good and the people rendering it to be genuinely friendly and concerned that I enjoyed myself. It is very seldom that you hear someone claim he was gypped on a western Wyoming vacation.

Even when they are not busy, which is during June, the first few days in July and all of September, dude ranchers don't welcome overnight guests. To show a profit they need guests who will stay at least three days and preferably a week or more. A week is really enough for most people to both relax and take in most of the activities a dude ranch has to offer. It is not a place for "singles" hoping to double up with some-one. Most of the guests are either well beyond their twenties or are the children of guests. There was a day or so at the Moose Head when I felt I was the only male guest who was neither middle-aged nor a millionaire. On such days I'd arrange to go riding with one of the young wranglers. Most of them said they had as much fun on the dude ranch as the paying guests did. I believe it.

Rates at dude ranches in 1971 were typically twenty-five dollars per day for children and thirty-five for adults. Adults traveling by themselves may be expected to be charged a premium of fifty dollars per day. These rates, which inflation seems bound to increase, make a dude ranch vacation one of the most expensive ways to visit in Jackson Hole. Some ranches offer scenic and fishing float trips on the streams as well as back-country pack trips at additional fees.

Certain people seem to vacation at dude ranches primarily to increase their social status back home. The overly sleek guest who slides into the public room of a lodge and begins talking about money inadvertently announces why he's come. Other dude ranches still fill their brochures with photos of grinning anglers holding up greedily filled strings of dead cut-throat trout. Such exhibitions of the grossness money can buy undo much of the substantial good other dude ranchers have done in the valley since Struthers Burt helped fight off the Idaho irrigators. While a dude ranch will supply an undemand-ing and unimaginative mind with a pretty shallow Jackson

Hole experience, a good one can also provide a wonderful experience that has no substitute.

For the person who is not sure about a dude ranch vacation, and is physically up to it, a trail ride into the back country may be the thing. Some dude ranches offer these trips. They may also be booked through organizations like the American Forestry Association and the Wilderness Society, as well as with outfitters who specialize in such trips. The Sierra Club has sponsored both pack trips and rugged hikes for backpackers in the area.

These trips last a week to ten days and cost from two hundred fifty to three hundred fifty dollars. Generally those trips operated by reputable outfitters and organizations are first rate. The one I took into the Gros Ventre was outfitted by Frome and Hyde of Afton, Wyoming, under the sponsorship of the American Forestry Association. I went along as a working guest of the outfitter and thoroughly enjoyed nearly every minute of the ten-day trip.

There were nineteen guests and nine employees who were either on salary or who, like me, worked their passage. When the trip began and ended the outfitter, L. D. Frome, was on hand with several more young men to help handle the stock and the mountains of equipment. Frome is one of the most active outfitters in Wyoming. He outfits a number of summer trail rides, runs a fishing camp on the upper Yellowstone, and in the fall has hunting camps and trips going all over Wyoming. It never fails to amaze me how this energetic young Mormon is able to keep so many activities running so smoothly for so many harried months.

Part of his secret lies with the staff Frome builds from around his home base in Afton, Wyoming. Some of them are completely unworldly kids from staid Mormon communities in Star Valley, where hard work has been a way of life. Other young employees come from all over America, accepting a small wage for the chance to get out into Wyoming's back country. For several years Frome's top packer has been a diminutive young fellow who grew up in Lebanon. Often there is a wayward boy in the crew who has been sent out in the hope that some hard work will straighten him out. Sometimes it does, sometimes not.

Frome's majordomo is a youngish man from Star Valley called Mont Harmon. Harmon has literally grown up in the wilderness of the upper Yellowstone country. He is, in my mind, the best all-around elk hunting guide in western Wyoming. He can pack six horses while I'm finishing my second. To watch him cape a big game head for mounting is to see an exhibition of incomparable skill and speed. Harmon is a superb handler of horses and can dress and quarter a big bull elk in the time it takes some men to clean a few trout. Over almost twenty years Harmon has learned how to run a wilderness camp to the satisfaction of both guests and employees—no mean feat. All these outdoor attributes combine in Harmon with his enviable strength and stamina. He throws a quarter of elk on a horse with dismaying ease. I guided with and for him during parts of two seasons, and it was embarrassing to always be huffing and puffing a step or two behind this rough-cut phenomenon.

The day we started our Gros Ventre ride there were unavoidable problems that delayed our departure from the Cow Creek trail head. But in expectation of delays and in deference to saddle-soft guests, the ride into the already established camp was purposely short. We were all in and unpacked long before dark. That first evening I noted, "After a prolonged session of saddling 50-odd horses we rode up Cow Creek about 8 miles to a beautiful swale overlooked by high red cliffs.

"From the downed log on which I'm sitting to write, I can see the Wind River Mts. We had a good camp dinner, Swiss steak, green salad, Dutch-ovened spuds, corn on the cob, etc. We will stay here 2 nights, taking a side trip tomorrow up on Sportsman Ridge and then pack up and go on Wednesday. The whole trip will cover some 50 to 60 miles.

"There are a number of older people in the group. Some, including the required physician, were well past 65. But they all took to the trip like kids—actually some of them did better than many kids would have."

The base camps consisted of a "kitchen," which was mostly

a fire pit, an iron grill, and a big, folding table secured to poles picked up near the site, all under a big, canvas awning. Pauline McCarty cooked, with the expert help of a grandmotherly gal named Gladys. They did it all over an open fire on bended knees that must have ached with fatigue. The food was simply superb. At mealtimes the long table was filled with an array that would have shamed many city buffets. When the guests had filled their trays they would take them over to the logs we had provided around a big campfire. There was virtually no class distinction—crew and guests ate when and with whom they pleased. After dinner John Montgomery, a young member of the staff, would play his guitar and sing for as long as anyone wanted to stay up.

The mountains of the Gros Ventre are of sedimentary rather than of granitic rock like the Tetons. They approach the height of the Tetons, but, instead of plunging away into vast chasms, these peaks often have great rolling, green uplands spreading out from their flanks. On the second day of our trip, we rode very easily to near the top of a ridge that aspired to be a mountain. Walking to the top we found a benchmark that gave the elevation as 10,655 feet. It was an area lush with succulent green vegetation while still liberally daubed with snow.

I had awakened early that morning in the camp meadow noting, "Woke up early to see a young buck deer passing a few yards outside my tent. After getting up and washing, I helped catch and tie the horses as they were brought in.

"Things moved leisurely after a good breakfast of ham, eggs, French toast, juices, and coffee. Then we, 21 of us, went up the creek to Sportsman Ridge. It was a leisurely ride. We stopped on the ridge below the summit previously mentioned and most of us walked up to the top. The view included far-off Mt. Moran and some of the peaks north of it. Parts of the Wind Rivers, including Gannet Peak and Fremont, were also visible."

Nearer to us, "the reddish cliff sides are striking and are eroded like a very early Bryce Canyon. To the south are rugged, barren peaks still covered with extensive snowfields.

"The many valleys (the one to the south seems to be glaciated) are often brilliant green meadows interspersed with darker stands of alpine fir and white-bark pine.

"While we rested one of the older riders took out a pack of cards and played a few games of solitaire." As the trip progressed I noticed that this man usually got in a few games of sol whenever the rest of the group took pictures or just relaxed and munched a sandwich. "The bugs are not too bad today— and have never been, although there are enough of them to go around."

While Frome provided comfortable, two-man tents for his guests, he had asked me to bring along my own. I have a lightweight miner's tent, a gem and irreplaceable, and relaxed in it to make my notes one afternoon. "A big, black, and very fleet spider has been rushing me for the length of my stay in here. I read some Gide; how nice it was to be for a few minutes with such a thoughtful man. I respect him—or some of what he wrote—even as a 20-year-old kid."

After the day's layover, in which the dudes took side trips, they would be fed the next morning and then asked to roll and deposit their tents, bedding, and duffle in a central spot near camp. Even as they were finishing breakfast, the crew, which had been up early, was saddling horses and breaking camp. The guests generally packed their own lunches from a trove of luncheon supplies on the table. When they had done this and then climbed aboard their horses, one of the wranglers led them out toward the next campsite.

Moving days were the hardest of all for the crew. We were expected to strike the camp, pack all the horses, move onto the next site, and have a hot meal ready for the riders when they came in. It was hard work for me, and I suspect it was even harder work for the women who had to ride a good distance (Pauline led a pack string), and then charge at another meal as fast as the crew set up their kitchen. They never failed, and the food was great.

At the close of a camp-moving day I wrote in my notebook, "9 P.M. A very long day with the usual irritabilities brought on by weariness. We moved the camp, 53 horses, over to the six lakes, and it is a beautiful spot.

"There are great, barren mts, turreted and minaretted, rising abruptly to the west. They are not craggy, but buttelike. The lake now after sunset is a deep emerald.

"All the gang has circled the fire under the fly and are singing old cowboy songs to the accompaniment of John's guitar.

"We rode about 9 miles today, crossing the ridge and riding up a beautiful green valley to a divide that was timbered and not too easy going. But no trouble with the packs, either.

"Pauline is tough and competent; cooking with a cigarette in her mouth and cooking very well, too. Hamburgers, Dutch-oven spuds, corn, vegetable salad, canned pears."

The next morning, while catching the horses, "I saw partly buried under a tree what looked like the base of a large skull. It was deeply imbedded in soil and duff." The gray rocklike color and texture of the almost hidden object, plus the lichens on it, led me to think it might be a petrifaction. Late in the day John Montgomery came back with me to the place, and by careful, tedious digging with a shovel, and finally with sticks, we unearthed a tremendous buffalo skull. Despite its long burial it was in fine condition, although the once black and shiny horns had begun to deteriorate. It was the skull of an old bull, no telling how long it had lain there in the high mountains. The old fellows used to quit the herd when they could no longer compete with the younger bulls, and spent their declining years alone in remote mountain valleys. Thanks to the packing skills of Eddie Lesoon and Morris McCarty, Pauline's husband, I was able to send the valuable find out to the road, where the McCartys packed it in my car.

On the same day I noted, "We rode to the top of the peak overlooking the lake below camp. On the side above camp and just under the summit there was a gradual inclination that became an abrupt drop for hundreds of feet to the talus slopes below. It was pleasant up there, even though there was a light overcast.

"There was a lot of oldish sheep sign on the mountain ridge.

It appeared that the bighorns may winter there at 10,000 to 11,000 feet.

"We descended and had a pleasant lunch in a meadow part way down the long ridge. After leaving the mountain we rode around the east shore of the lake to the north of camp. There was nothing to travel on but game trails. The ride wasn't very productive, although young David [one of the guests] found a rock bearing fossil shells.

"After dinner we caught the packhorses. I felt particularly sorry for a little blue roan with terribly bad hobble sores. I had difficulty getting the hobbles off him, and even more in putting Corona grease on the chaffs. The horse struck and cow-kicked even though Eddie had him 'earred down.'

"We had another good dinner, pot roast and boiled spuds, onions, and carrots."

Due to the heavy and still-lingering snows of the previous winter the trip had to be arranged to avoid the worst drifts. But toward the end of it we had to cross a high divide at the head of the Gros Ventre River. "Eddie Lesoon woke me at 5 A.M. It was hardly light. We mustered around the campfire drinking coffee for a few minutes before going out after the horses.

"There was a heavy mist hanging in among some of the mountain crags, and the sight of the horses coming in across the still, gray meadows was enchanting.

"But from then on it was work breaking camp and packing up. Four of us left with the kitchen and nine packhorses and rode up to the divide at the very head of the Gros Ventre. It was awesome looking back down the long, sloping valley and then looking up at the great buttes and pinnacled mountain ridges rising all around. At the summit we were crossing through some very pink snowfields. Then we turned down Crystal Creek and began a long descent that finally brought us to a timber-studded meadow in the canyon." Part way down we had overtaken the guests at their lunch site. The trail into the bottom of the canyon had been obliterated by drifts and slides, making it necessary for us to work our way down the best we could. At one very steep place on the canyon side the earth was so soft and treacherous that I remember just easing my own horse through and not having the nerve to look back to see if my pack string was going to make it. But make it they did.

Crystal Creek is a lovely, clear, but booming stream that grows ever larger as it moves down to its junction with the Gros Ventre River. It was the last leg of our ten-day looping trip through what many hope will soon be designated a wilderness area. As we rode down the creek we came upon a charming glen, where the only other party we had seen was camped. Their pack burros brayed and trotted excitedly around on their stake ropes in the meadow. As we passed we visited with the guide and his small party for a few minutes, and then plunged on across the creek. Near the Red Rock Ranch, L. D. Frome was waiting with a crew, three big stake-body trucks, and a couple of smaller vehicles. As quickly as the packs were jerked off, the gear was packed away in the trucks and then the horses were led up ramps and tied to the stake bodies. The guests said hasty good-byes, before being put aboard a bus-like van and whisked away to showers and soft beds in Jackson. As she had promised to do, one of the young ladies shed a few tears at the end. I really couldn't blame her—it had been a marvelous trip.

Part way through the Gros Ventre ride Pauline McCarty and her husband had been replaced by Eileen and Bruce Johnson. The McCartys were sent in twenty-eight miles to the upper Yellowstone to manage Frome's fishing camp at Hawk's Rest Mountain. This camp and another, about eighteen miles east, which is set up in September, also serve as hunting camps.

There are more than sixty of these camps in the Teton Forest. They cater almost exclusively to nonresident hunters who come from all over the world to hunt for elk, moose, bear, mule deer, and even bighorn sheep. The location of these camps is more or less static. The sites have been designated and special use permits issued to the outfitters by the Forest Service.

They are generally so located as to provide forage for horses and a good campsite without being too close to any other outfitter's camp. In practice there is some fudging into adjoining hunting territories. Most outfitters, if they haven't reached boundary agreements with their neighbors, tolerate this with better humor than they do "spike camping."

It is against forest regulations for professional outfitters to roam the area with their customers, hunting and camping where they please. But if their prescribed area lacks game, some outfitters will spike camp—move their hunters into another outfitter's territory. Often the trespassing outfitter will have a licensed moose hunter in his group whom he uses as an excuse to be out of his district. I've seen spike campers virtually ruin an area for the season. And this is even more infuriating to the legitimate outfitter when you realize that his special permit for a camp may be worth a hundred thousand dollars. In 1971 I knew of a camp being offered for two hundred thousand.

As game populations in other western states decline or hunter numbers increase beyond endurance, big-game hunters have increasingly come to Wyoming. Wyoming has for many years restricted the number of nonresident elk hunting licenses it sells. It is also virtually the last state requiring nonresidents to obtain a licensed resident guide before hunting on national forest, park, or refuge lands. These two requirements have helped keep Wyoming's nonresident hunter success extremely high.

There are some residents, however, who feel that Wyoming game officials are often confusing dollar signs with game animals. This ever-increasing pursuit of nonresident license monies has led to catastrophic results to game herds in adjoining western states. About fifty-five hundred nonresident big-game licenses are sold each year in Wyoming—to an ever-increasing demand. Each one of these licenses allows its holder to kill a bull elk. There are not anywhere near that many trophy bulls in all of Wyoming. I have a letter written by a Wyoming state game warden in 1968 that says, in part, "You are probably correct in assuming that the quality of [elk] hunting will decrease if you base quality on a high hunter-success of mature male animals, because in offering more people recreation and the opportunity of hunting, the hunter-success will naturally go down."

Today a nonresident big-game license costs one hundred twenty-five dollars, and it is a bargain, but the resident elk license in Wyoming is only *five* dollars. It is so cheap that many unscrupulous hunters buy one for every member of their family. They fill as many of them as they can in the course of a long season. Another ploy is to simply shoot all the elk one can and then run down to town and buy enough licenses to cover them.

A pack-in elk hunting trip in the Jackson Hole back country costs from six to eight hundred dollars for ten days. In the better areas a hunter has eighty-five to ninety-five percent chance to kill a legal elk, and a few outfitters still guarantee a fair shot at such an animal. The guarantee is not for a refund, but for the right to stay in camp and hunt until the hunter gets his shot or a reasonable opportunity to shoot. After a week or ten days of rugged back-country hunting, most hunters, successful or not, have had enough and go home.

Also after a few hard days, one of the most important things a camp has to offer is its food and dry, warm tents. Many times I have heard Eileen Johnson rattling stove lids in her icy cook tent at 3 A.M. to build fires and begin preparing breakfast for twenty, or even more, guides, packers, and hunters. She has also stayed up past eleven at night to fix hot suppers for me and my hunters when we came in late.

Not only was she a good cook—Eileen prepared wonderful roast turkey dinners in her small wood-burning range—but she wrangled, too. She loved all the horses and mules and was the only person in camp who could walk out and catch any one of fifty or sixty often cantankerous animals. One day on the Gros Ventre ride, Eileen caught and then brought up pack animals while her husband Bruce and I packed them. It was like an assembly line, with Bruce tying off one hitch after another. We made about fifteen miles that day and never had to touch a pack.

Betty and Merritt Egan ran Frome's Pass Creek Hunting Camp east of the one on the Yellowstone. The year I guided there, Betty was the only woman in camp for weeks. I remember how she beamed when the packer finally brought her in word of a new grandchild. Merritt, as camp boss and guide, treated all the help like sons, coming in each morning to light our fires and lanterns so we wouldn't have to dress in the cold and dark. In the cook tent Betty performed miracles. Frome had lots of good cooks, but Betty Egan was exceptionally good. One day she handed me my lunch bag and apologized because the candy bars were all gone. Far down the trail I opened the sack, and in addition to the homemade cookies and lush sandwiches I'd come to expect, I found a homemade apple turnover in lieu of candy. Never ate a better one.

Not all of the dozens of hunters seemed to appreciate the bone-grinding efforts made on their behalf. Some would tip and others wouldn't, and a guide learns to recognize a tipper as fast as he does a bull elk. Younger hunters are notoriously stingy tippers, and no hunter tips as well if he kills an elk the first day as he does if he has to hunt for a while. Some guides will quickly learn a hunter's occupation and size him up accordingly. The hunter who starts off a trip by complaining about how expensive it is is also likely to be a poor tipper. Naturally, there is competition among the guides for the hunters who seem most likely to tip. The younger, less experienced guides usually wind up with the deadbeats. Most guides don't expect a tip unless his hunter kills an elk. Then twenty dollars is a minimal tip, but for a really exceptional bull a guide may receive one hundred dollars. Not only does a tip mean more tangible appreciation than a handshake at hunt's end, but it supplements a very modest wage.

Some camps are lazy affairs, but I've never worked in one of those. Depending upon the time of year a guide rolls out at 3:30 to 4:30 A.M. The first one up lights the lantern and builds a fire in the tent's little stove. If there is time he may wait in his sleeping bag a few minutes for the tent to warm. Then he gets up and dresses. I used to clump out in cold-stiffened boots and brush my teeth. If you use toothpaste you don't really need any water at all. Then I'd go next door to the cavernous combination cook and dining tent and wash and have coffee if it was hot. After that I'd clump back to the tent and put on my heavy coat before walking back to awaken my hunters in their tents. Often I'd build them a fire and light their lanterns. Then I'd hurry up to the corral, where Mont and the other guides would be or soon appear to catch and saddle the day's mounts. Not knowing all the horses I often had to depend on Mont or Bruce to point out good, gentle horses for my hunters. Then it was catch and tie them before going into the pitch-black tent to find my hunters' saddles. Once the horses were saddled, they'd be fed half a bucket of grain pellets.

At times the horses were left tied by the corral to eat, and at other times we'd lead them down to the tie line near the tents. Then we would go in and eat our breakfast—very fast if we were running late. Outside again, the bridles hanging on the saddle horns were fitted on the horses; then heads and the lead ropes, attached to their halters, were fastened to the horns. It was still dark, and a wrong move by an impatient guide somewhere along the line of horses could and did start a chain of horseflesh moving that sometimes got you stepped on or even kicked. Finally, the sleepy, stubbly-faced hunters would come along, stuffing all manner of what was often junk into the saddlebags and then stuffing their lunches down on top of that.

Before they mounted I would tighten the saddle cinches, and on particularly cold mornings we led our horses down the trail a hundred yards to let them work the kinks out before we got on.

In October the mornings are so cold that you bundle up to a point where mounting a horse, especially a tall, shifting horse, is no easy trick. I used to hold a lot of my hunters' horses to preclude accidents, and once Mont had to hold a nervous mare for me.

In late October of 1971 southern Wyoming was wracked by some of the worst blizzards in years. In the back country of Jackson Hole it did not snow so much as it blew—fierce, icy winds that froze the rivers solid in a single night. I rode across the frozen Thorofare Creek, the morning after a big blow, on ice that never so much as cracked.

If there is a way to get colder than sitting on horseback in a biting wind, I don't know it. That cold day I wore: cotton briefs and undershirt, heavy woolen longhandles, wool shirt, down vest, woolen sweater, and a heavy down coat. Over my thick woolen pants were a pair of cowhide chaps. I had on a light pair of wool socks under a second, heavy, hand-knitted pair. Over them were leather boots and rubber overshoes. I wore medium-weight woolen gloves under a heavy, insulated pair that were also waterproof. My hat was a stocking cap that could be pulled down to form a face mask. I think I wore a bit more than some of the other guides, but not much, and I was at least fairly comfortable, if only slightly mobile. Hunting that day was poor.

In two seasons of guiding hunters on the Yellowstone I met many men that I enjoyed being with. Many of the crew were indefatigable workers and a welcome revelation in this lazy day and age. I also met a genuine and perfect clinical example of a sadist, and another guy who spent the golden, expensive days trying to show me his penis. I saw a man lose his reason and then the queer look of foreboding in his eyes that followed. I saw a lot of greed. I got painfully weary of seeing animals killed. But guiding is a vicarious experience that interweaves itself with feelings of love and hate. In November you say you'll never do it again, but, by the first of next September, you're not quite so sure.

16 / *Not Wisely But Too Well*

For me, one of the less attractive features of hunting elk on the Thorofare is the proximity of the south boundary of Yellowstone Park. More than once I've sat in the timber with hunters and waited for a bull elk to step across the line. My feelings were always a queer mixture of dread and rapt anticipation. There were times when I was sure the elk could read and understand the park boundary signs, which stud the meadows and extend through the timber at lock-step intervals. At other times the animals innocently wander by the protective markers and into the valley of death. A part of my ambivalent feelings about "hunting the line" lay in the knowledge that if I got overeager and let a hunter shoot an elk inside the park we would both be in trouble with the park rangers.

A few outfitters and hunters disdain "park" elk, never realizing that most of them are also Jackson Hole elk. Depending upon the hunting season and the routes the elk migrate along, these animals run a long gauntlet of danger before they finally reach the safety of the Jackson Hole Elk Refuge. One trip down that long, perilous slope ought to educate any elk that survives it to the dangers presented by men. The only "friends" the elk have along their way are a very thin red line of game wardens and a somewhat thicker green and gray one made up of park rangers.

It is the fashion in certain quarters to take verbal potshots at the rangers. Some hunting guides call them "Yogis," after the cartoon bear in the comic strip. Nevertheless they all respect the rangers, who have deserved reputations for their tough but fair enforcement of park regulations. These rangers may be called on to determine from a blood spore where an elk was shot or who was tapping the till of a certain cash register. They are expected to know what kind of rocks are in a particular mountain and "what kind of bird is that black one with the red wing?" (The public never seems satisfied to learn that it is a red-winged blackbird.) For a job of such diverse requirements it is surprising to know that there are still men around who can do it.

Many of those who serve in the ranger force are "seasonals" —employees who work only part of the year. Some of them, depending upon their skills, are assigned to the naturalist branch, while others specialize in park protection. Many of the summer rangers and naturalists are college professors or teachers in secondary schools. On the other hand, Joe Shellenberger, who works a long season at Grand Teton, gave up the aerospace industry to become a professional silversmith. Joe is also a trained botanist and a fascinating leader of nature walks.

The Park Service furnishes housing for its permanent staff at a sort of Levittown West at Moose, and also at the Beaver Creek enclave. Summer help is put up in old dude ranch cabins scattered throughout the valley. Most of the cabins are good enough for a two-week family vacation, but some are a little too primitive for a summer-long stay by rangers and their families. This need for new employee housing is just one of many problems facing park managers, who generally strive to prevent such problems from interfering with the good time of the vacationing public.

Despite the housing situation Grand Teton Park attracts some of the country's best-educated and most willing part-time help. We can all be grateful when men like these are accused of having possessive feelings toward the national parks.

But having a national park in your back yard is not a completely positive thing. A resident of Jackson Hole recently told me that, like "damyankee," "GoddamParkService" is one, indissoluble phrase. There is little doubt that the Park Service has been high-handed with some individuals in order to further what the service considered the overall public good in Jackson Hole.

The basis for much of the old animosity toward the Park Service and its now successful attempts to enlarge Teton Park was money. People who were barely making a living on marginal ranches in the valley hated the thought of some nebulous "rich dude" taking over and playing on their land. Some also hated to imagine that "outsiders" might be successful on lands where old-timers had failed. But now, more than twenty years after the fact, nearly everyone realizes that the park has made Jackson Hole rich. Teton County has the highest per-capita income in Wyoming. The flood of tourist dollars surges through the valley in a golden stream that rises higher every summer.

To a lot of people, the establishment of a national park begins with a big political hassle and some congressional hearings. After some give and take the park is established, and many people think the battle ends there. It is not true. There are incredible pressures put on the parks and their staffs all the time. In this chapter I hope to explain some of the pressures, and possible ways of reducing them, in Grand Teton National Park.

In finding out about the park I did not seek out spokesmen, superintendents, or chief rangers. Instead I tried to spend my time with the field men, seasonal rangers, and trail crews who not only know the score but are not afraid to give you their interpretation of it. If every park visitor could be treated with the openness, courtesy, and generous hospitality that I received in Grand Teton the Park Service would have an even greater circle of friends than it has now.

One of the seasonal rangers helped me to find a camping

place where I could stay for longer than the normal limit without infringing either on other campers' rights or the park environment. In return for my isolated campsite I promised to let the ranger know of any untoward activities in the area. Poaching is more common in the park than many visitors realize.

One evening this obliging ranger stopped by my camp and during our visit told me about a strange young man who was camping along a wild section of Pacific Creek. The young fellow was on foot, and he was furtive. Being on foot he found it easy to slip into the park without passing through the entrance stations. His camp outfit consisted entirely of a sleeping bag and several bottles of cheap liquor.

I passed this young camper once on the Pacific Creek road— at least I think it was he. His long hair was weedy, his jeans were faded and floppy, and he had on a lightweight, short-sleeved shirt that was shapeless and slightly grubby. Except for his peculiar behavior he was much like thousands of other young people in the park at that season. From time to time he would move his liquid camp, always hiding it away somewhere in the brush.

Each time the boy moved his camp the ranger would have to hunt it out. The secretive boy wasn't doing anything particularly heinous; maybe he just had some thoughts or problems to work out by himself. But because the problem of thefts and vandalism is a growing one in all the parks, the ranger had to keep an eye on the boy. He did it unobtrusively. Finally, the boy, his sleeping bag, and liquor bottles just disappeared; apparently he had not harmed anyone or anything. Hopefully, he had found what he was seeking in the park, and hopefully, too, the ranger's circumspect efforts to observe without interfering were justified.

Of necessity the rangers are becoming increasingly strict about things like camping in unauthorized spots and feeding bears, but most of them bend over backward to avoid spoiling a vacation.

A young ranger recently told me about a camper who absolutely refused to move his huge motor home from an unauthorized camping spot. "I paid fourteen thousand for this unit," said the camper, "and it seems to me that I ought to be able to park it where I please." I know this ranger to be an extremely reasonable man, but he could not make the camper see the error in his reasoning. So he delivered an ultimatum: "I'll be back in two hours. If you haven't moved your truck I'll have it towed away—at your expense."

The camper refused to move his rig and it was duly towed away.

By themselves such park visitors are funny; when they become hundreds and even thousands they can menace the park itself. Grand Teton is one of the most popular of the western parks. In 1959 an estimated 1,400,000 people visited there. In barely a decade this figure more than doubled to 3,000,000; by 1979 estimates are for 5,000,000 visitors a year at Grand Teton.

Most of these will be drive-through visitors. While they have a relatively light individual impact on the park and its facilities, together they present a substantial problem. Roads and parking areas are already clogged during the peak of the season. We have also learned that building more roads and parking lots only compounds the problem and that too many facilities actually help to destroy the park.

Not everyone in Jackson Hole sees it this way. At last count there were more than thirty businesses in the Jackson area offering auto sales and service. The town of Jackson seems to be upholstered with filling stations. But to a lot of people this seeming glut is also what provides some twelve percent of Teton County's total income. So, even though climbers on top of the Grand Teton can now hear the roar of the automobile traffic below, to stop that traffic completely would work a substantial hardship on a lot of people.

Because of this and many other serious problems affecting the park, a recent and highly commendable effort has been made to establish a park master plan. The plan has as a corollary a proposal to designate certain areas of the park as wilderness. The plan is really only a part of the first rational attempt to develop a beneficial management policy for the vast, publicly owned area that includes part of southeast Idaho, the southwest corner of Montana, and a great chunk of northwestern Wyoming.

An equally commendable effort has been made to give this master plan as wide a public hearing as possible. And despite some nattering on fine points, conservationists have generally applauded the Master Plan for Teton Park. One of the plan's specifics was "to develop a means of transportation that will relieve motor-vehicle congestion in the Jenny Lake–String Lake area and extend their application to other sections of the Park, in keeping with the results."

This is in direct line with the then Park Service Chief Hartzog's avowed intention of getting rid of the automobile in crowded national parks without getting rid of the people. It is a very big intention. Right now it seems to devolve upon a system of quiet buses transporting people from their cars through the worst areas of park congestion. This may not be the most popular solution, but it does seem to be the only practical one. The opposition to the busing proposal came in the form of a spokesman for the Jackson Chamber of Commerce, who felt "the traffic problem is due to bicycle riders . . . and to large vehicles . . . to restrict cars is to restrict a man raising a family."

A woman at the same meeting declared, "They come in their brief allotted time to drive through the park . . . if they are not permitted to drive through the Jenny Lake area, I see nothing in the park for them. . . . I agree with Governor Hathaway [of Wyoming] that what we need is a wider highway with parking space."

What these opinions ignore are the rights of the hiker to enjoy the park *his* way and also the fact that because of the isolated location of Jackson Hole most people who wish to visit there will still have to come at least part of the way in automobiles. The Jackson firms catering to motorists do not stand to lose very much to a busing program.

Even most of the hikers get to Jackson Hole in automobiles. And their numbers, too, are creating some problems. In 1970, the last year for which figures were available, hikers registered for 116,000 trips into the back country of Grand Teton Park. This is a minimal figure, for many other hikers do not register. Many of the hikers are also mountain climbers, and the number of registered climbs in the park jumped forty percent in one year.

The problem of human waste and garbage disposal is so acute, as a result of all this use, that helicopters have been proposed to ferry the human waste out of the mountains. It is prohibited to bury garbage in back-country sites, but anyone who tries it will likely find that someone has already buried trash on the chosen spot before.

Just south of the Colter Bay complex, at the far end of an open sage clearing, is a strange-looking earthwork—you can see it from the highway. I walked down there one summer morning in 1970. In my notebook I wrote, "There are two long pits 4 to 5 feet deep. They are 359 by 320 normal steps [this would be about nine hundred feet in each dimension] and at the north end are 2 smaller pits within the large ones. These, in contrast to the others, are filled with green, thickish-looking water. In the center of each is a large electric pump. The banks of this pit have been sprayed with instant mulch vegetation, but with very little resultant germination.

"The rangers at the Colter Bay Visitor's Center were not very helpful in identifying the exact purpose of this excavation. One opined that it might have 'something to do with sewage.' "

Despite all the varying opinions as to how the park should be developed, or left alone, virtually everyone will agree that sewage is not a balm to recreation. The Park Service is on record as wishing to "design sewage treatment facilities to prevent the discharge of any effluent directly into the streams or lakes of the park, as well as to avoid the disruption of the area's ecosystem through the pollution or alteration of the ground water."

Considering the proximity of the Colter Bay sewage lagoons to Jackson Lake, and the porous nature of the gravelly soil in which the lagoons have been built, I have to be dubious of the service's ability to implement their aim. The sewage lagoons below Jackson Lake Lodge have already caused serious problems. And these lagoons are even closer to the lake and the Snake River than are the Colter Bay facilities. Engineering estimates for sewage treatment plants assume an input from such tourist facilities at one hundred gallons per person per day. This means that the amount of effluent from the Lodge and Colter Bay complexes, where many of the park's overnight accommodations with flush toilets are, can reach the proportions of the sewage outfall from a good-sized town.

This is why park planners are talking about "gateway cities" around the parks rather than encouraging still more overnight accommodations within the parks. It is also why, despite the parks' present status as natural areas, attempts are being made now to set aside permanent wilderness areas within the parks. Already because of human activity in Teton Park there is much land that cannot meet the technical classification of "wilderness."

I get the impression from much of what I read these days that it will not be too many years before national parks will constitute some of America's very last undeveloped lands. In proportion the parks are just a tiny bit of this country, and it saddens me to think that a way of life that westerners, especially, have taken for granted is ending. The new way of life may not be bad, exactly—I know a lot of young people now who accept urbanization and enjoy it. But to me it will never be as good as the untrammeled freedom I came to Wyoming to find.

One evidence of the growing urbanization, even in Jackson Hole, has been the controversy over the airport just north of the town of Jackson. An airport existed there even before the park was created. It seems a logical place for an airport to be. It is the summertime perch for many private aircraft, as well as the facility used by the only scheduled commercial carrier,

Frontier Airlines. Other than a limited bus service, the airline offers the only public transportation in and out of Jackson Hole.

Frontier has not been a particularly profitable airline. Recently they published a statement that reported that their annual loss was much less than it had been the year before. The release read like Frontier was announcing a simultaneous stock dividend and split. Nevertheless, Frontier hangs on in Jackson Hole because it makes money there despite a weather-dictated, landing cancellation rate of thirty-five percent. Most of these cancellations occur in the winter.

Former Park Service Chief Conrad Wirth sweetened the Jackson Hole ante for Frontier by authorizing a seventeen hundred-foot extension of the landing strip. Current Park Director Hartzog then decreed that three hundred feet of the increase will be permitted to the north and deeper into the park, while the other fourteen hundred feet must be extended to the south and away from the park.

Under the aegis of Wyoming Senator Clifford Hansen, Congress appropriated 2.2 million dollars to extend the runway two thousand feet, specifying that seventeen hundred feet of the extension be to the south. Frontier claims it needs the longer strip for 737 Boeing jet planes. Originally it had requested the extension for its Convair 580s, which are now, according to the airline, becoming obsolete.

Some people in Jackson have objected to the extension because of the noise and air pollution a jet port seems likely to increase. They have also objected on grounds that airports don't really belong in national parks. Others have supported the proposal but asked that the extension be north, thus preserving for subdivision some potentially valuable private land at the south end of the airstrip.

While the debate has gone on, Frontier has steadily increased its estimate of needed runway length. In March of 1972 they were asking for 10,500 feet, almost two miles, to "allow the 737 to operate at maximum efficiency." This means, really, to allow the jet to operate at maximum passenger loading levels.

Hot days and the high altitude combine to reduce the plane's lift and, ultimately, its payload.

Proponents of runway extension have sometimes waved the bloody shirt of air safety to win their point. But the thing that would make the airport safer, relatively, is an instrument landing system (ILS). This system would also sharply reduce the number of landing cancellations at Jackson due to bad weather. What had not been publicized, at least until it appeared that the environmentalists opposing extension might win, was that an ILS would work very well on the present airstrip. Frontier Airlines has announced that it not only intends to stay in Jackson Hole but that it expects to service the valley with its present Convair 580 prop-jet for two to five more years.

What seems to be creating the heat under some of the proponents of runway extension is the 2.2 million dollars. Offsetting all other arguments in favor of the longer strip are Frontier's already superb safety record in Jackson Hole and the fact that passenger space is usually available on flights into Jackson Hole. The whole project underwent an ecological assessment of the effect the extension might have on the park. Then, late in the summer of 1972, the extension was approved just about as its proponents had long wanted.

Such problems, real as they are, have a way of stultifying the average park visitor, who has come to a park to put aside old problems, not find new ones. But it is precisely because of the inspiration that can be gained from the parks that we need to do our best to see that they are managed wisely. I remember a wilderness trip I took and the Jewish fellow I met in the course of it. For fifty weeks out of a year he worked in a store in a huge eastern city. But he told me that it was the two weeks he could spend in the wilderness that made those other fifty weeks bearable.

Since the back country is more familiar to me, I probably did not appreciate it with the intensity that this Jew did. What I sought in our first talks together was information about the shows, libraries, and music that my friend could take almost for granted on the East Coast. And as he talked about the things I wanted to hear, another, unique feeling passed over me like a cold wave. I thought, "This is the kind of man people burned. This sweet, sensitive, appreciative member of the human race who is being so kind to me could have been shoved into an oven or covered with lime in a mass grave."

Perhaps my unsummoned thoughts were an outgrowth of another feeling that wild places instill in me—rather, it is what they take out. Meanness. The wild country just takes it out of you. Some of the most miserable human beings I've ever encountered were hunters who had not killed in the course of wilderness hunts and let that empty failure spoil the real fullness of their experience. I think this is also why many of us who live in this country are inclined to be supercritical of the average tourist. He spends a lot of money getting out to this country and then tightens up his soul so only a tiny bit of the amount possible can get in where it might do him some real good.

Sometimes I think that if more park visitors would attend the campfire lectures and nature hikes offered free by the Park Service it could help to solve problems. During the 1970 season Andy Kardos gave an outstanding slide-illustrated lecture on the destruction of the environment. In notes I made after the talk I wrote, "Most of the slides were fine, except for those of pollution which were meant to shock, and I wonder if they did. Halfway through his talk 4 girls, 15 to 18 years old, got up and walked out on Mr. Kardos—he did not deserve that. They needed him far more than he needed them."

Another of the outstanding campfire talks has been given for years by Dr. Richard Shaw, who was my botany professor at Utah State University. Shaw was a seasonal naturalist at Grand Teton even before I became one of his students. His colorful booklets on wild flowers and other plants of the park are standard works for interested visitors. My notes following Shaw's talk state, "The weight of his fine slides combined with his knowing sincerity made it an excellent talk. I only wish he had shown more pictures of wild flowers, although I know he must please and pace his audience with 'relief' shots.

"He had one shot of a bumblebee on a flower, only it wasn't a bumblebee, but a butterfly whose outward appearance has evolved into this example of mimicry for self-protection.

"But the sad thing and the thing that sent me home angry and disgusted was the rudeness of the audience. They were noisy and whispering throughout the lecture, and a few even walked out in the middle of it."

The day after the lecture was the Fourth of July, and then-Interior Secretary Hickel was winding up a visit to the park. Before his departure he had agreed to hold a press conference. It was held in warm sunshine on the lawn adjacent to the park superintendent's handsome quarters at the Beaver Creek enclave. I made these notes during and after the conference.

"Hickel was dressed in a new-looking pale gray western shirt, bolo tie, and dark blue or black saddle pants. He had on new boots of the Wellington type, and was wearing a crushed-looking version of the LBJ hat.

"Senator Hansen who was acting as the Secretary's co-host was bare-headed, wearing a brown, peek-a-boo western shirt, neutral saddle pants, and black, somewhat worn-looking cowboy boots. Hansen is a trim but not a big man, 150-160 lbs. and 5′10″.

"The only *real* reporter there, a man named Holloway from AP, was given the first question, and it was one I'd planned to ask. It was about park congestion and what could be done to alleviate it.

"Hickel said that the auto was fine for getting to the parks but means had to be found for moving visitors into the less-used, but not primitive, areas of the parks. He mentioned several times the necessity of determining the highest and best uses of the public lands, and he wants to inventory and catalog them in this way." It is well to note here that it depends upon what interest does such cataloging as to what becomes the highest and best use of land.

"Hickel did not appear to be a man of pretensions or illusions. He did not try to give us a conservation lecture. In fact, he seemed rather a silent man. He did say he was mildly in favor of plans to lengthen the Jackson airport's runway, but withheld his feelings about jet use and is against sonic booms in the area. He has obviously done a lot of homework."

I asked the secretary if he liked his job. He smiled, seemed a bit relieved, and said, yes he did. He said he was happy as long as he had something to do.

Soon after his Wyoming visit Secretary Hickel leaked a letter to the press in which he criticized the Nixon administration's position toward young people. It gave the President the excuse he seemed to want for firing this strange public figure, who had alternately been fought, then loved, by the nation's conservationists.

For a time it had been thought that Wyoming Senator Hansen might be Nixon's first Secretary of the Interior. He had backing from both the oil and livestock industries. But Hansen went on record as refusing the job even before it was publicly offered. As a former president, and still a member of the executive committee of the Wyoming Stock Growers Association, Hansen's nomination to a cabinet job would not have pleased environmentalists. And while Hansen has changed some of his positions about the uses of the public lands, he is still remembered as a bitter enemy of early proposals to enlarge Grand Teton National Park. He was photographed with gun-toting actor Wallace Beery and some ranchers as they drove a bunch of cattle across the new monument's lands in an empty gesture of protest. (Stock driveways had already been promised the ranchers.) At last report Hansen still opposed increases in the modest fees ranchers pay for grazing their stock on federal ranges.

Cliff Hansen grew up in Jackson Hole. He is loved there and well liked throughout Wyoming. Hansen comes from pioneer stock, and is probably the only real ex-cowpuncher in the United States Senate. He is certainly a lot more authentic in the saddle than Lyndon Johnson ever was. The Hansen ranches are located on some of the most beautiful lands in Jackson Hole. They are prosperous holdings, and Hansen is a millionaire because of them and his interest in the Jackson State Bank. But, for all his success, the senator is still the sort of fellow who stops his car and offers a ride to an old hunter plugging along at the side of some back road. From a back-country ranch boy who stuttered, Cliff Hansen has become a suave, articulate mixer. He was plainly more comfortable at the Hickel press conference than was the secretary. He ably bailed Hickel out when the secretary floundered on minor points.

Hansen had a commendable record as governor of Wyoming. He is backing an effort to establish a Gros Ventre Wilderness Area and also one that is supposed to safeguard the corridor area between Yellowstone and Teton parks. His old position against the enlargement of Teton Park has apparently undergone a complete reversal. So, when a former park employee named Bernard Shanks wrote a letter criticizing Hansen to a Friends of the Earth publication, all hell broke loose in Jackson Hole.

According to Shanks's letter, Senator Hansen had illegally acquired grazing permits on the public domain in Jackson Hole during World War II. These permits, along with some held by other Jackson Hole ranchers, were in the Pothole-Moran area. The ranchers' grazing privileges were acknowledged when the area was included in Grand Teton Park. According to a 1950 law the permits were to be honored for the next twenty-five years, "and thereafter during their [the holders'] lifetime, and the lifetime of their heirs if these heirs were members of the immediate family on that date."

Grazing permits have a usual life of ten years but in reality they normally remain the holder's for as long as he wants them. So while it may appear that Hansen and his fellow ranchers made a suspiciously sharp bargain with the Park Service, they actually were not doing anything extraordinary. It must be remembered, too, that while the bargaining was going on to get an enlarged park, many concessions had to be made to area residents. What might be a bad bargain today was probably a necessity when it was struck. When Hansen became a senator his grazing permit was legally transferred to his wife. This was a rather meaningless gesture to the conflict of interest statutes.

For a few years after 1950 the senator's cattle and those of two other ranchers continued to graze in the Pothole-Moran area. Then, according to a letter written by one of the graziers whose cattle ran with Hansen's, "In about 1954, Rockerfeller [*sic*] decided to develop the area at Colter Bay and build the Jackson Lake Lodge. As tourism progressed the clientele at the Lodge and those living at Colter Bay did not exactly enjoy hobnobbing with the cows who came to graze the newly developed lawns."

At the Park Service's request all of the several hundred involved cattle were removed from the Potholes to an eleven thousand-acre parcel embracing the old Elk Ranch property —a holding Rockefeller had purchased and later turned over to the government.

Teton Park Superintendent Chapman wrote, "The graziers, of which Senator Hansen was one, accepted this proposal. To accomplish the grazing relocation, irrigation systems had to be redeveloped, fences built and cultivation revitalized."

To "revitalize" the cultivation, and so on, has so far cost the taxpayers over a quarter of a million dollars. The Park Service irrigates the meadows and maintains the fences. For this the ranchers pay a seasonal fee of sixty to seventy cents per cow. Calves less than six months old run free of charge, and are normally considered part of the cow and not counted against the ranchers' allotment. This may explain the disparity between Shanks's statement of cattle numbers and the Park Service's much lower figure.

The controversy died down in Jackson Hole after the above explanations were made, but Michael Frome, conservation editor for *Field & Stream*, revived it in his March 1972 column. "Bernard Shanks was assigned to study domestic grazing within the Park. He concluded that several permittees, including a United States Senator, Clifford Hansen, had acquired grazing rights illegally and that a key winter range of moose, elk, and deer was being subjected to serious environmental change as a result of heavy stock usage. Though ramifications of the case are clouded in legalism, Mr. Shanks's competency was personally vouchsafed to me by Dr. Adolph Murie, the distinguished wildlife ecologist. . . . But what Shanks got from the Park Service was disavowal of his findings. . . ."

Even Jackson Hole's environmental group, ENACT, disavowed the charges made in Shanks's letter. I have ridden the range in question and do think some of it is heavily used by cattle. But I cannot agree that it is "key" wildlife winter range. Deer do not winter in the area in significant numbers. The snows are terribly deep, and the only animals I have seen wintering there in any numbers are moose.

When the cattle were pulled off the Pothole-Moran district they were leaving a publicly owned range of some eighty thousand acres to come to one of eleven thousand acres. And because some of the former range had been on national forest lands, upward grazing adjustments were made in the ranchers' favor in order to compensate them for loss of territory. In retrospect it appears that the Park Service may have been both careless and naïve in spending such a whopping sum to graze a relatively few head of cattle. The senator, too, might be justly criticized for adhering so strongly to a remarkably good bargain at the expense of his current employers, the taxpayers.

The area where the cattle now graze in the summer is southeast of Moran Junction. The irrigated meadows have been enclosed with picturesque buck and rail fences. Basket exclosures are located in the meadows as a gauge for checking overgrazing. The water to irrigate this land is stored in the Elk Ranch Reservoir. Late in the season, when the water level is low, the reservoir's mud flats are a dismaying sight. Fortunately, they cannot be seen from the highway.

I have seen Canada geese grazing in these meadows and, at certain seasons and times of day, many elk also use them. But to the ordinary summer tourist driving by, the fenced lands dotted with Hereford cattle look exactly like a private holding and not part of their national park.

The government has long contended that grazing permits on its lands have no cash value. But in reality they do have considerable value, and in a few cases the government has officially admitted this by paying to recover permits. It might behoove everyone involved to simply sell out the permits to the Park Service and end a problem that otherwise could grind on another fifty years.

Like most bureaucracies, the Park Service's higher echelons tend to be a lot happier and more comfortable without boat rockers like Bernard Shanks in their midst. This prickly sort of employee is exactly the kind all public agencies need more of.

In making the agencies more sensitive to their shortcomings, real or imagined, the Bernard Shankses also make the agencies more valuable to us. This is exactly what has happened to the valley and the town of Jackson—the park has enriched them both. In addition to its higher per-capita income, Teton County also has a higher educational level than surrounding areas. And this level shows in Jackson's higher cultural level.

*Night life in Jackson gets off to an
entertaining start each evening with
the public hanging . . . Boardwalk
Stomping is one of the favorite evening pastimes as nearly all the shops
remain open until 10 p.m. seven days
a week. . . . Rodeos provide real
whoopin' and hollerin' on Friday and
Saturday nights. . . ."*

WHAT TO DO IN JACKSON,
excerpted from a tourist brochure

17 / *Two-Season Town*

For the traveler, especially the one motoring in from the
north or south of town, Jackson's cultural side is well-nigh invisible. On the south, the town is bounded by propane depots,
a drive-in movie, trailer parks, and a vast used-car lot. But all of
this is made comparatively innocuous by a roaring sand and
gravel business standing close by the roadside. Adjacent hills
have been permanently defaced to extract this sand and gravel.
North of town is a long array of practical proofs of H. L.
Mencken's admonition to "never underestimate the bad taste
of the American public." Here entrepreneurs have bulldozed
a trailer park into the side of the East Gros Ventre Butte overlooking the elk refuge. There are strident gas stations, cutesy-
vomitous taco barrels, and phony barns dispensing gasoline
plus do-it-yourself car washes. This is the natural habitat of the
hamburger of micron thinness and the lank, foot-long hot dog.
Some of the West's most woebegone-looking ponies stand broil-
ing in the August sun and obviously not relishing the tourist
children who kick them to the top of the butte and down again.

For years all this and more was announced far in advance by
a myriad of billboards on the highways leading to Jackson.
Residents who had long protested these signs to little avail

were delighted recently when some group began cutting the signs down. Operating with power saws late at night, these citizens treated their fellows to an almost pristine look at the approaches to Jackson. The sheriff warned against such lawlessness. But, by the time his warning was published, nearly all the signs had been leveled. No arrests were ever made.

In its ambivalence between protection and profit Jackson is a microcosm of Wyoming. Half the citizens are clawing and scratching to encourage and attract business that may ruin the natural values the other half are struggling to save. But there most similarities end. The town of Jackson is unique, and has been for years. In 1920, just six years after it was incorporated, the citizens of Jackson elected a full slate of ladies to run their town. They did a good job, too, and were reelected in 1921. The press tended to make light of the "petticoat rulers" with limericks and spoof interviews with the sheriff. But under the women's administration Jackson's streets improved and steps were taken to install a water system. This tradition has continued, and the women, native-born and expatriate alike, have consistently led in the successful effort to make Jackson a rewarding place in which to live. The excellent hospital, the wonderful library, the fine summer symphony program, the town square, and even the ski hill behind the town have all greatly benefited from the ladies' fond attentions.

Grace Miller, Jackson's first and only lady mayor, was the wife of nabob Robert E. Miller. Mrs. Miller deeded a block near the present center of the town to the areas' children. A 4-H building has been put on the site, but, by and large, the land remains undeveloped. The ever-encroaching business and residential developments will eventually prompt the complete fruition of Mrs. Miller's gift.

Unlike many western towns with outskirts reaching to the horizons, Jackson has been forced to confine much of its growth. The surrounding mountain slopes and buttes require it. And it was not until after World War II that growth was much of a factor in Jackson. Just what life there was like before the boom has been wonderfully told by Donald Hough in *Snow Above Town* and also by Mardy Murie in *Wapiti Wilder-*

ness. The books describe the days when Teton Pass was a formidable obstacle to the civilization "outside." In winter mail came over the pass in horse-drawn sleds, and high freight rates doubled the cost of merchandise by the time it reached Jackson.

In recalling earlier days in Jackson, Floy Tonkin wrote, "No longer do pinnacles of smoke in the winter mean someone's water line has frozen up. No longer does a saddle horse tied outside a bar mean that the master is in a poker or solo game.

"We recall the furor that was raised when an 'outsider' bought the Cowboy Bar and proceeded to deck it out in neons and running light. The old Cowboy, with its bearskin rugs and sagging sofa in front of the fireplace was no more.

"The Log Cabin, Wally Beery's favorite hangout, was a rendezvous for cowmen, and the fact that it was next door to the Chili Parlor made it especially popular with the late crowd.

"The Wort was the place to eat breakfast after a night on the town."

Miss Tonkin was recalling a time when the snow fell and stayed where it had fallen until a thaw came. There were few snowplows, and "breaking out" a road meant driving a team of horses over an untracked expanse of snow. The roadways, by spring, were often high-mounded berms with a beaten traveling surface along their tops. To win a bet over getting into the valley a businessman named Amoretti sent a crew of coal miners to shovel open the road across Togwotee Pass early one spring. Amoretti owned the original Jackson Lake Lodge, and Slim Lawrence, who supervised the shovelers, said the road was opened and the bet won. Years later when Jackson Holers thought they could shovel open the roads after the terrible storms of 1948–1949 they found the canyons choked with snow. Ever since, state, county, and Park Service road crews have done an outstanding job of keeping roads and highways open all winter long. Also in those earlier days the town's electricity was homemade and unreliable, and the municipal water system could be shut off by a few errant pine needles. Since then the times and living conditions have vastly changed.

The town of Jackson today has an annual budget of over

six hundred thousand dollars. It is not seriously in debt, and at the end of some years has shown a cash reserve. Community boosters no longer need feel they have to brag about the "four-year high school"; even though the present Jackson-Wilson High School is infinitely superior, there are enough other civic attributes now to slide the school system pretty well down on the boosters' lists.

There has long been a lot of justified pride in the community's medical services. Old-timers still fondly remember their beloved Dr. Huff, who, as a freshly graduated physician from Johns Hopkins, came to Jackson in 1916. With his help the town built a hospital of logs that served it well for many years. Marion Budge wrote about Dr. Huff and this hospital in 1928: "It is because of his reputation as a physician and surgeon and because of good hospital service, that millionaires from all over the United States are willing to bring their families and remain an entire summer so far from a railroad."

Unlike so many small western communities where doctors are in desperate demand, today Jackson has a bevy of excellent physicians and a modern hospital that is still good enough for millionaires.

Over the years, Jackson has had a lot more newspapers than it has had hospitals. In the early days when winter weather shut off the supply of newsprint, an enterprising editor substituted brown wrapping paper to get his edition out on time. In the Jackson Hole Museum you can see one of the original copies of this unique paper.

At this writing there are two weekly papers in Jackson. Both are good. In addition to these there are underground papers and sheets of short duration that come and go like the wild flowers in Jackson Hole. According to one yarn Floy Tonkin started the *Jackson Hole Guide* because she had a press and was printing flyers for cutter racing anyway. The *Guide* has since changed hands, and editors there come and go even faster than the wild flowers, but nearly all of them have left a spot of color behind.

One editor attempted to attend a law enforcement meeting

in the City Council Chambers uninvited. The then county attorney, further identified in the paper's account as "an ex-amateur boxer" threatened to throw the editor out. This fearless fellow kept his seat, however, and later wrote that the attorney, "shoved back his chair and stood up.

" 'All right godamit, I told you once and if you don't leave I'm going to throw you out,' he said . . ."

The editor said, "You don't give me much choice. . . ."

The County Attorney whom the article described as weighing "an estimated more than 200 pounds," then grabbed the editor, "who weighs 142 pounds soaking wet, by the left shoulder, jerked him off the chair and dragged him across the floor and shoved him through the door."

More recently the paper carried this display advertisement:

Wanted: A Bachelor Rancher

A liberated attractive blond woman of 37 seeks career change from a museum exhibit designer to rancher's wife. Likes children, cooking, outdoors, carpentry, and animals. Owns home in the country, college educated in the East, has been a Wyoming resident for three years, and has traveled extensively throughout the world. Are you interested?

Earlier, an ad appeared in the lost and found column:

Found: A lady's purse in my airplane. Owner may have by identifying and paying for this ad. If owner can satisfactorily explain it being in my airplane—I'll pay for the ad.

Following the summer season a correspondent from Moose annually revived her column called "Moose Droppings." And during Leap Year an attempt is made to identify Jackson Hole's "bachelor herd" for fun and for the edification of unattached ladies. Perhaps this latter feature stems from the fact that in its early days Jackson Hole had a surplus of bachelors—lonely men who gambled and boozed away the hours between cattle feedings or even the months between departure and arrival of the summer dudes.

It should be noted, however, that both papers concentrate a

lot more on local news than they do on frivolity; there aren't many Bill Nyes in the boondocks any more. News is also broadcast over the small voice of KSGT, Jackson's lone radio station. This station sometimes departs from the ordinary programming by broadcasting a morning reading from a worthwhile book. Twice a year *Teton Magazine* is published by a Jackson advertising firm. This is a handsome magazine with fine photographs, many in full color, of Jackson Hole subjects. Most of the articles are also interesting accounts of a wide variety of area-related topics.

The average tourist driving through the town does not usually see the magazine or read Jackson's sprightly weeklies. He sees instead a commercial district that is a jumble of architectural dissonance. Individually some of the buildings are attractive, but in combination they mostly clash in a loud paean to the tourist dollar. One or two of the stores owning the very best locations specialize in the sleaziest sort of tourist souvenir—plastic sculptures of vomit, horse manure in little bags, and miniature privies and water closets. The stores stocking this junk remain in business season after season, so someone must be buying it.

In a few of the stores stocking higher-quality merchandise an average-looking customer may be greeted with a haughtiness that jars old standards of western hospitality. One day, after my wife and I had been out tramping around the country, we stopped into a handsome Jackson sporting goods store in hopes that we could find my father a fancy gift knife. I don't doubt that we looked as though we'd been outdoors, and this may be why the proprietor sniffed, "There's nothing in that case under fifty dollars." He was the same fellow I had observed earlier selling the fishing rod cases that were supposed to go with the rods at no extra charge.

If you look, you can also find storekeepers who'll insist you buy a pair of boots whether they fit or not. You'll also find a snotty little artist or two whose behavior doesn't match the happy names of their shops. On the whole, however, the merchants of Jackson treat their customers with a lot more consideration and courtesy than they might expect to get at home. There is a hardware store on the square, Benson's, where I have never failed to get a warm, attentive, and interested welcome— even though my purchases run in the "fifteen-feet-of-halter-rope" brackets.

Benson's competitors, kitty-corner across the town square, are equally nice, and their gift shop is one we head for first when we want something extra special. The Valley Shop, under its new management, is fast becoming the best source of western books in the region. There are other stores where you can try on boots or shoes until you find a pair you both like and find comfortable; if you cannot find such a pair the clerk will probably send you to a store he thinks will have something to suit you.

And, along with a tempering of my criticism of a few Jackson stores, I should mention that laments for the disappearance of the town's frontier architecture are not entirely valid. Some of the first permanent buildings in town were made of brick from a nearby kiln. This building influence was spare, Bible-belt gothic, and is no more missed today than some of the stuff that has replaced it would be missed.

When I first came to live in western Wyoming, all of Jackson's commercial gaudiness withered, died, and was crated up after Labor Day. The summer help rode the tourists' coattails out of the valley and the residents had their town to themselves for another nine months. Nowadays retired visitors follow the summer families, these older couples are followed by hunters, and they, in turn, are replaced by skiers. More and more businesses now stay open year round to cater to this new trade. But Jackson is still a two-season town and, in my opinion, is most enjoyable during its off-tourist season.

The operators of the Teton Village ski area believe that their "hill" can eventually accommodate 12,500 skiers. So far this number has never been remotely approached—because, while skiing in the Tetons is a scenic extravaganza, the snow conditions are not always ideal. Furthermore, Jackson Hole is on the remote side in comparison with skiing areas in surrounding states. To make up for the skiers who do not come or come but prefer to stay nearer the slope at Teton Village, Jackson has also welcomed the cutter racer, the sled dog driver, and, lamentably, the snowmobiler.

I have never been able to enjoy cutter racing. From what I've seen of it, it is just an equine drag race, slow to start but quick to finish. Dog racing is something else again. The races were very popular for a time prior to World War II, but interest declined and only recently has it shown signs of reviving. Dogs cannot pull a sled over the snow as fast as a team of horses can pull a cutter. But from a participant's standpoint, as well as from that of the spectator who wants to both watch awhile and know who won, sled dog racing could be the most fun of all. Also, at intervals throughout the winter there are ski races and limited jumping on Snow King. Watching the skiers zip skillfully down this hill leaves me wondering how they can stop before crashing into a Jackson living room. The slope is that close to the town.

Snow King is a medium-sized mountain. Skiing there was pioneered by the children of Jackson. Over the years the slope was improved by the parents of the skiing youngsters until it eventually became a commercial hill, and one of the first chair lifts in this part of the west was built there.

Recently Snow King has been a kind of pawn in a contretemps over three retail liquor licenses. The liquor laws in Wyoming are comparatively liberal—as might be expected in a state where per-capita consumption has been tops in the nation. Liquor is sold from a state warehouse to Wyoming bars, which are also the only legal retail source of bottled liquor—called "package goods." Beer is also sold in these combination bar-liquor stores, but not in grocery or drugstores.

In addition to regulating the flow of liquor, Wyoming's licensing system makes any business holding a retail liquor permit especially valuable, particularly in a resort town like Jackson. For many years there were only four such licensed establishments in Jackson. Then business interests convinced Teton County's remarkable young representative, John Turner, that more liquor permits were needed in the town. In due course the permits, three of them, were authorized, and then the dam burst. To a bystander it seemed that everyone in this part of the state wanted to go into the whiskey store business. At least seventeen applications were filed for the permits. The town council, which had the right to issue the permits, may have done a little preauthorization planning, but it could not cope with the deluge. The first permit was issued to the new, and big, Virginian Motel. The then mayor announced that the two remaining permits were going to applicants who could use them to the best financial advantage for the town of Jackson—whatever that meant. For some reason this announcement seemed to immediately put most of the local license applicants out of the running. Council votes were taken, then repudiated, meetings were held in secret, one councilman resigned in a huff and another refused to vote at all. Finally, the town got itself sued. That ended the indecision—one of the remaining permits was issued to the motel chain, which has plans for developing Snow King. The other permit, much to the consternation of some council members, went to the Pink Garter Plaza, which is right across the street from the license-holding Wort Hotel.

In the midst of all this confused wheeling and dealing, which a town cynic claimed would only spread the drinker's dollar, not increase it, the terms of Jackson's mayor and some councilmen expired. The town voters were apparently weary of the license boondoggling, and an even more nettlesome fight over zoning, for they turned out all the incumbents.

Some people claim that the real power in Jackson belongs to the Mafia. One story has it that some years ago the Mafia bought a Jackson bar in order to gain a foothold in the town. They then used this foothold to shut down Jackson's wide-open gambling so that people who wished to wager would be forced to go to the Mob's Nevada operations. When the unorganized gambling in Jackson was closed down, the story goes, the Mob sold out. Other people will tell you that certain businesses in Jackson are now run by "the syndicate."

As might be expected, the FBI will neither confirm nor deny the presence of the Mafia in Jackson Hole. Local law-enforcement officers all told me they doubted the stories, but added, "When there's a lot of money around, as there is in Jackson, you can never be entirely sure who's behind it."

Hoping for a more definitive answer about the Mafia, I wrote to Gay Talese, whose book, *Honor Thy Father*, qualifies him as a leading lay expert on the Mafia. Talese wrote back, in part: "I really doubt that the Mafia is in Wyoming in any capacity."

There is certainly a paucity of Mafia-type crime in Jackson. The police laughed when I asked about prostitution. "There's so much free stuff around here that a man would have to be crazy. . . ." And while there is a drug problem in Jackson, it is mainly one of marijuana and LSD, not heroin or cocaine. Police say LSD runs a very poor second in popularity to pot. And, to the townspeople's relief, most of the drug users are transients. When a drug problem did erupt in the area it was quickly met by an enlightened officialdom and the problem retreated.

There is some gambling in Jackson, but it is neither organized nor a serious problem. Officers I talked to said it was unlikely that a person could find any establishment in the area that would accept a bet on an average ball game or horse race. It is fairly common in this area during the World Series, which coincides with hunting season, to ask, "Who won the game?" and be answered, "What game?"

Police keep "hippies" moving through and out of town in response to demands of local businessmen. In all the times I have been in Jackson, I have seen only one person on the streets who seemed to be "high" on something other than alcohol— and he was desperately trying to hitch a ride out of town.

Jackson is not a haven for perverts, and those who are there are pretty circumspect about their predilections. The last fag I saw in Jackson was remarkable only because he was unusually polite. The town police seem to handle these and other potential problem-causers with quiet skill. When a scruffy California motorcycle club made tentative motions toward taking over the town, the police were expecting them. The gang was allowed to stay but on the town's terms, and no trouble ensued.

The biggest nights of the tourist season are those around the Fourth of July. Purely in response to the demands of this book I visited Jackson on a recent Fourth. During the afternoon I noted, "I walked around the town. It is thronged but there was no air of holiday excitement. The town's business area is loaded with art galleries. An artist was painting pictures of the Tetons, apparently from memory, in the Pink Garter Plaza. He was whipping them out so fast that I could smell the oily paints. His lowest prices ran $8 and went up to $20. His stuff was as good as a lot of that being sold indoors at much higher prices.

"Most of the other crafts, pictures, leather goods, pottery is just crap being offered by bearded bums wearing vests with no shirts. The odds-on ghastliest object offered for sale was a beige-pink plastic toilet seat imbedded with silver dollars—some of which had been given a gold wash."

Later that afternoon I drove out to the Federal Fish Hatchery just north of town. Except for a maintenance crew the place was empty of people, and I was able to have a nice chat with one of the employees. After that I went back to my camp in the northern end of the valley and had dinner. In the early evening I drove back into Jackson.

It was nearly dark, and the lack of markings, save the center line, made it difficult to see the highway. A few miles from Jackson the difficult driving grew worse as I met cars streaming north out of the town; a couple of them felt the highway was wide enough for passing even though the oncoming lane was in use. My notes continue:

"The shows, there are three theaters in Jackson, plus the rodeo and a 10 P.M. fireworks display, all contributed to the worst congestion I've ever seen in Jackson. Around the square the wooden sidewalks were thronged, and it took me a couple of turns around several blocks to find a parking space. Some of the restaurants were still serving, and the bars were beginning to fill up.

"After parking I took a walk around the town's commercial area. The theatergoers were fast disappearing, and the streets and sidewalks were being taken over by teen-agers. Most were not bad kids, at least when I saw them; only a few were drunk, although a few more were roistering and apparently wanting to be drunk. A big bunch of them were knotted outside the Cowboy Bar peering wistfully in at what appeared to me to be a God-awful western combo.

"This scene was the same outside the Wrangler. When I passed, a man in his forties was asking a fatuous-looking blond boy, 'Where are your shoes?' The boy was barefoot.

"I could not feel that most of the kids were having a good time. They were milling and yelling and seemingly trying to find courage and strength in their own numbers. Some kids were sitting alone or in pairs on darkened curbings or in unlit building entrances. It was quite dark north of the Jackson Trading Post, but two boys there were taking pictures with expensive-looking 35mm cameras.

"Beer cans and the remains of the litter of eating were appearing all along the streets. The square itself was a kind of no-man's-land. A few kids were sitting on the grass there, others were hanging in the trees, shooting off firecrackers or just sitting in morose-looking rows under the elk horn arches. It was a night of skin, hair, suede leather, and denim."

Before the night was over I was to see that while the police had not been in evidence on Jackson's streets that night they were very much in readiness for any trouble. To my knowledge nothing particularly violent happened that night. I noted, "The whole thing of the kids' seemed so fruitless and senseless that I went back to my car and started for camp." On the way there I further noted, "In the turnouts beside the elk exhibition pasture cars were parked and the people were shooting off several varieties of rockets, fountains, etc. I felt sorry for the poor elk out in the fenced meadow who had to suffer through this moronic display."

Later an officer told me that the summer kids caused less trouble, per capita, than the ones who came in winter. Many of the wintertime kids, the officer felt, were dropouts from school who had no goals and seemed to reflect their lack of direction in an increased use of drugs. The officer also said that the area is still small enough so that the authorities can keep tabs on transient vehicles that seem out of the ordinary. The police said they thoroughly check out all suspicious newcomers.

I'm not at all sure I would enjoy being broke and under suspicion in Jackson. I know I wouldn't enjoy it if I were also black. One Jackson Hole officer with considerable previous experience in a large metropolitan area said, with satisfaction, "We've got no minority problem here. Most of the people here are upper middle class and middle class—there's no lower class." This is largely true. Jackson and Jackson Hole have a tremendous population turnover, but it is not of low- and poverty-class people. They are often people who arrive in the romantic summer and find the bitter winters and the lack of substantial employment more than they bargained for. Those who do find work often complain that wages are low and prices, especially those for rents and food, are high. People in lower-income groups have got to like the area very much in order to make the economic sacrifices necessary to live there.

There isn't enough year-round work in the valley to hold a large labor force that would require a substantial, moderately priced housing development. And there is no local incentive to develop low-cost housing when any housing in Jackson commands premium rents and sale prices. It took my wife and me a long time to weigh Jackson Hole's advantages and disadvantages before we decided we wanted to live there. It took us even longer to adjust to the idea that our housing dollars were worth about half in Jackson Hole what they were in other places.

But despite these drawbacks the valley's population is growing. And, while only a few are speaking publicly about it, Jackson and its surroundings have a finite carrying capacity. The power blocs in the area should now, if they aren't already, begin making some concrete decisions about how many people

can live the good life together in Jackson Hole. Most environmentalists believe the area is a lot nearer saturation now than
some real estate developers apparently do.

All one has to do is drive through the residential areas of
Jackson to see the effects of largely unregulated growth. Mold-
ering cabins that once made the area charming are now sagging
cheek by sagging cheek with aging bungalows. In a few
sections small businesses detract from older but still handsome
homes. A big junkyard lies smack in the middle of what
otherwise might be a pleasant residential area. The town has
engaged planners and tried to zone its often malevolent growth,
but these efforts have not been completely successful except in
comparison with some of the horrible things perpetrated outside town in the county.

Although a lot of Jackson is crass and commercial, a lot of
it is not. The place has a cosmopolitan aura that in many ways
reminds me of San Francisco. This is what redeems it for me
and also what helped my wife and me decide we wanted to
live on the edge, if not right in the midst, of Jackson's many
activities. For example, at almost every season there is a film
festival running somewhere. In the summertime the Grand
Teton Music Festival lives up to its slogan that only music
could make Jackson Hole more beautiful. First playing at
Jackson Lake Lodge, the symphony orchestra has since been
moved to a big blue tent at Teton Village. I think the tent's
acoustics and the proximity of the audience to the orchestra
explain the heavy reliance on stringed instruments. But despite any apparent imbalance the overall effect is good, and
often much better than good. Performances are deservedly
sold out week after week, and the only sure way to get a seat
is to buy a season ticket.

Although the show bars in town lean overwhelmingly toward
guitar plunkers and country-western music, and the star acts
seldom rise above the level of Homer and Jethro, the town does
get good live entertainment. People are still talking about the
jazz band that entertained at a library benefit a year ago, and
the favorably reviewed Laubins perform authentic Indian
dances throughout the summers.

For many years summer melodramas at the old Pink Garter were high camp and great fun. Performing such things as a musical version of *Tom Jones* and the *Princess and the Pea,* the young and exuberant cast filled the old theater all summer long. But then a seemingly slicker organization leased away the old Chevrolet garage that had been the Pink Garter's home and renamed it the Diamond Lil Theatre. Some of the towns-people welcomed the new company, but others joined together to save their Pink Garter company and its producer. It was decided to house the company in a huge tent until a new theater could be built for them. But the spell of success seemed to have been broken, and from that time on all of Jackson's campy shows fell into a decline. Good casts got bum scripts and vice versa. Recently wintertime residents revived a community theater group, and their efforts in the new Pink Garter Theatre have helped to make up for the lacks of the summer presentations.

In addition to the community theater there are wintertime adult education classes in a multitude of interesting subjects. People teach courses in painting, silversmithing, anthropology, and physical fitness. In addition the Park Service has begun offering some really splendid snowshoe hikes to various parts of the park. These are free, but there are commercial ski-touring and snowshoe trips available, too. For me the nicest month in Jackson *Hole* would likely be the last two weeks in August and the first two in September. But the nicest month in Jackson *town,* for me, is probably March.

The long winter of isolation causes the usual attrition on marriages, but, at least in one case described to me, a rather widespread exchange of splintering couples. A few other sybaritic types pass part of their winters by swimming in the nude at Granite Hot Springs.

Many of those who have learned to live more sensibly with Jackson Hole's long winters do so with a wonderful zest. They are too busy with life to do anything but take people as they come. When they have fun they have a lot of it. Recently my wife and I attended a Jackson Hole gathering, and not a superspecial one, whose drop-in guest list fairly sparkled. There were four or five writers whose work was nationally known, plus show people and at least one respected photographer. No Jackson Hole gathering is complete without its painter. There were also teachers, wilderness guides, and one of the world authorities on grizzly bears. There was even a cowboy and one fellow who had done some exploring. Another member of the group was contemplating a float trip down Africa's Blue Nile. When a question arose about this still mysterious river, its prospective navigator called on another guest, one who had already rafted down the Blue Nile. It is amazing to find a community so limited in population yet so filled with talented people who are doing things.

Jackson is still a town where a millionaire or a cowhand can walk into the coffeeshop of the Wort Hotel in dusty range clothes and have a hamburger without attracting a second look. One day the film actor, Rock Hudson, drove into town for a short visit, and his appearance, which would have been page one news in most small towns, was only briefly noted deep in a Jackson paper. Not only are the residents accustomed to visits from celebrities, but many of them seem to realize that anyone needs a rest from being famous and they are given that rest in Jackson Hole.

A lot of people seem to feel that being an old-timer in Jackson Hole is a lot better than being famous. Great store is placed on length of time spent in the valley. Being a damn sight older now than when I began this book, I can't hope to ever be an old-timer in Jackson Hole. I won't live that long. And there was a goodly period of time when I never thought we'd live there at all.

For months that became years my wife and I looked at the relatively few places that were for sale and even made a couple of hopeful offers, but had them refused. Eventually we got close enough to one spot to put money down on it, only to see the deal fall through. And all the time we were looking for something we both liked and could afford, the ever-dwindling properties that were for sale dwindled even more and their prices went up.

One day I was in Jackson in connection with this book, and finding I had some extra time, decided to call a couple of realtors who had placed interesting ads in the paper. The first property was nice, but it was both too expensive and too close to the airport. The other place had been advertised as having a "Big View of the Tetons." I doubted that we could afford a big view, but my wife and I let the realtor drive us out to the site anyway.

We went past the elk refuge headquarters and north by the spot on Miller Butte where Ed Thompson was supposed to have shot it out with the posse. In some of the surrounding meadows hay was lying baled, waiting to be picked up and stacked away for the elk next winter. Beyond the grasslands there was the promised big view of the Tetons, as well as a panorama of the Gros Ventre Range with the elk pastures lying in its lap.

As we drove through the gate and into a meadow that was gold and green with the first streaks of Indian summer, I knew it was the place we'd been looking for. When my wife agreed, we drove back into Jackson and bought the land.

Sitting in the realtor's office I said, "I never expected to be buying any land today."

The realtor smiled. "I knew you would. In fact, when you called on the phone this morning, I knew you were going to buy."

Probably I shouldn't have been surprised. That clairvoyant realtor also plays polo in the summer and makes striking and original drawings for his Christmas cards in the winter. Like so many other residents of Jackson Hole, I think he came there for deeper reasons than those of making a living.

Slim Lawrence said it best one wintry, blizzarding afternoon when I was bundling up prior to leaving his snug home overlooking a frozen Jackson Lake.

"I probably won't make much from this book," I said.

"That doesn't matter. You have to love this country to write about it. What matters is that you love it."

Slim Lawrence was right.

Reading List

I have listed here a number of books, pamphlets, and periodicals that will be useful to those wishing to know more about Jackson Hole. In addition to the material listed, the Western History Research Center at the William Robertson Coe Library at the University of Wyoming has many more published and unpublished documents. There is also a small but helpful collection at the National Park Service Library at Moose, Wyoming. W. C. "Slim" Lawrence of the Jackson Hole Museum also has a useful private collection of papers relevant to the area.

Alter, J. Cecil. *James Bridger: Trapper, Frontiersman, Scout, and Guide.* Rev. ed. Norman: University of Oklahoma Press, 1961.

Bailey, R. G. *Landslide Hazards Related to Land Use Planning in Teton National Forest.* Ogden, Utah: USDA Forest Service, 1971.

Beal, Merrill D. *The Story of Man in Yellowstone.* Rev. ed. Yellowstone National Park: The Yellowstone Library and Museum Association, 1960.

Bonney, Orrin H., and Bonney, Lorraine. *Battle Drums and Geysers: The Life and Journals of Lt. Gustavus Cheney Doane.* Chicago: Swallow Press, 1970.

————. *Bonney's Guide: Grand Teton National Park and Jackson's Hole.* Houston: Privately published, 1966.

Brown, Dee. *Bury My Heart at Wounded Knee: An Indian History of the American West.* New York: Holt, Rinehart and Winston, 1970.

Bryan, Harry. *Teton Trails: A Guide to the Trails of Grand Teton National Park.* Moose, Wyo.: Grand Teton Natural History Association, 1969.

Burroughs, John R. *Guardian of the Grasslands: The First Hundred Years of the Wyoming Stock Growers Assn.* Cheyenne, Wyo.: Pioneer Printing, 1971.

Burt, Struthers. *The Diary of a Dude Wrangler.* New York: Scribner's, 1925.

Chittenden, Hiram M. *The Yellowstone National Park.* Edited by R. A. Bartlett. Norman: University of Oklahoma Press, 1964.

Coutant, C. G. *The History of Wyoming from the Earliest Known Discoveries.* Ann Arbor: University Microfilms, 1966.

Craighead, John J., Craighead, Frank C., and Davis, R. J. *A Field Guide to Rocky Mountain Wildflowers.* Boston: Houghton Mifflin, 1947.

DeVoto, Bernard, *Across the Wide Missouri.* Boston: Houghton Mifflin, 1947.

Doane, Gustavus C. Manuscript copy of Doane's journal of his winter expedition of 1876–1877. Library, Grand Teton National Park.

Driggs, B. W. *History of the Teton Valley, Idaho.* Rexburg, Idaho: Eastern Idaho Publishing Co., 1970.

Ewers, John C. *The Blackfeet, Raiders on the Northwestern Plains.* Norman: University of Oklahoma Press, 1958.

Farb, Peter. *Man's Rise to Civilization.* New York: E. P. Dutton, 1968.

Ferris, Warren A. *Life in the Rocky Mountains.* Edited by P. C. Phillips. Denver: The Old West Publishing Co., 1940.

Fosdick, R. B. *John D. Rockefeller, Jr.* New York: Harper & Bros., 1956.

Fryxell, Fritiof. *The Tetons: Interpretations of a Mountain Landscape.* Berkeley: University of California Press, 1938.

————. Collection of Fryxell's papers in the Archives at the Western History Research Center, Coe Library, University of Wyoming, Laramie.

Gilette, Bertha C. *Homesteading with the Elk*. Idaho Falls: Mer-Jons Publishing Co., 1967.

Goetzmann, Wm. H. *Exploration and Empire: The Explorer and the Scientist in the Winning of the American West*. New York: Alfred A. Knopf, 1966.

Grand Teton Natural History Association, ed. *Campfire Tales of Jackson Hole*. Moose, Wyo.: Published by the editors, 1960.

Hafen, LeRoy R., ed. *The Mountain Men and the Fur Trade of the Far West*. 8 vols. to date. Glendale, Calif.: A. H. Clarke, 1965.

Hagen, Harold. *A Fishing Guide to Jackson Hole*. Cheyenne, Wyo.: Pioneer Printing, 1954.

Hampton, H. Duane. *How the U.S. Cavalry Saved Our National Parks*. Bloomington: Indiana University Press, 1971.

Harris, Burton. *John Colter*. New York: Scribner's, 1952.

Hayden, Elizabeth W. *From Trapper to Tourist in Jackson Hole*. 2nd ed., rev., Jackson, Wyo.: 1963.

Hayden, Ferdinand V. "Sixth Annual Report . . . for the Year 1872." Washington, D.C., 1873.

Hebard, Grace A. *Wasakie*. Glendale, Calif.: A. H. Clarke, 1930.

———. Collection of Hebard's papers in the Archives at the Western History Research Center, Coe Library, University of Wyoming, Laramie.

Hough, Donald. *The Cocktail Hour in Jackson Hole*. New York: Norton, 1956.

———. *Snow Above Town*. New York: Norton, 1943.

Irving, Washington. *The Adventures of Captain Bonneville, U.S.A.* Norman: University of Oklahoma Press, 1961.

———. *Astoria: or Anecdotes of an Enterprise Beyond the Rocky Mts.* Norman: University of Oklahoma Press, 1964.

Jones, W. A. *Report Upon the Reconnaissance of Northwestern Wyoming in the Summer of 1873*. House Exec. Doc. #285, 47th Congress. Washington, D.C.: Government Printing Office. Out of print but available from Library of Congress. 1874.

Kelly, Charles. *The Outlaw Trail*. Rev. ed. New York: Bonanza, 1959.

Larson, T. A. *History of Wyoming*. Lincoln: University of Nebraska Press, 1965.

Leigh, Richard. Writings of Richard "Beaver Dick" Leigh of Jackson Hole, Wyoming. Transcription from the Original Diaries and Letters on File in Archives and the Western History Department of the University of Wyoming, Laramie, 1956.

Love, J. D., and Reed, John C., Jr. *Creation of the Teton Landscape.* Moose, Wyo.: The Grand Teton Natural History Association, 1968.

Mattes, Merrill J. "Jackson Hole, Crossroads of the Western Fur Trade, 1807–1840," *Pacific Northwest Quarterly* 37 (April 1946) and 39 (January 1948).

McDougall, W. B., and Baggley, H. A. *The Plants of Yellowstone National Park.* Yellowstone National Park: Yellowstone Library and Museum Association, 1956.

Morgan, Dale L. *Jedediah Smith and the Opening of the West.* Lincoln: University of Nebraska Press, 1953.

———. *The West of William Ashley.* Denver: The Old West Publishing Co., 1964.

Mumey, Nolie. *The Teton Mountains.* Denver: The Artcraft Press, 1947.

Murie, Margaret E., and Murie, Olaus J. *Wapiti Wilderness.* New York: Alfred A. Knopf, 1966.

Murie, Olaus J. *The Elk of North America.* Harrisburg, Pa.: Stackpole Co., 1951.

Owen, Wm. O. Collection of Owen's papers in the Archives at the Western History Research Center, Coe Library, University of Wyoming, Laramie.

Paul, Elliot H. *Desperate Scenery.* New York: Random House, 1954.

The Rajah: or the Great Presidential Sporting Excursion of 1883. n.p.: Privately Published. Out of print but available from Library of Congress.

Rajender, G. R., et al. *A Study of the Resources, People, and Economy of Teton County.* Laramie: University of Wyoming, 1967.

Raynolds, Wm. F. *Report on the Exploration of . . . 1859–60.* Washington, D.C., 1868. Out of print but available from Library of Congress.

Rollins, Phillip A., ed. *The Discovery of the Oregon Trail: Robert Stuart's Narrative . . . Wilson Price Hunt's Diary of His Overland Trip Westward in 1811–12.* New York: Scribner's, 1935.

Ross, Alexander. *The Fur Hunters of the Far West.* Norman: University of Oklahoma Press, 1960.

Ross, Marvin, ed. *The West of Alfred Jacob Miller.* Norman: University of Oklahoma Press, 1951.

Russell, Carl P. *Firearms, Traps, and Tools of the Mountain Men.* New York: Alfred A. Knopf, 1967.

Russell, Osborne. *Journal of a Trapper, or Nine Years in the Rocky Mountains, 1834–1843.* Edited by A. L. Haines. Lincoln: University of Nebraska Press, 1955.

Saylor, David J. *Jackson Hole, Wyoming: In the Shadow of the Grand Tetons.* Norman: University of Oklahoma Press, 1970.

Simpson, William L. Collection of Simpson's papers in the Archives at the Western History Research Center, Coe Library, University of Wyoming, Laramie.

Spaulding, Kenneth A., ed. *On the Oregon Trail: Robert Stuart's Journey of Discovery.* Norman: University of Oklahoma Press, 1953.

Stone, Elizabeth. *Uinta County: Its Place in History.* Laramie, Wyo.: Laramie Printing Co., 1929.

Sunder, John E. *Bill Sublette, Mountain Man.* Norman: University of Oklahoma Press, 1959.

Swain, Donald. *Wilderness Defender: Horace M. Albright and Conservation.* Chicago: University of Chicago Press, 1970.

Teton Magazine, Jackson, Wyo. Published by Teton Advertising twice yearly.

Trenholm, Virginia C., and Carley, Maurine. *The Shoshonis: Sentinals of the Rockies.* Norman: University of Oklahoma Press, 1964.

Tilden, Freeman. *Following the Frontier with F. Jay Haines, Pioneer Photographer of the Old West.* New York: Alfred A. Knopf, 1964.

Victor, Frances F. *The River of the West.* Columbus, Ohio: Long's College Book Co., 1950.

Warner, Matt, and King, M. E. *The Last of the Bandit Riders.* New York: Caxton Printers, 1940.

Wilson, Elijah N. *Among the Shoshones.* Salt Lake City: Book-Craft, 1969.

Wister, Owen. *Owen Wister Out West: His Journals and Letters.* Edited by Fanny Kemble Wister. Chicago: University of Chicago Press, 1958.

A Note on the Author

Frank Calkins was born in Portland, Oregon, and took a B.A. at the University of Utah and a Master's Degree at Utah State University. After a two-year hitch in the Navy, he joined the warden service for the State of Utah and subsequently became editor of *Utah Fish and Game*. Since 1963 Mr. Calkins has been a free-lance writer. He is the author of *Rocky Mountain Warden* and has also contributed articles to *National Wildlife, Sports Afield, Field and Stream,* and other outdoor magazines. He and his wife, Rodello Hunter (author of *A House of Many Rooms*) live in Wyoming's Jackson Hole.

A Note on the Type

The text of this book was set on the Linotype in a type face called Baskerville. The face is a facsimile reproduction of types cast from molds made for John Baskerville (1706–75) from his designs. The punches for the revived Linotype Baskerville were cut under the supervision of the English printer George W. Jones.

John Baskerville's original face was one of the forerunners of the type style known as "modern face" to printers—a "modern" of the period A.D. 1800.

Composed, printed, and bound by
The Haddon Craftsmen, Inc., Scranton, Pa.

Typography and binding design by
Virginia Tan